Blank Comic Book

This book belongs to...

_____

Notebook to Create Your Own Comic Book
140 blank pages to draw your own comics, super hero comic, variety of templates and designs

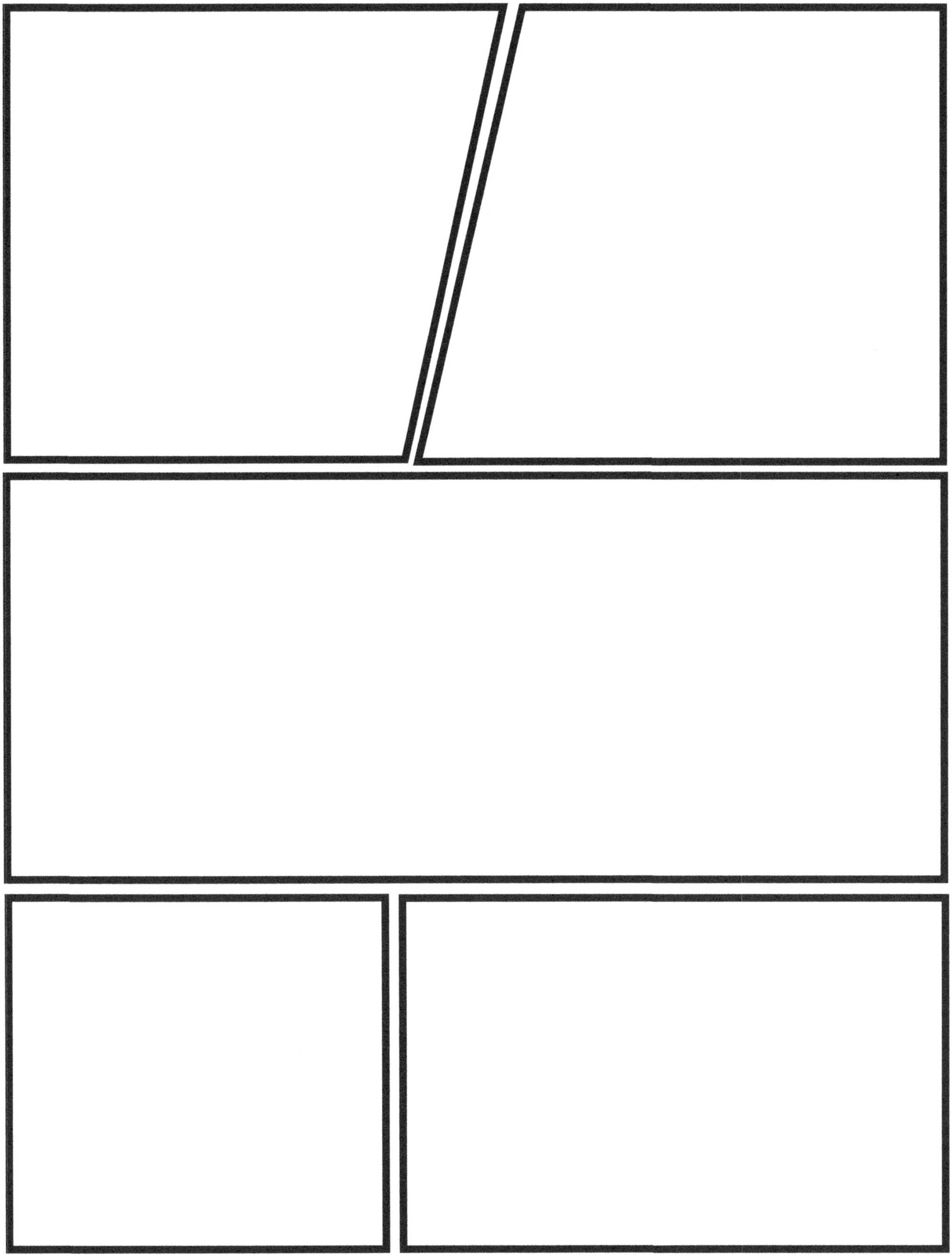

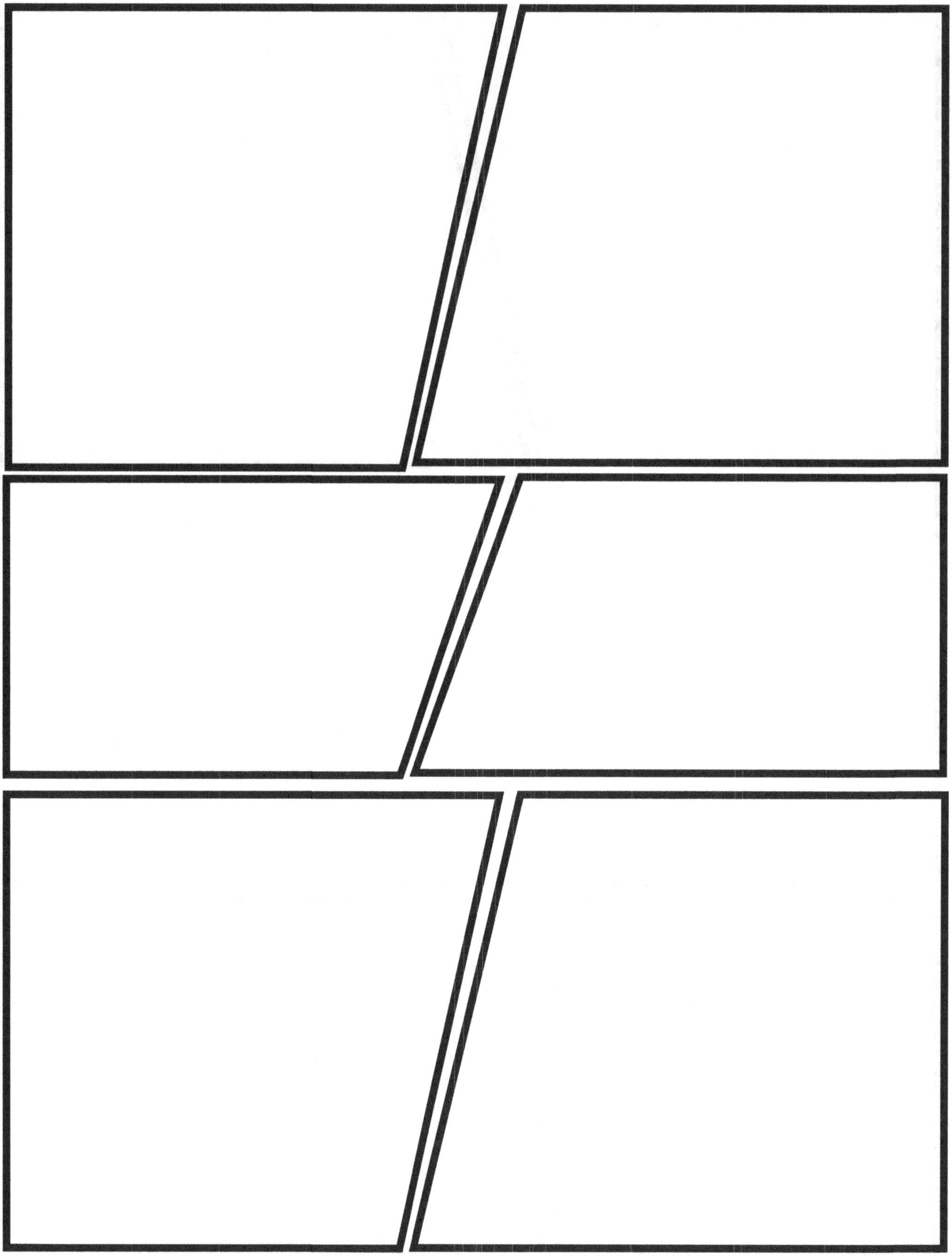

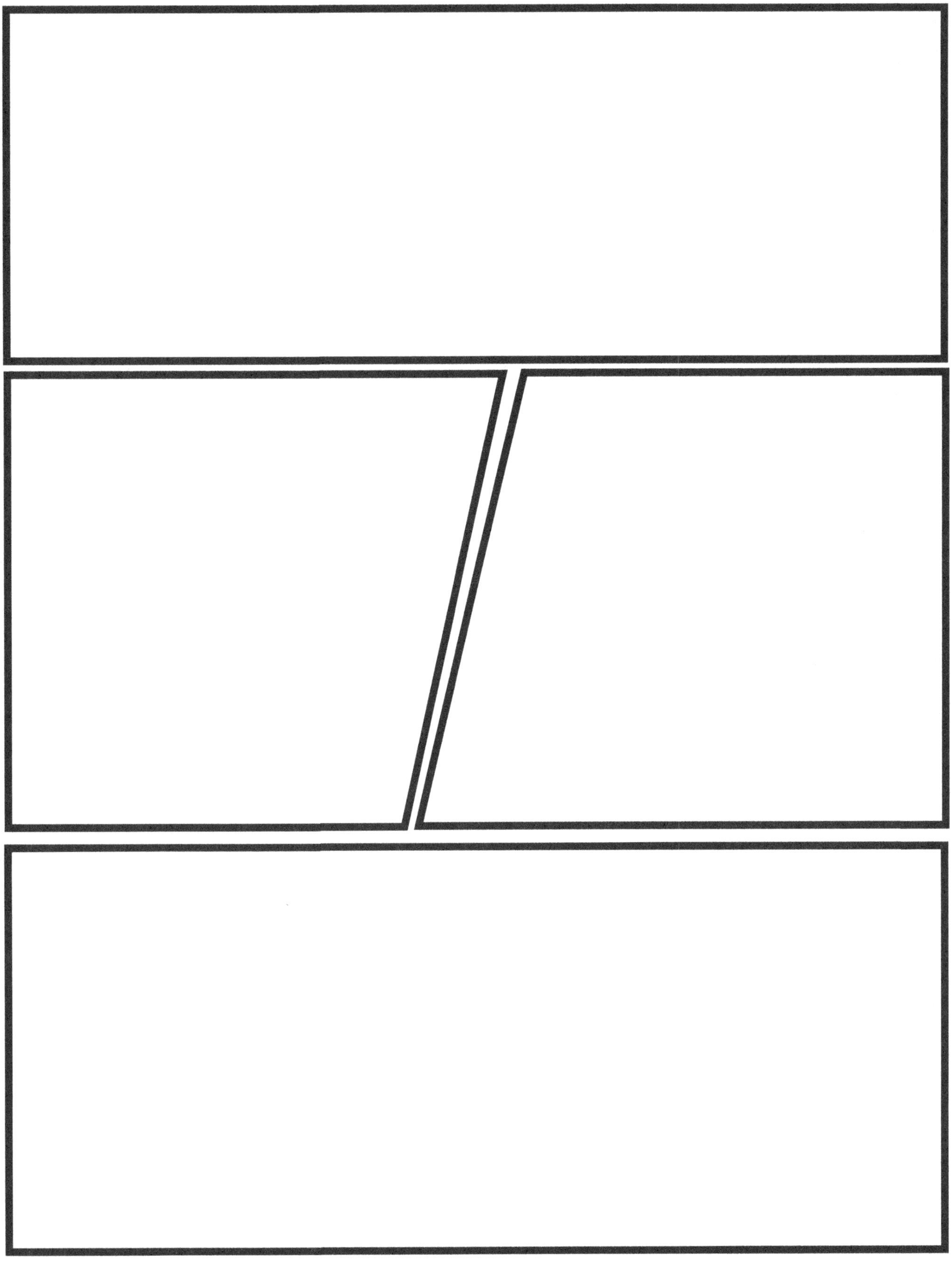

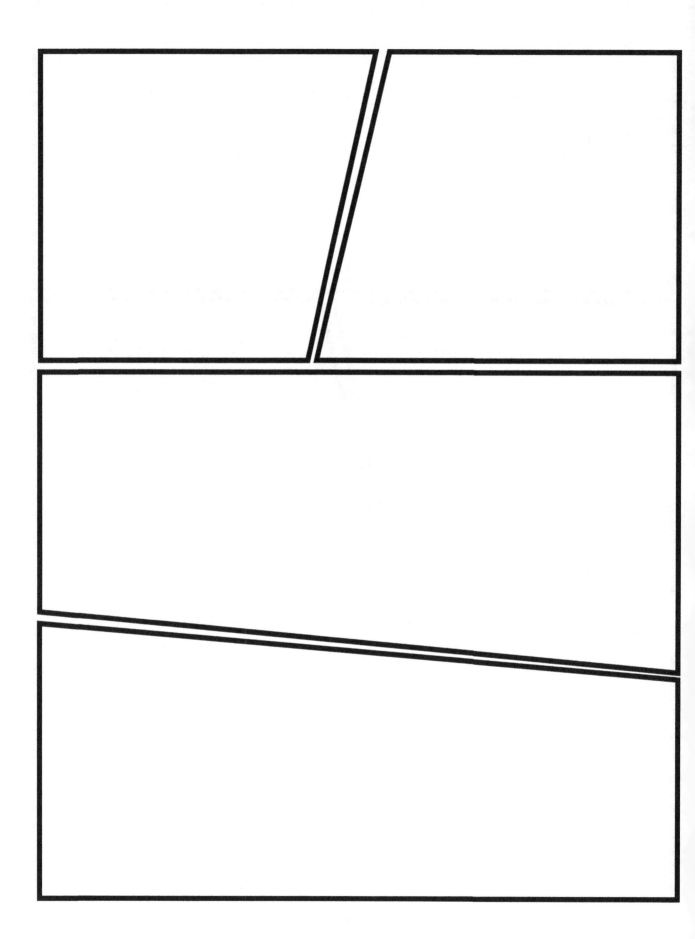

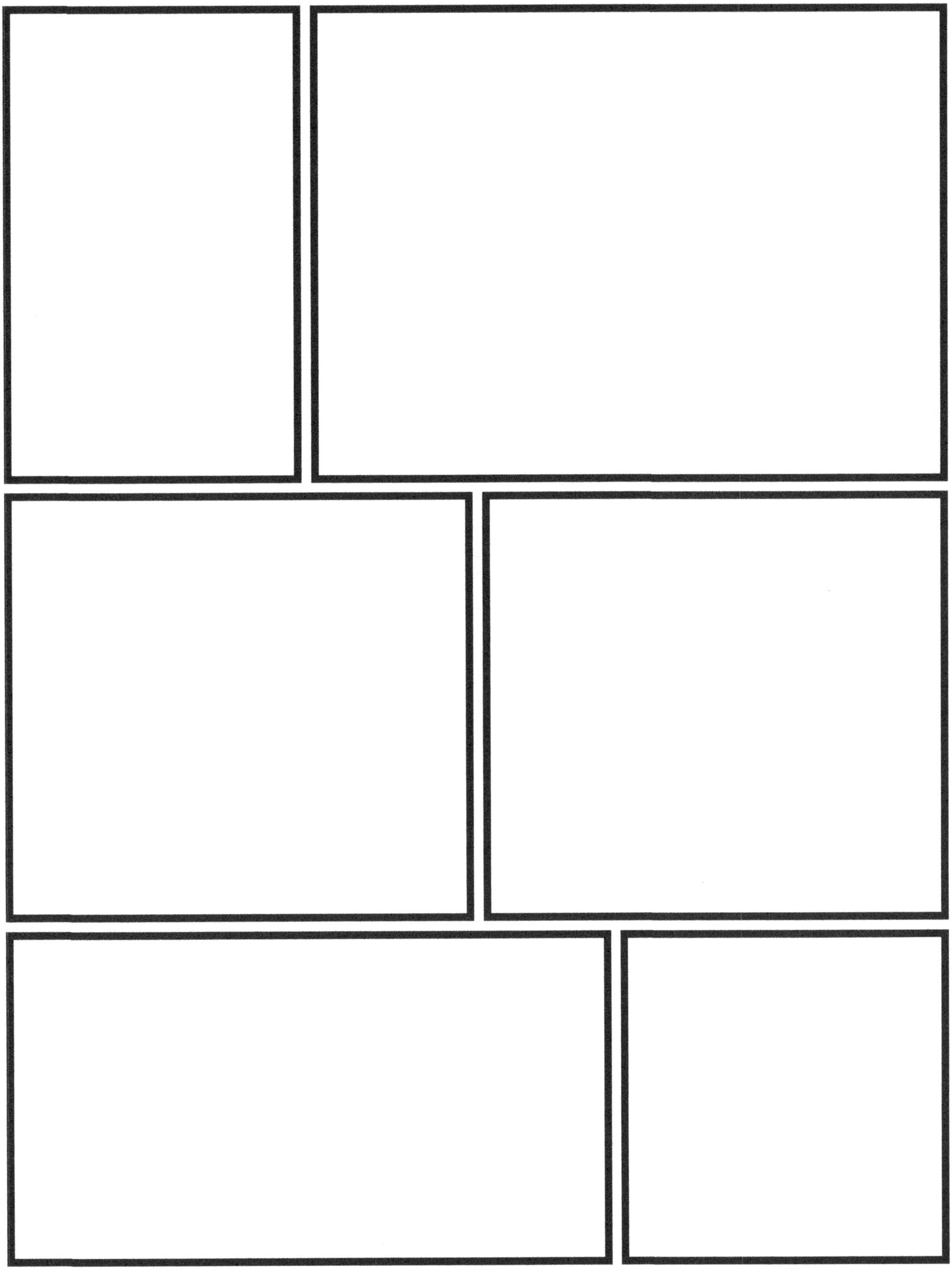

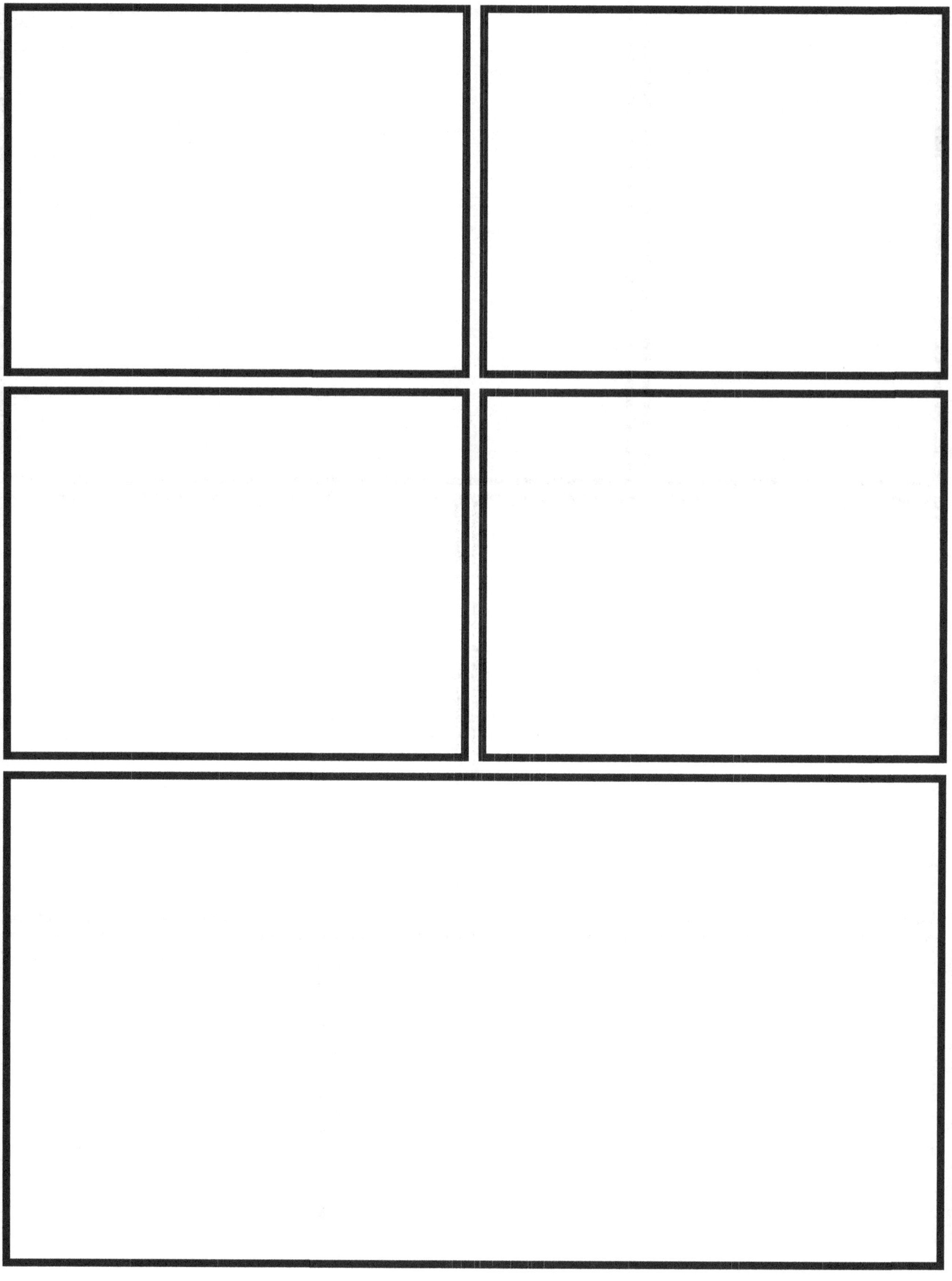

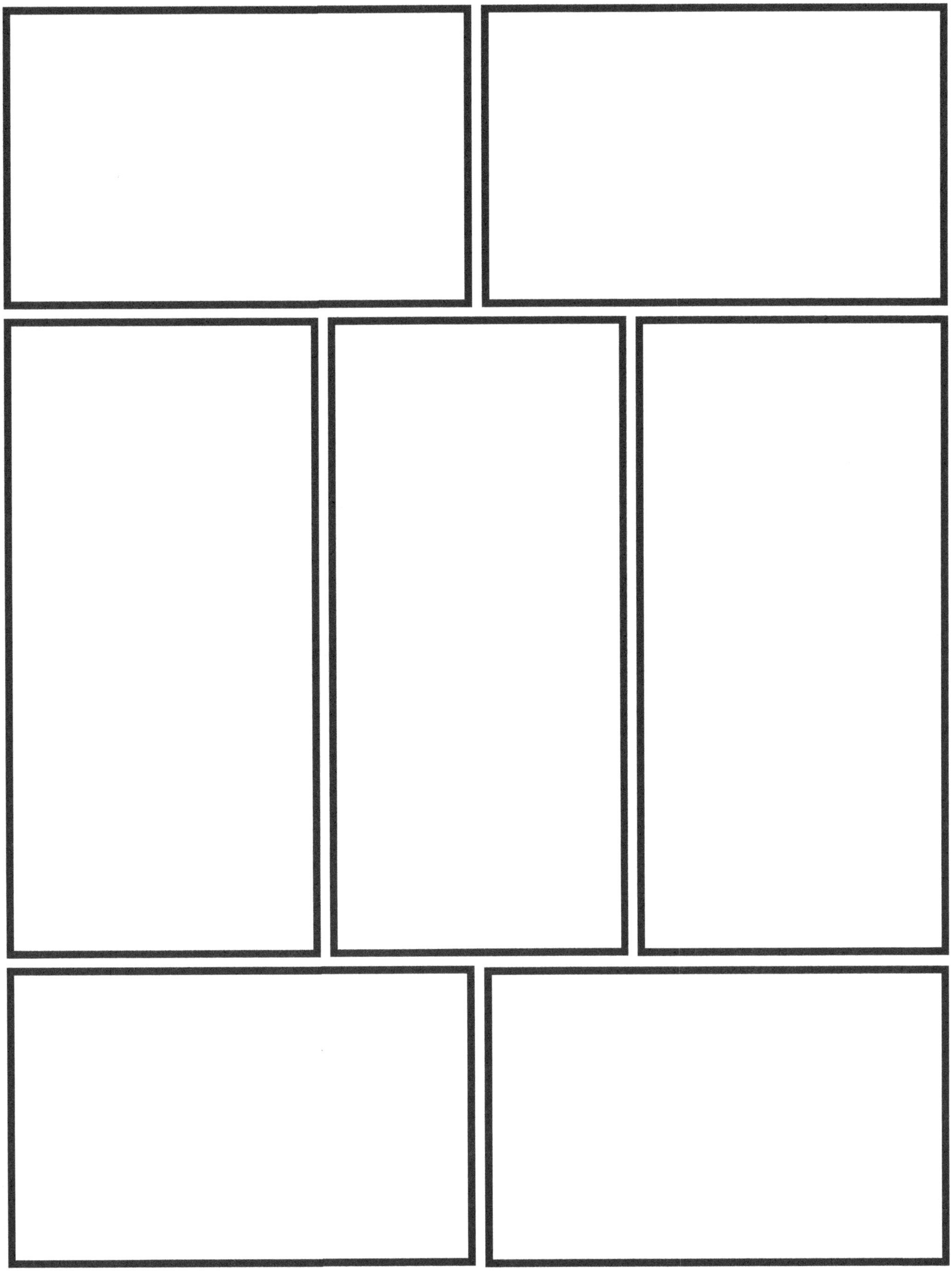

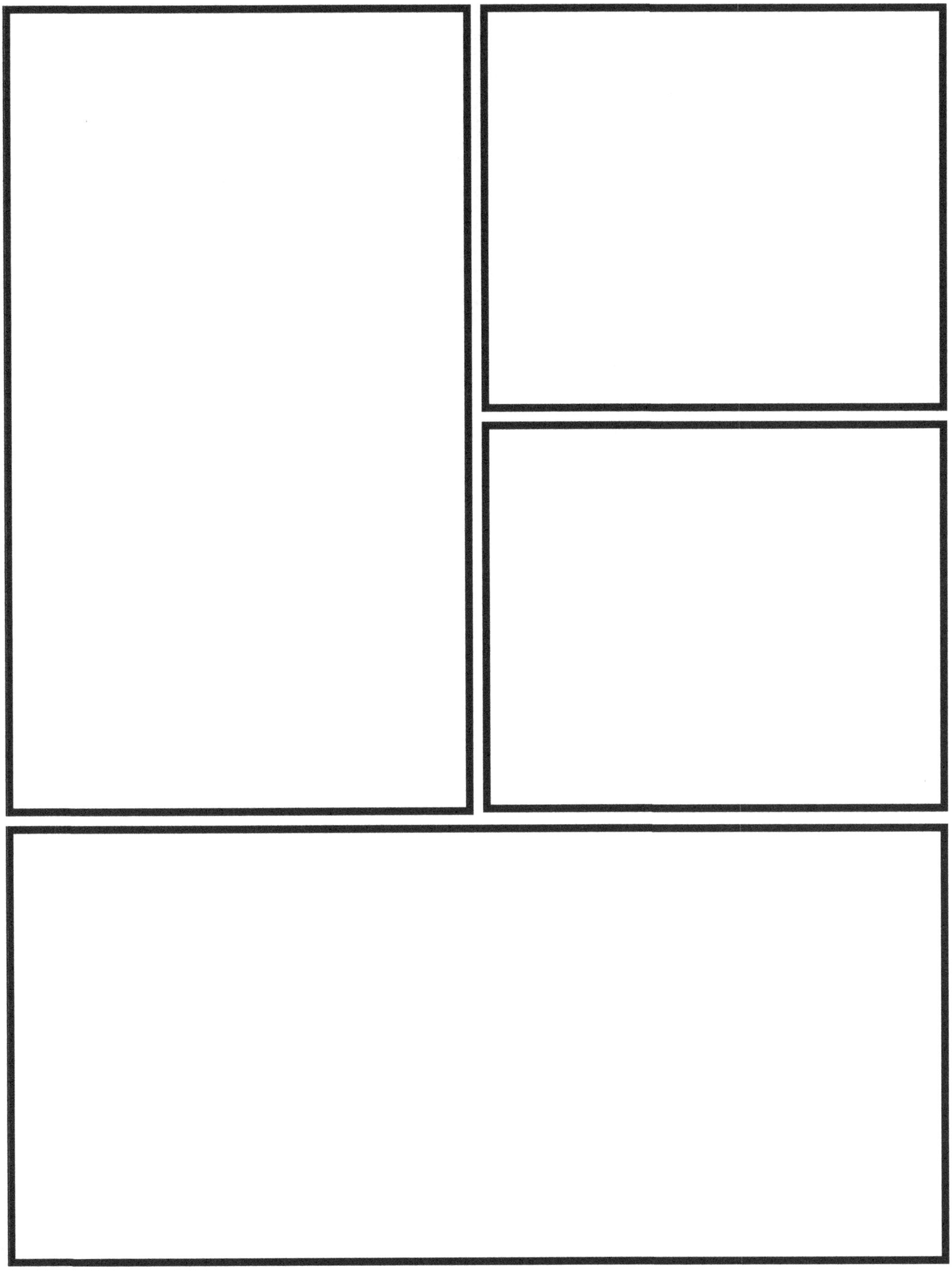

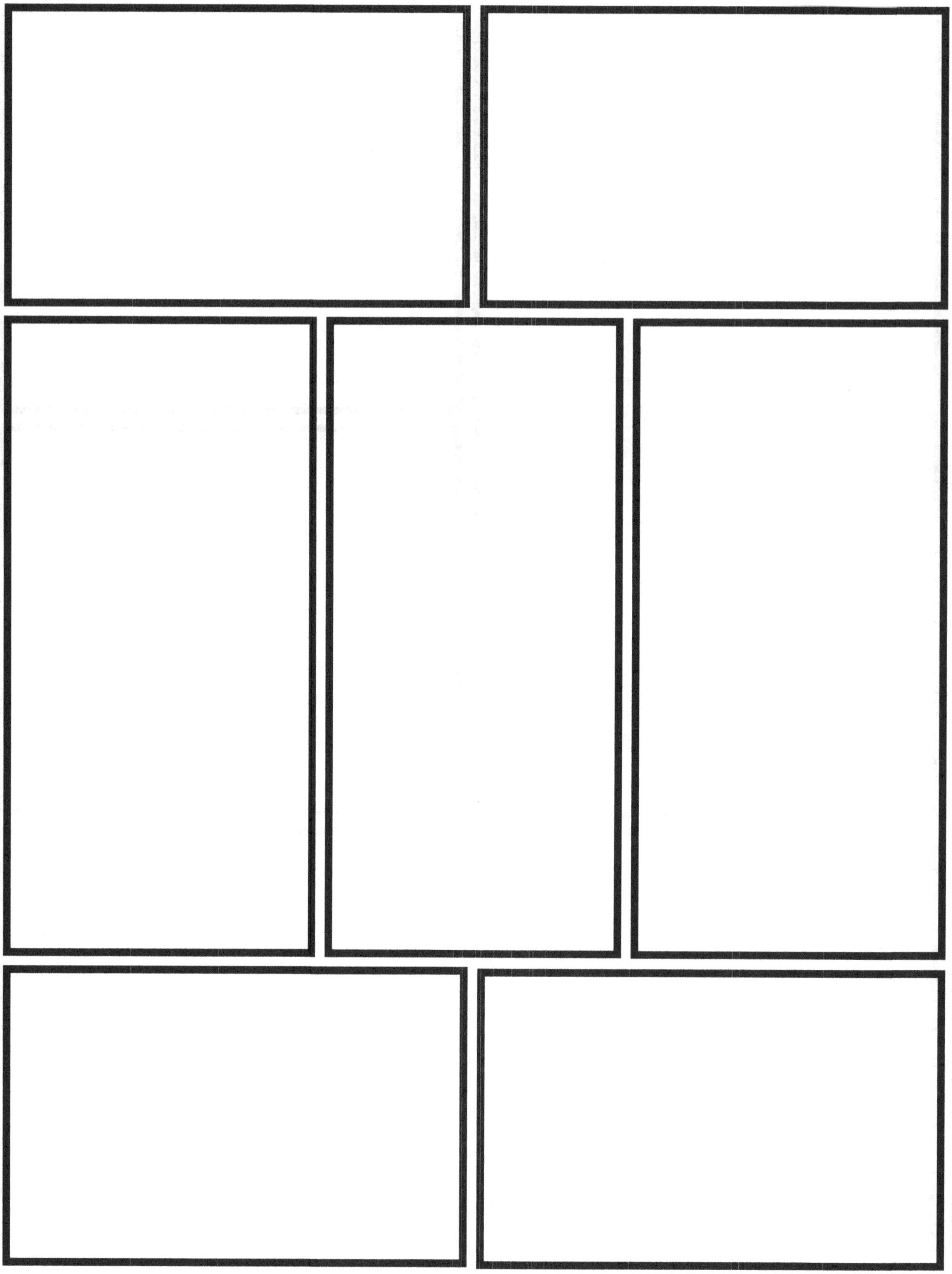

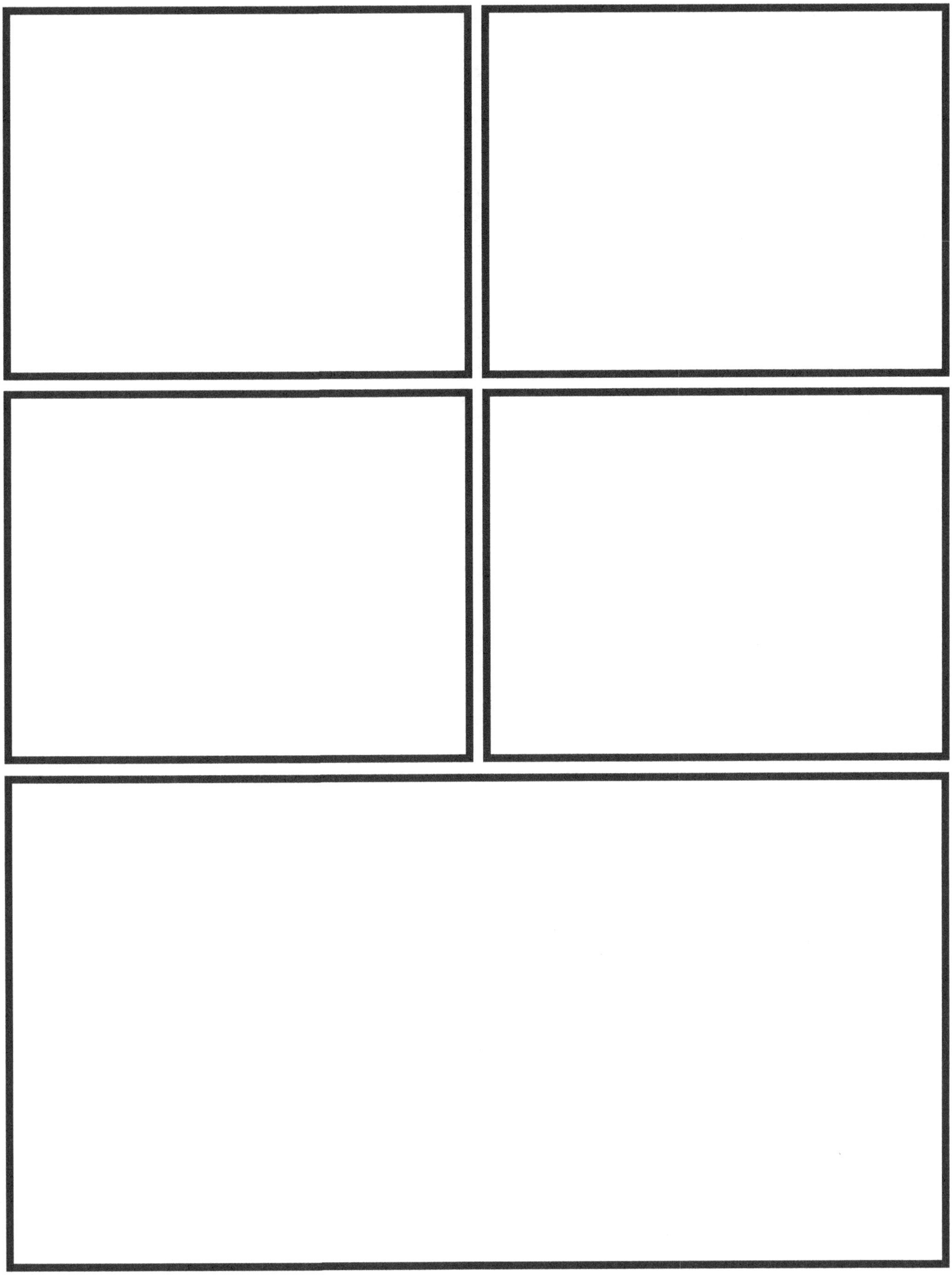

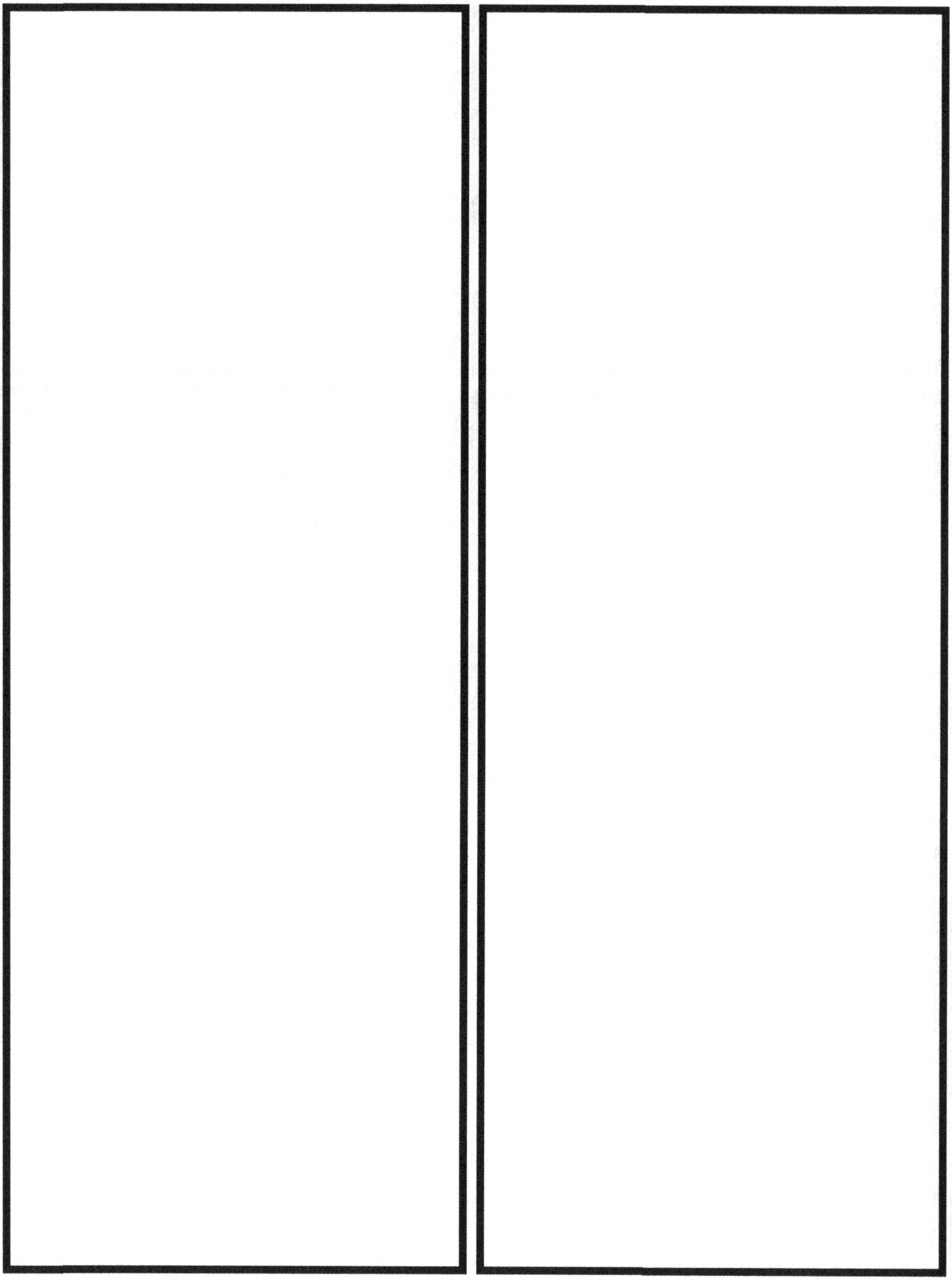

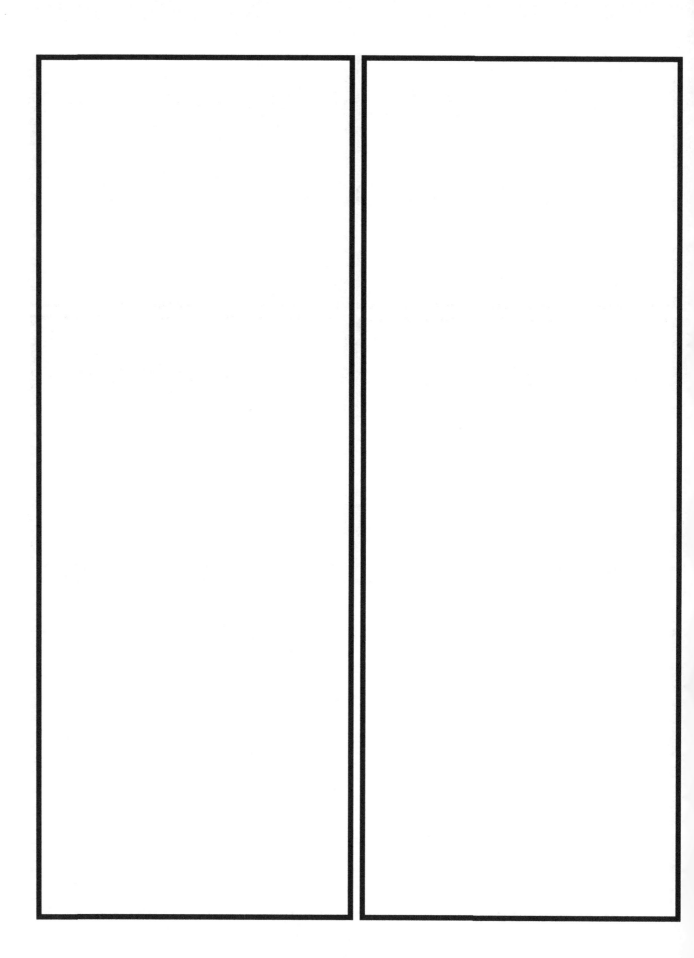

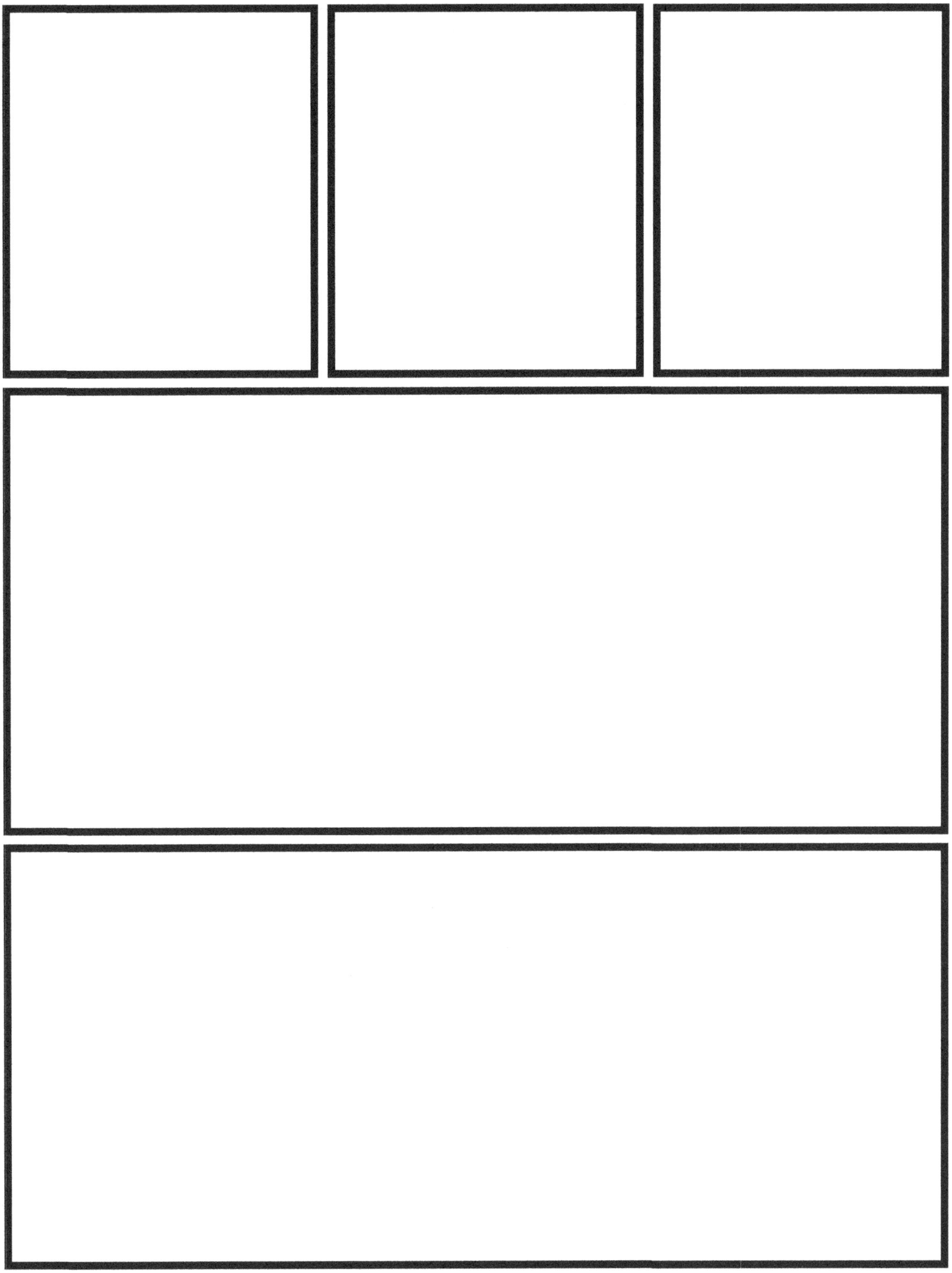

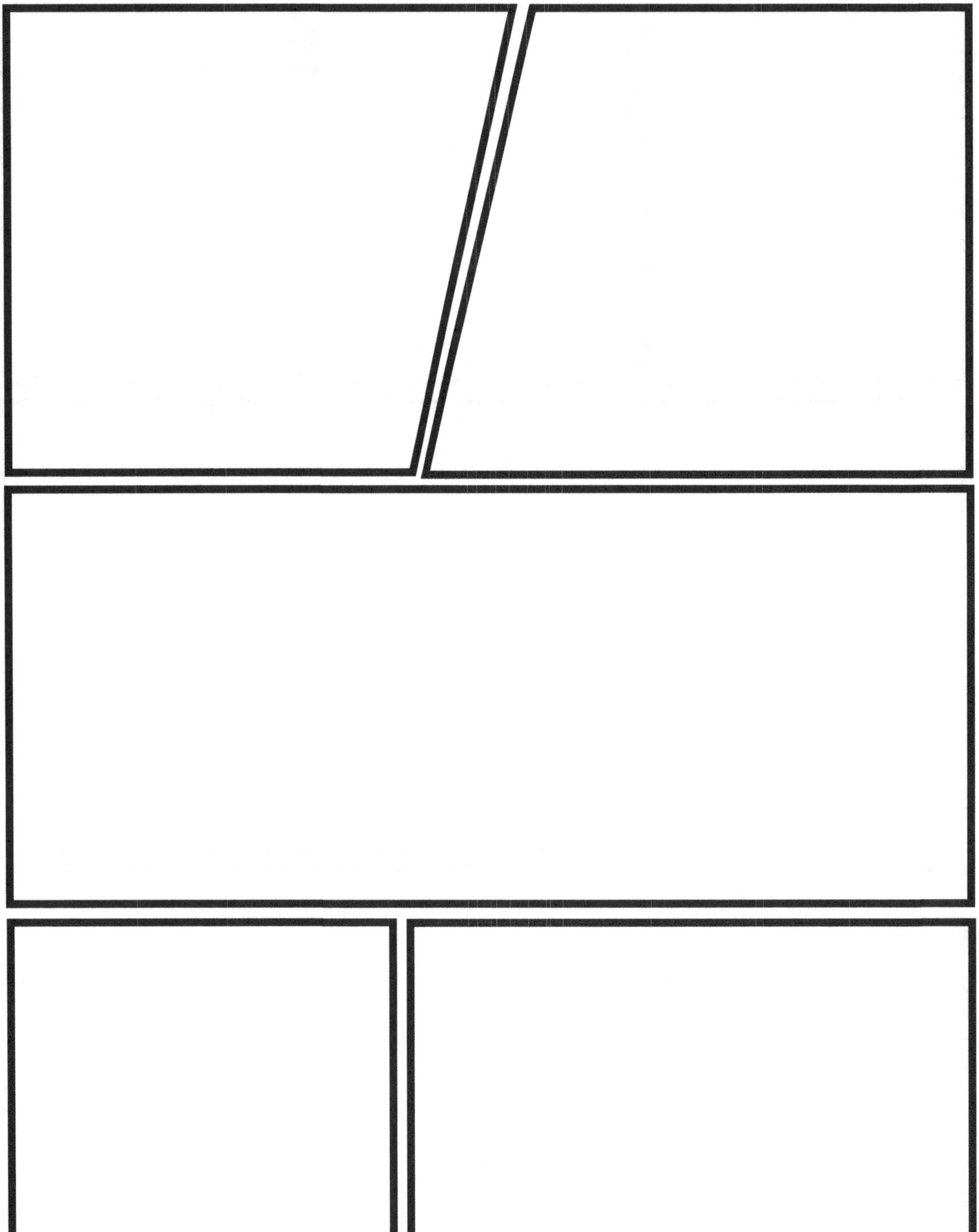

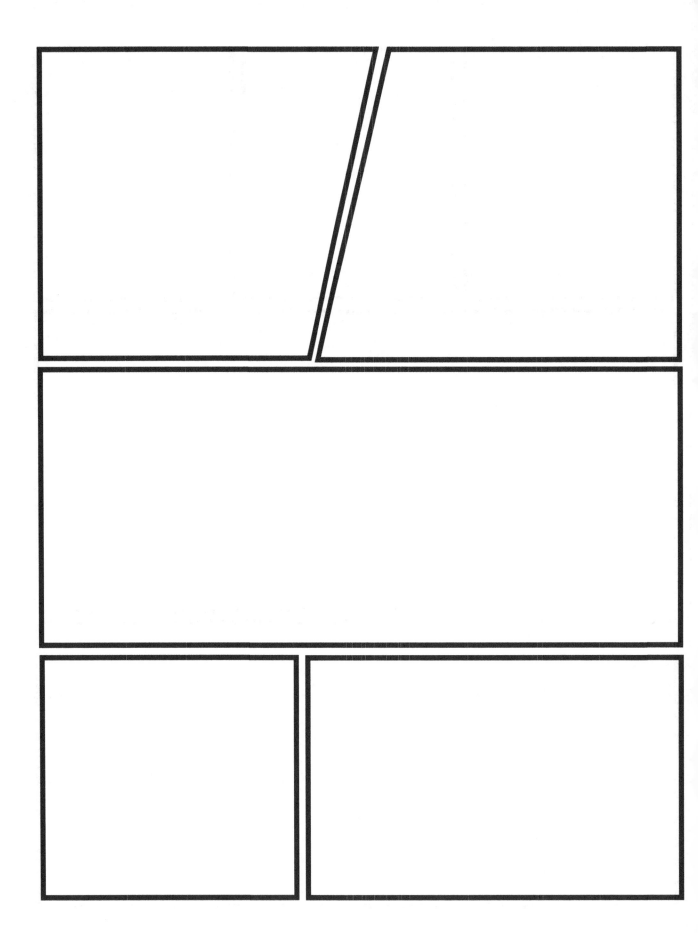

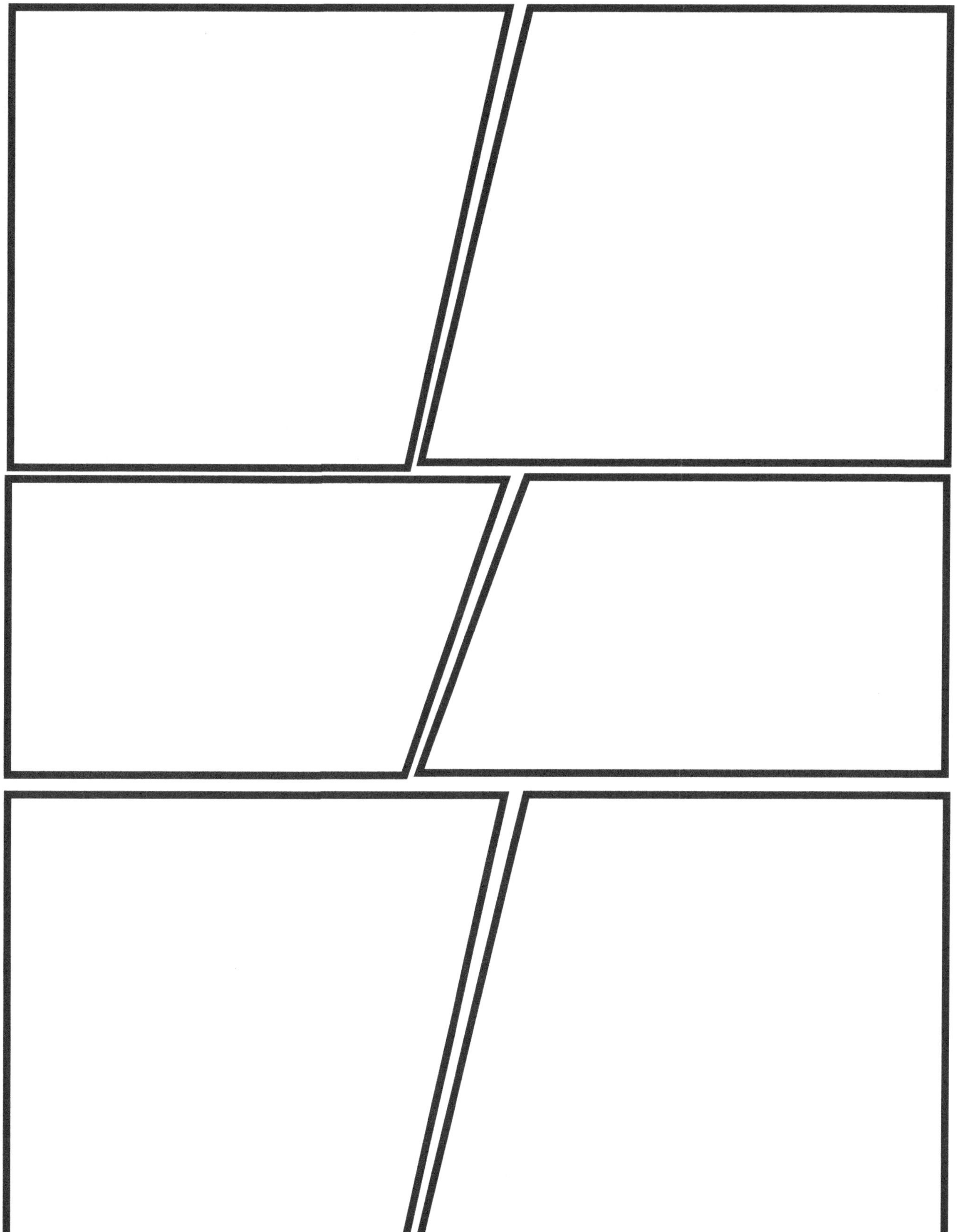

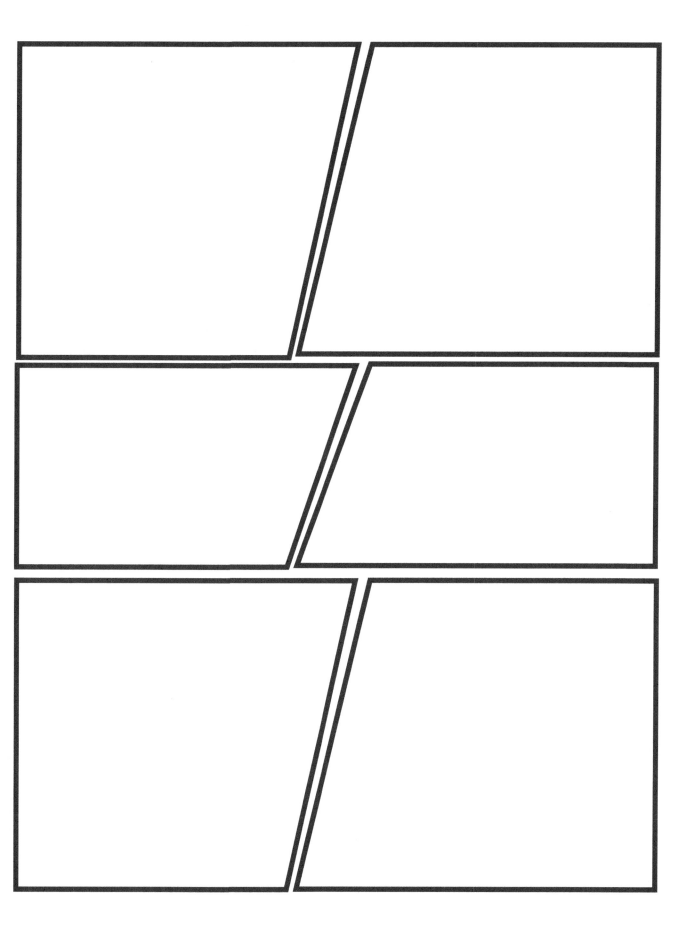

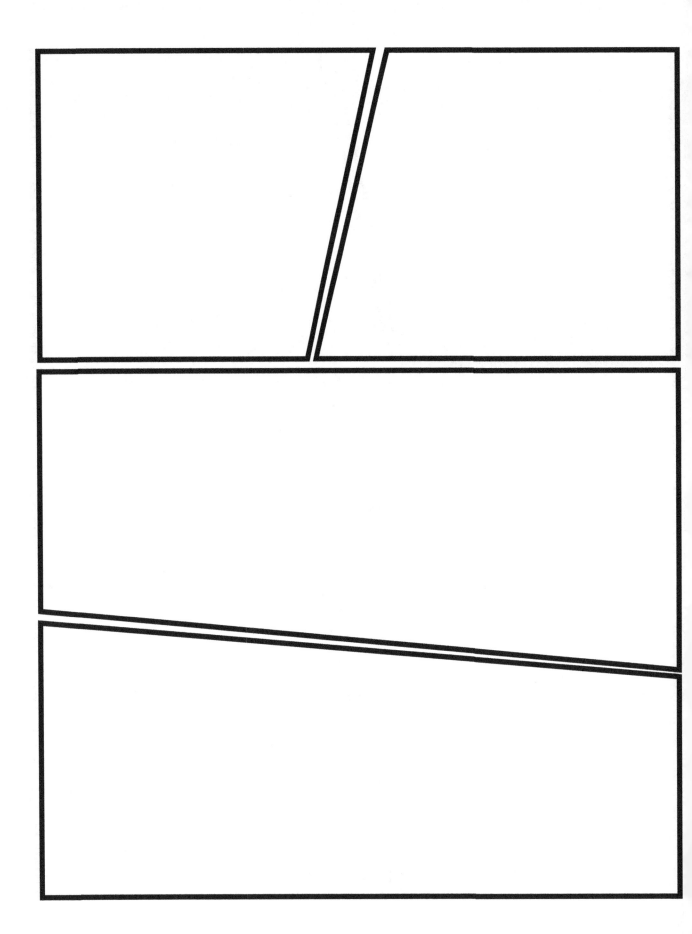

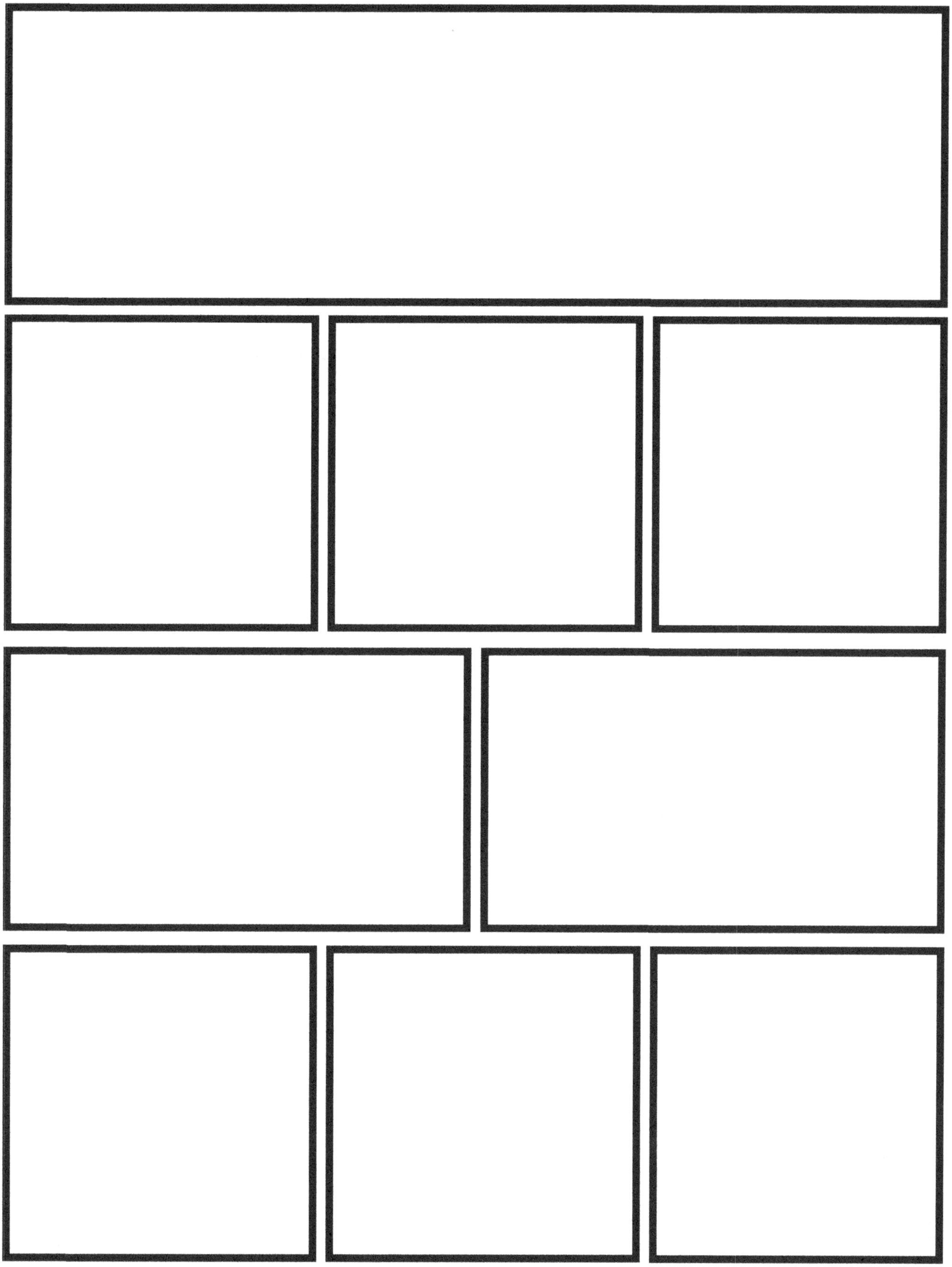

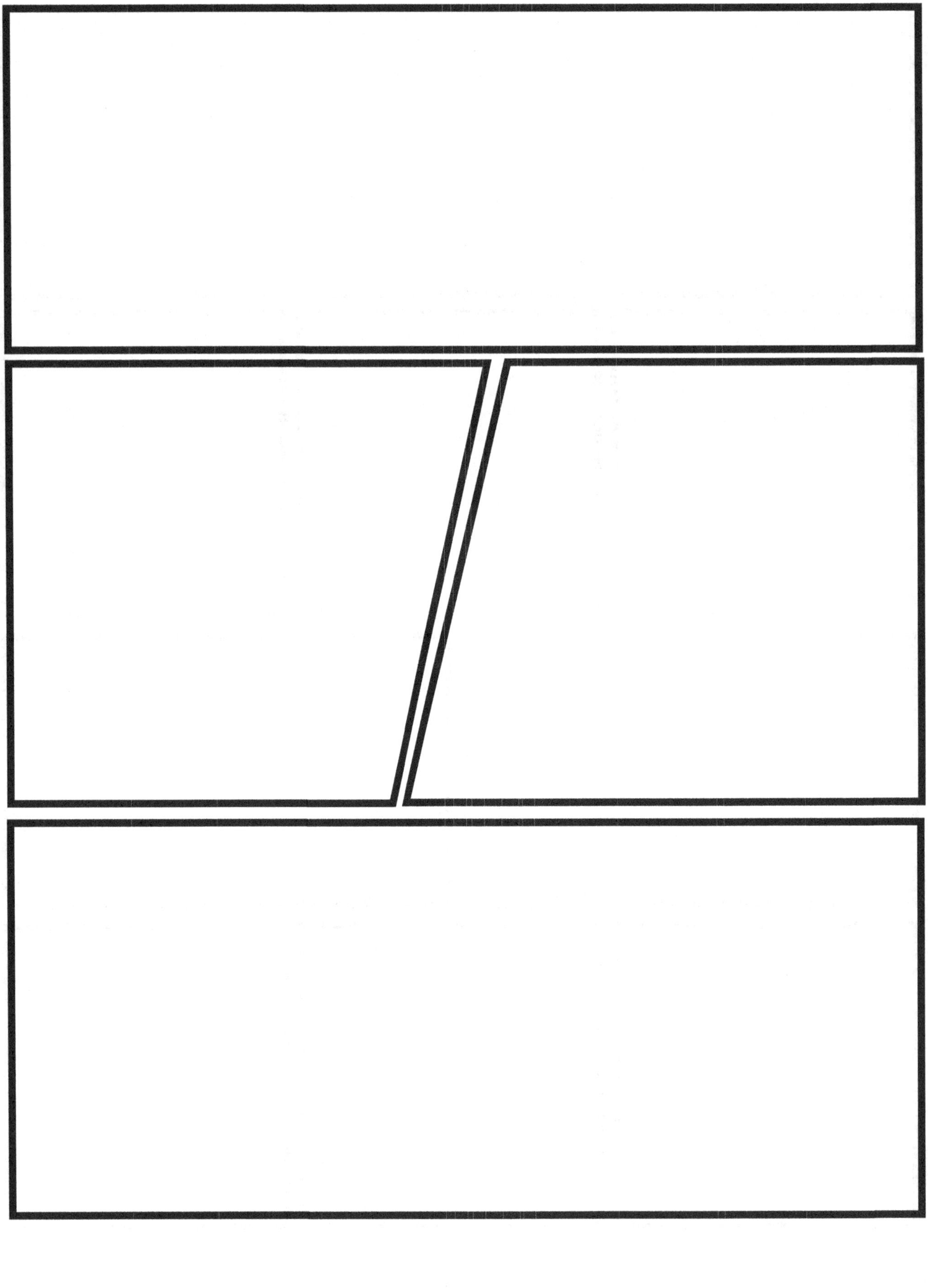

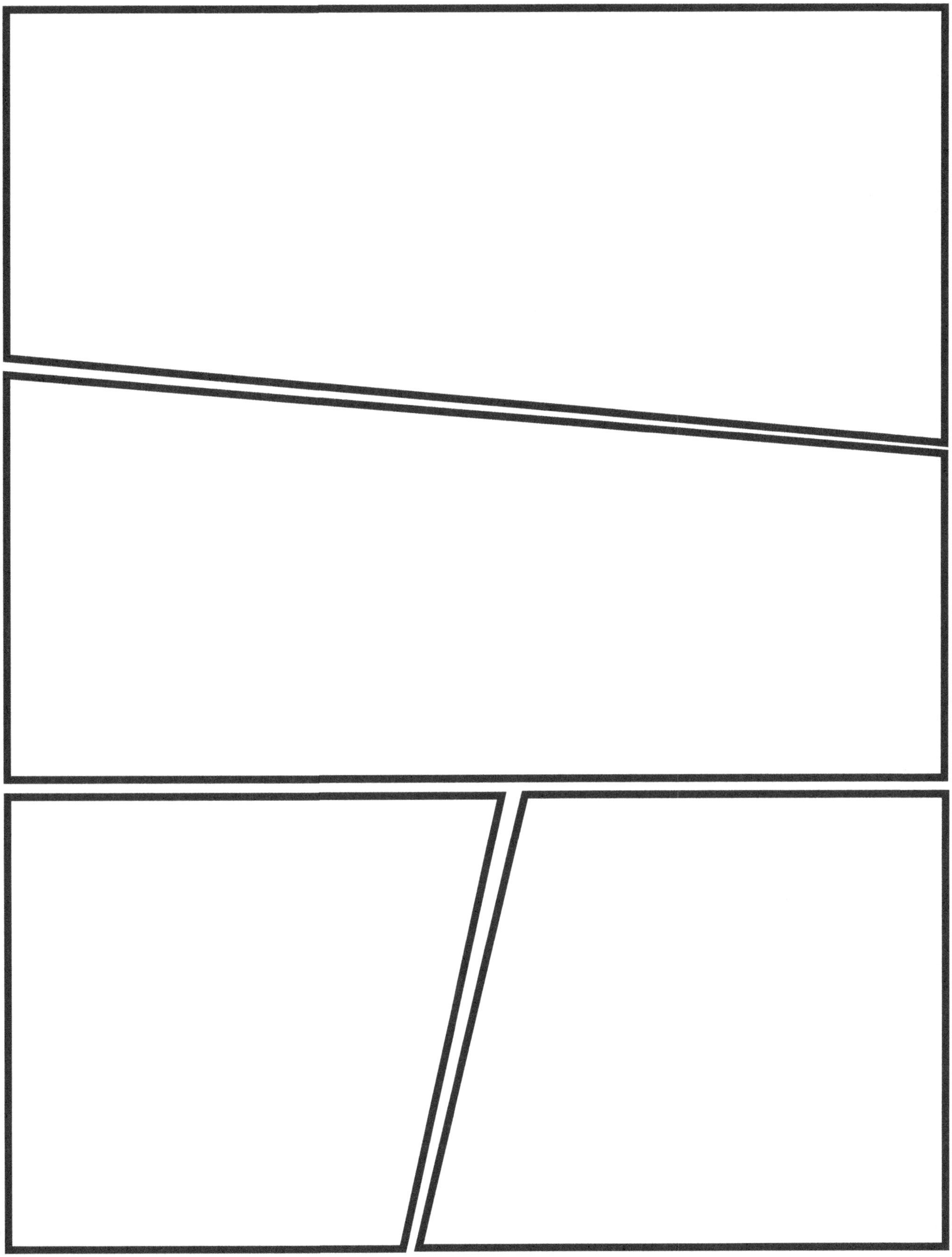

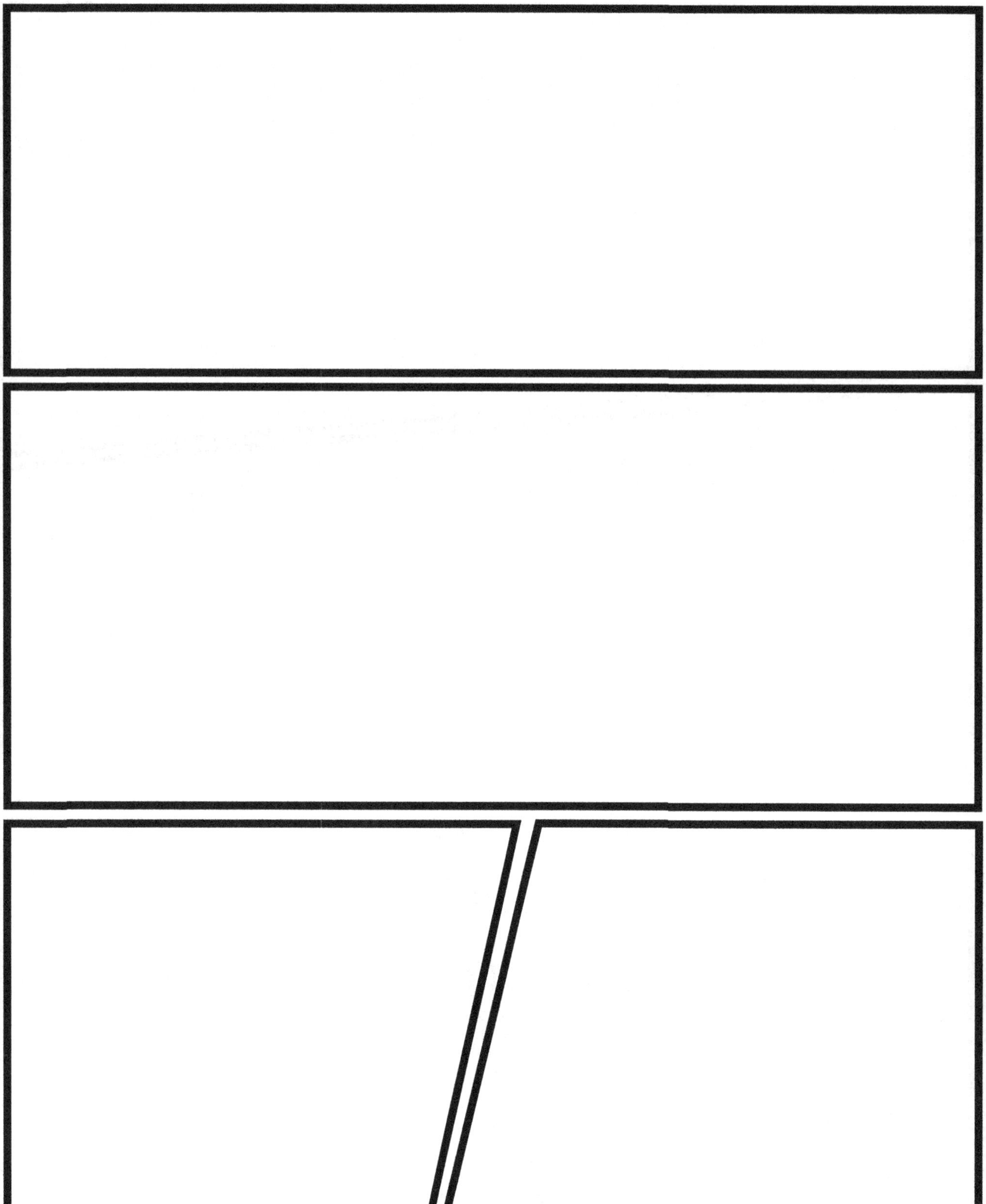

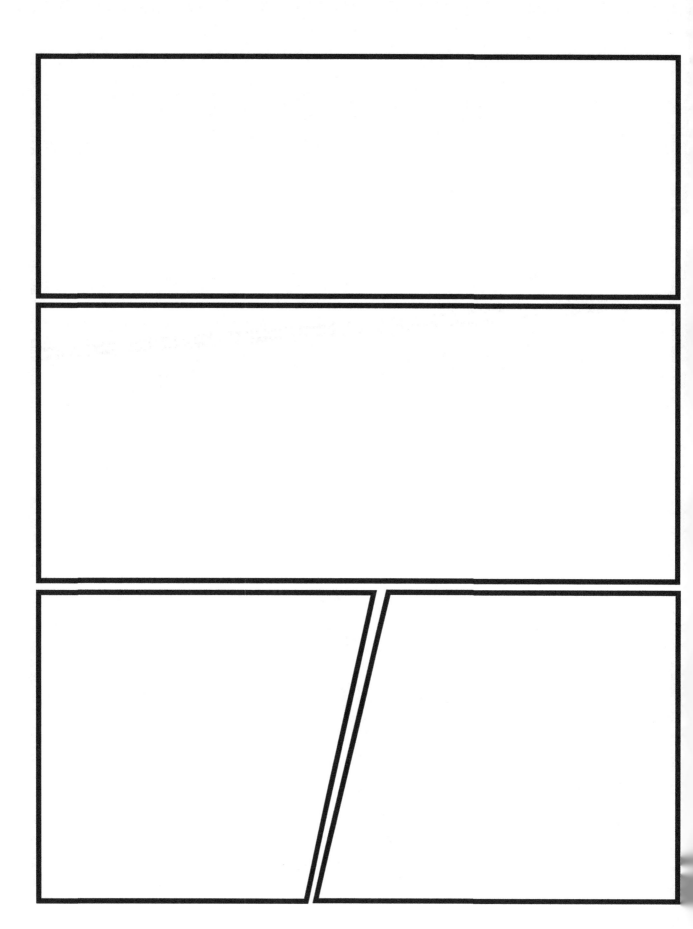

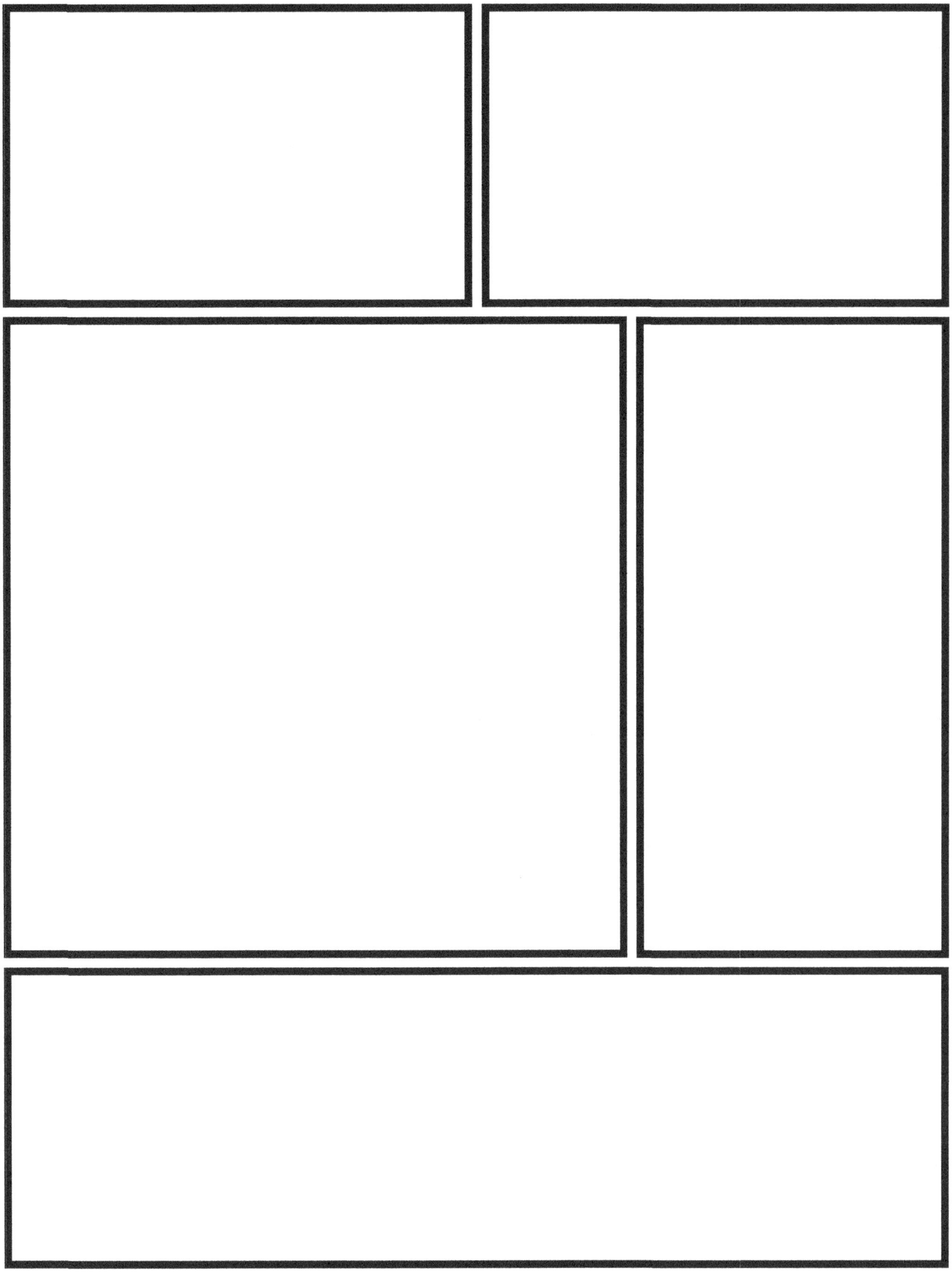

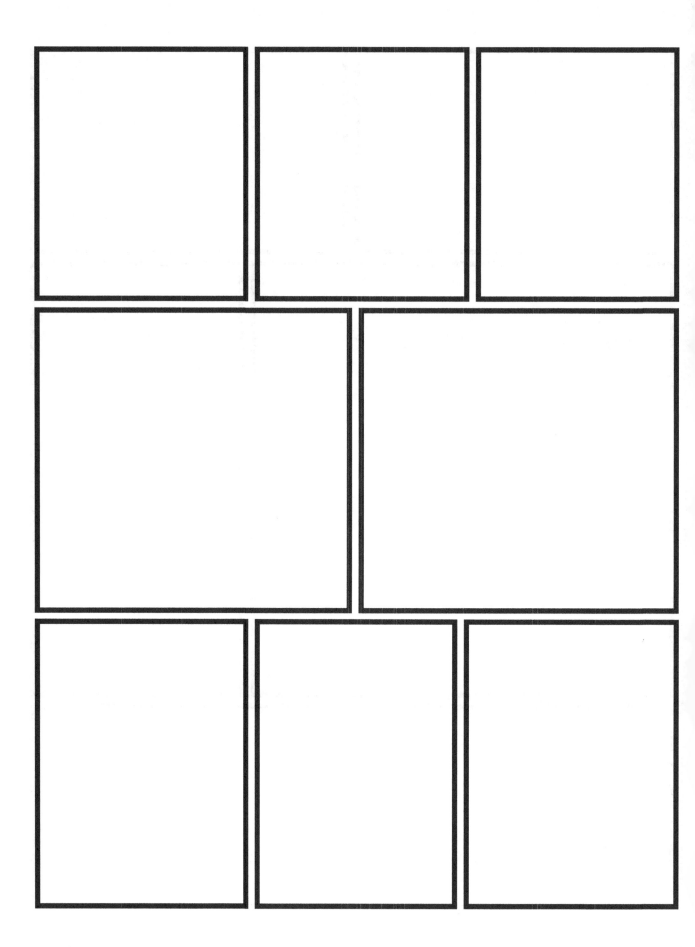

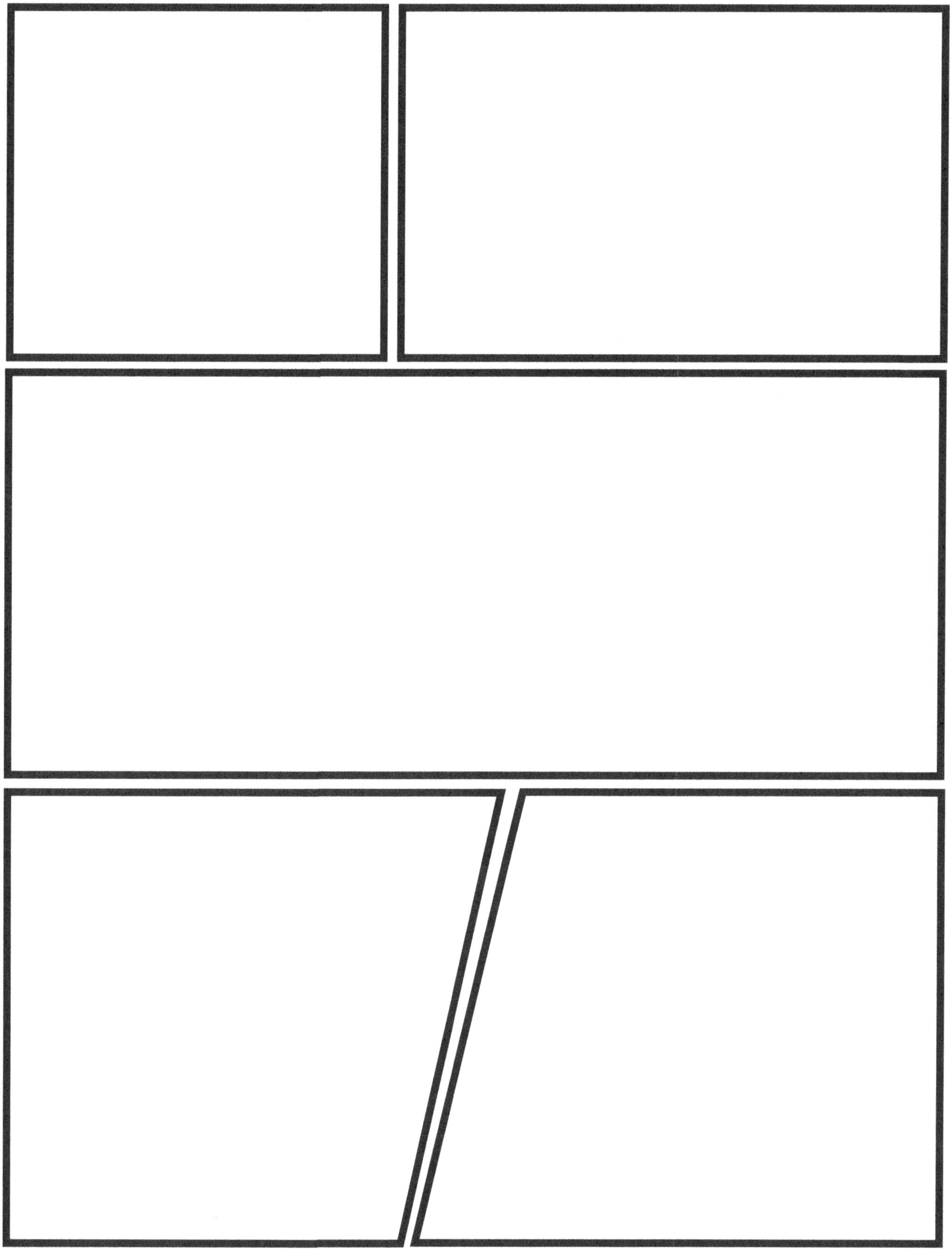

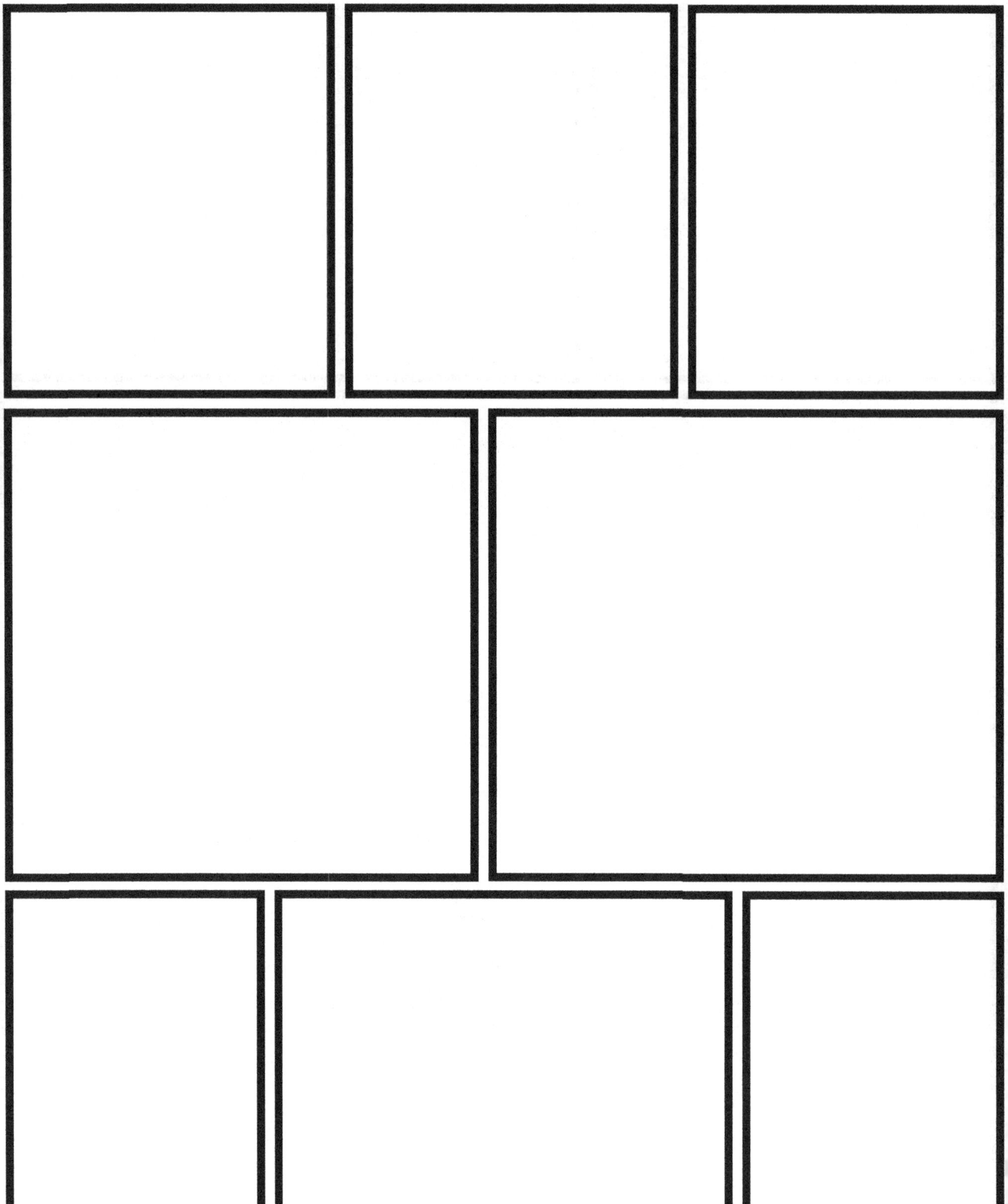

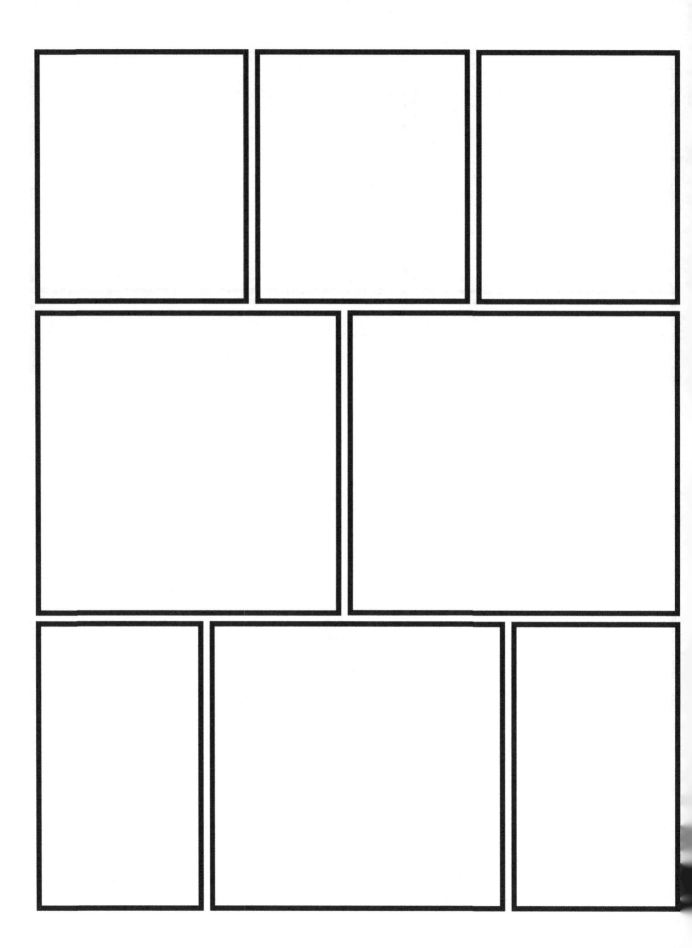

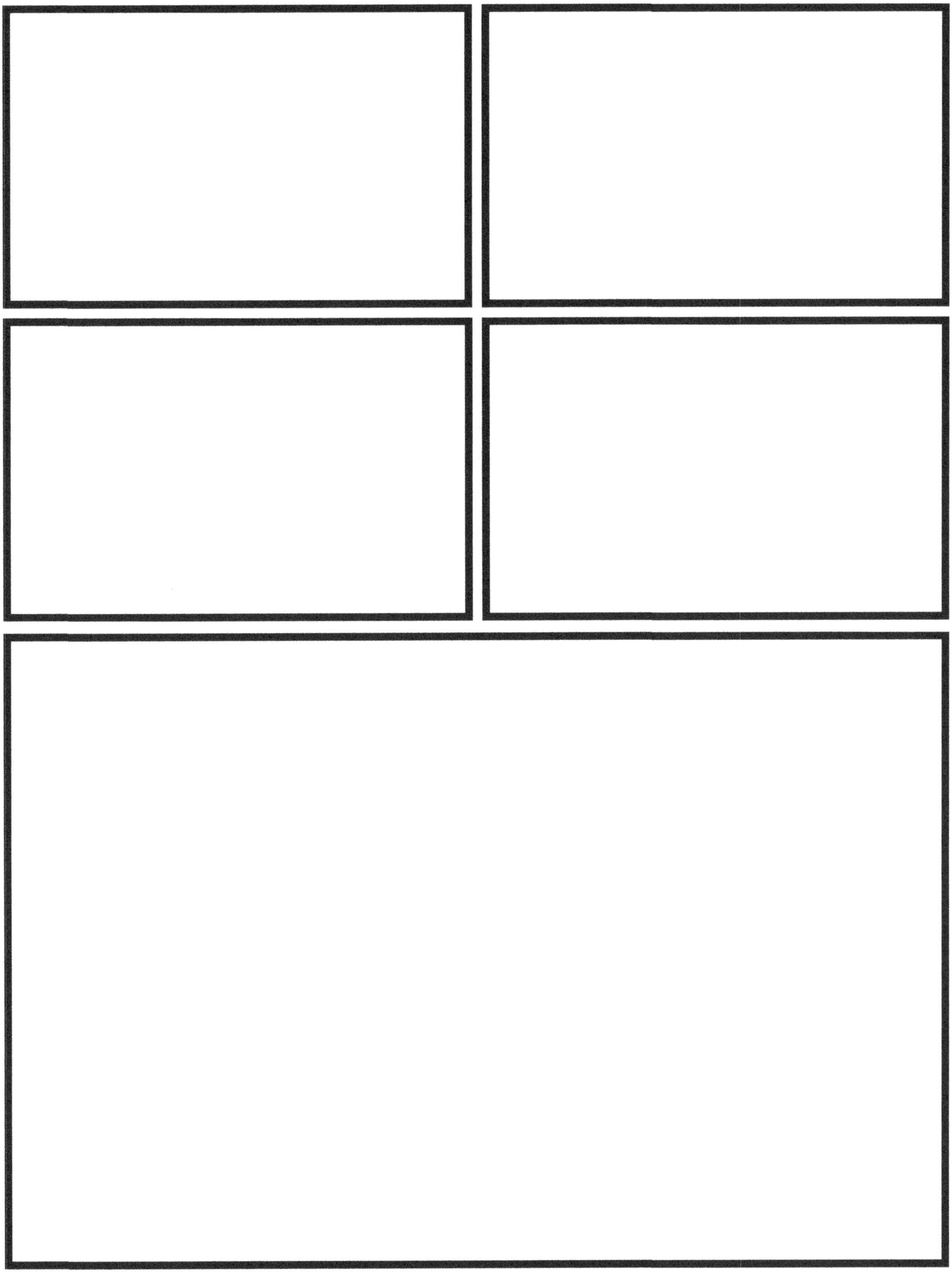

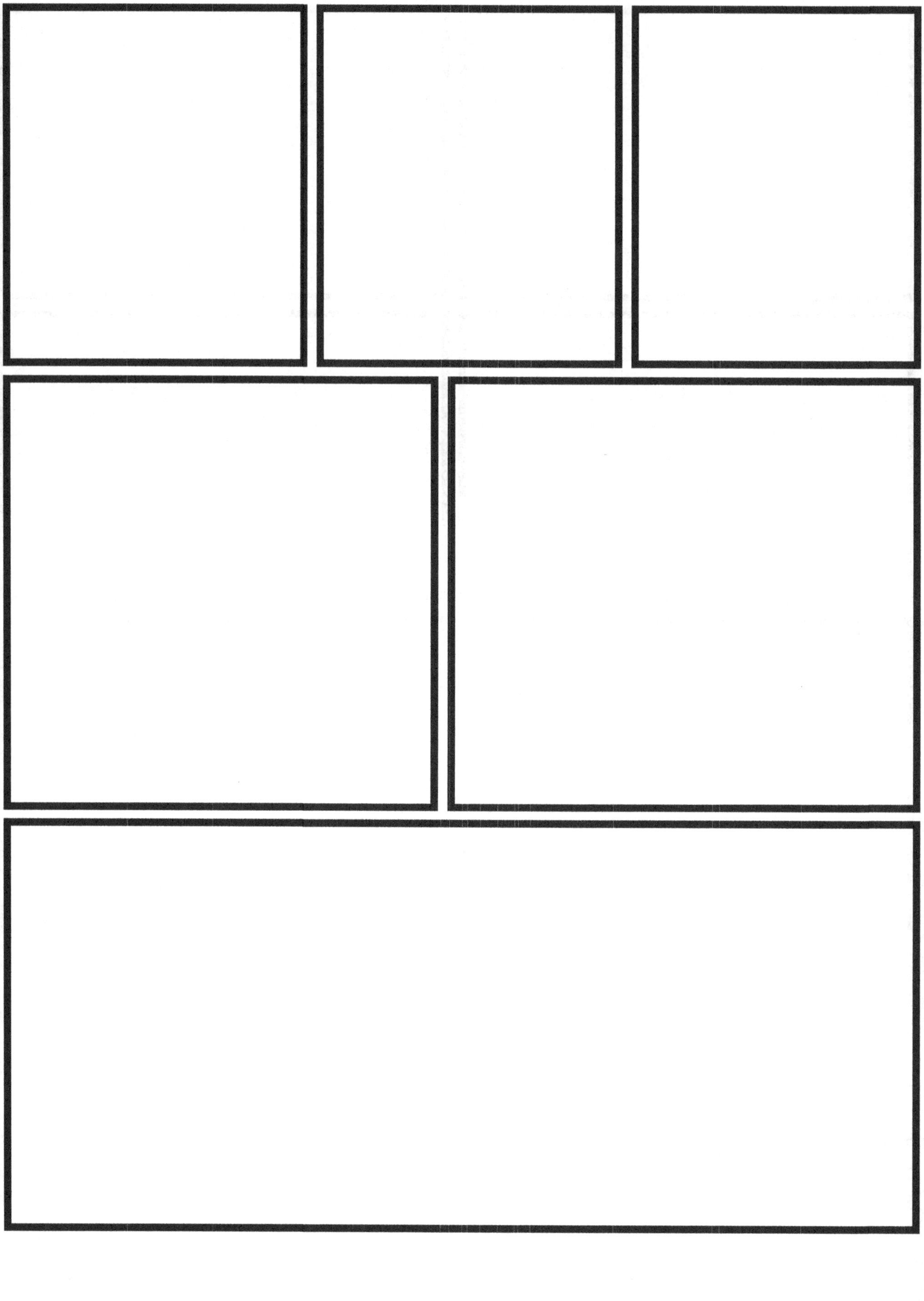

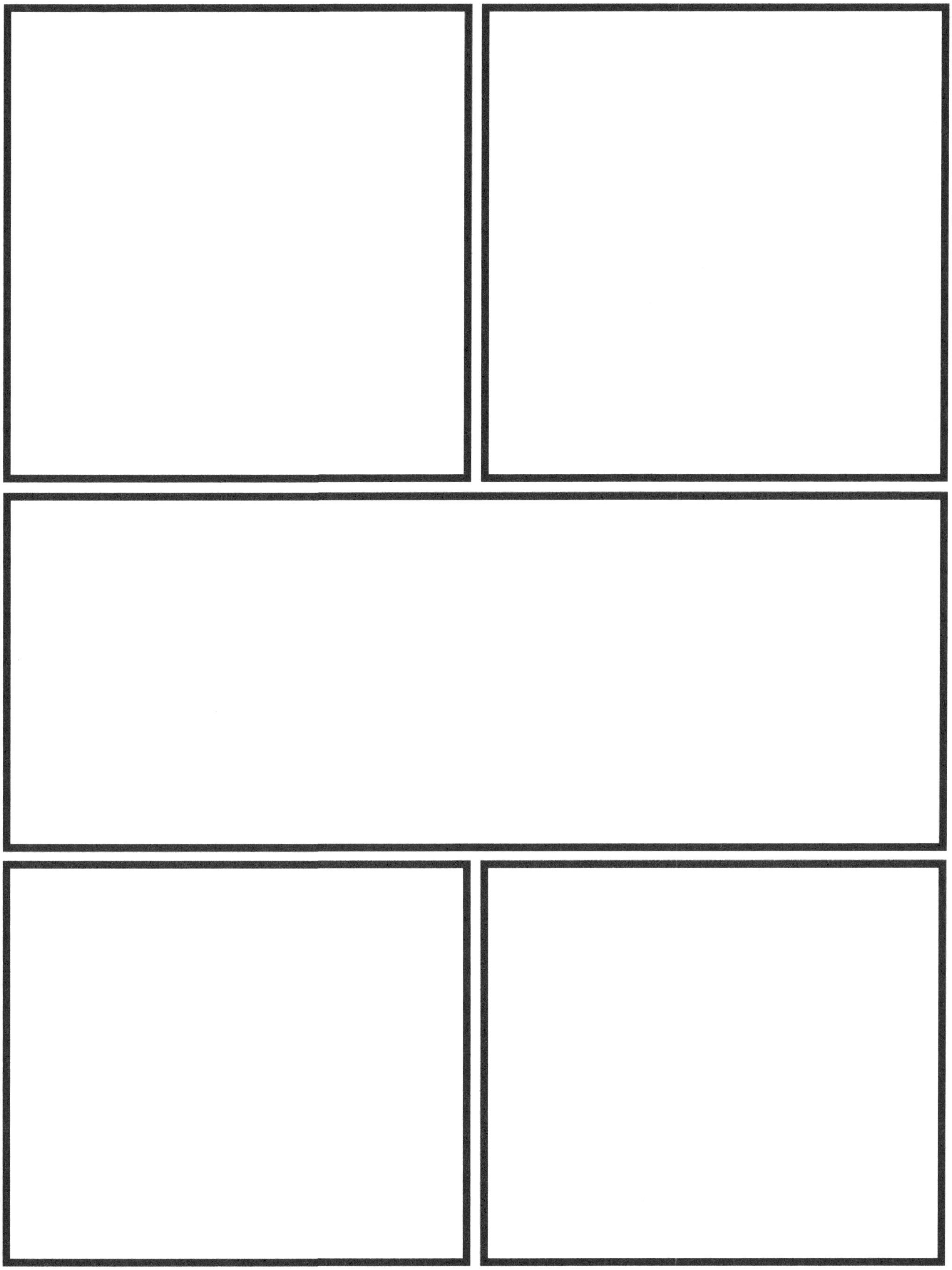

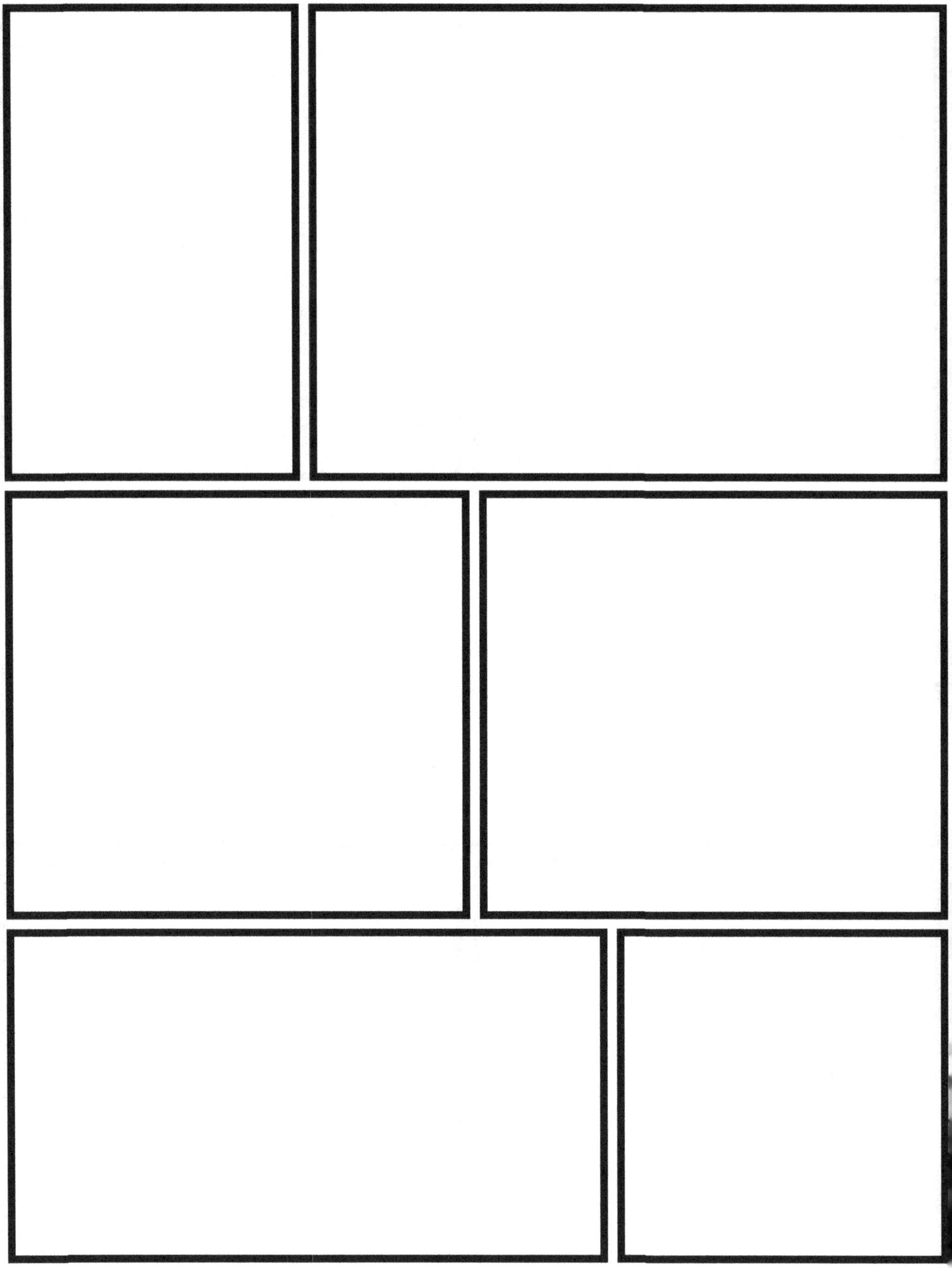

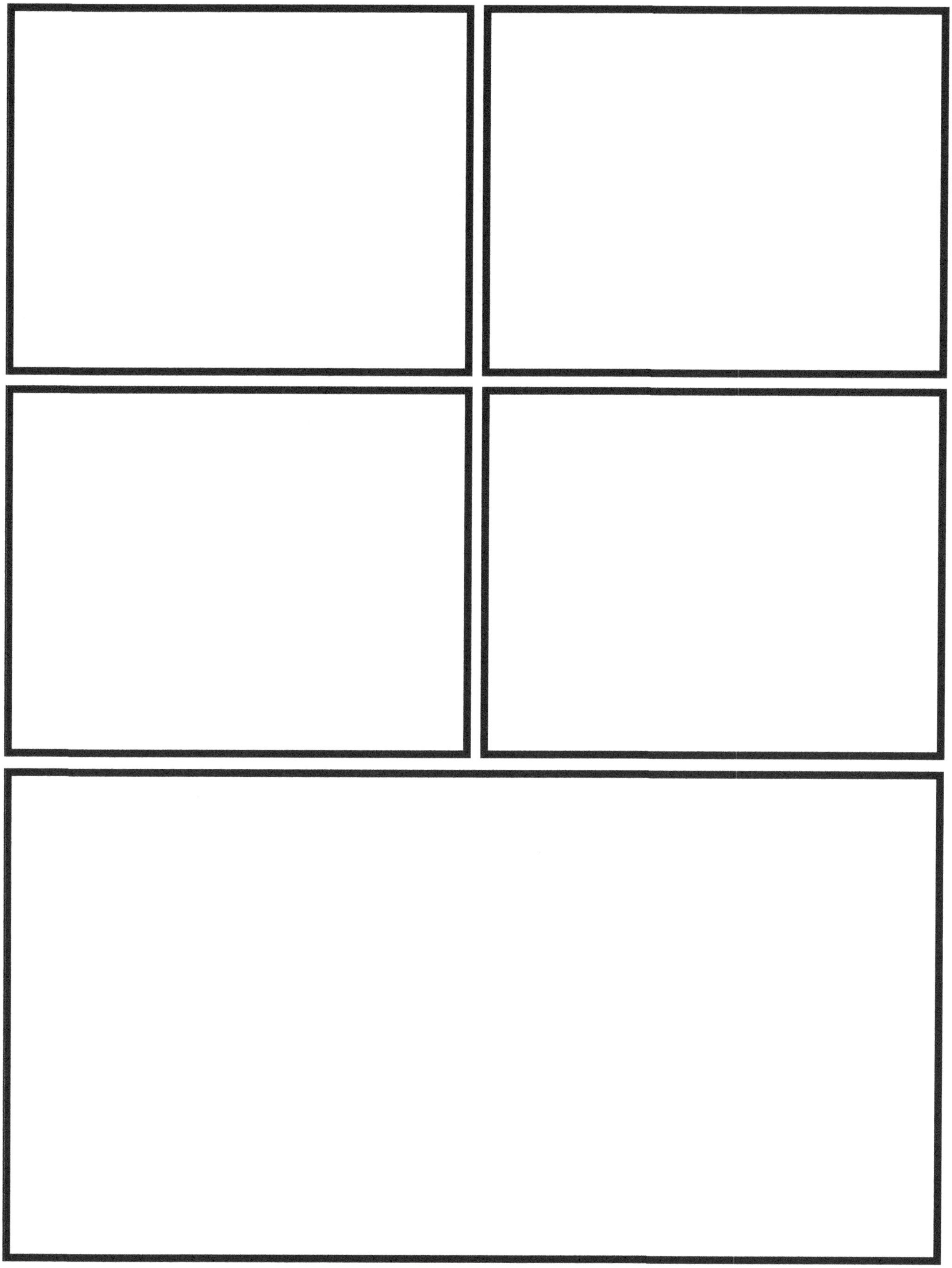

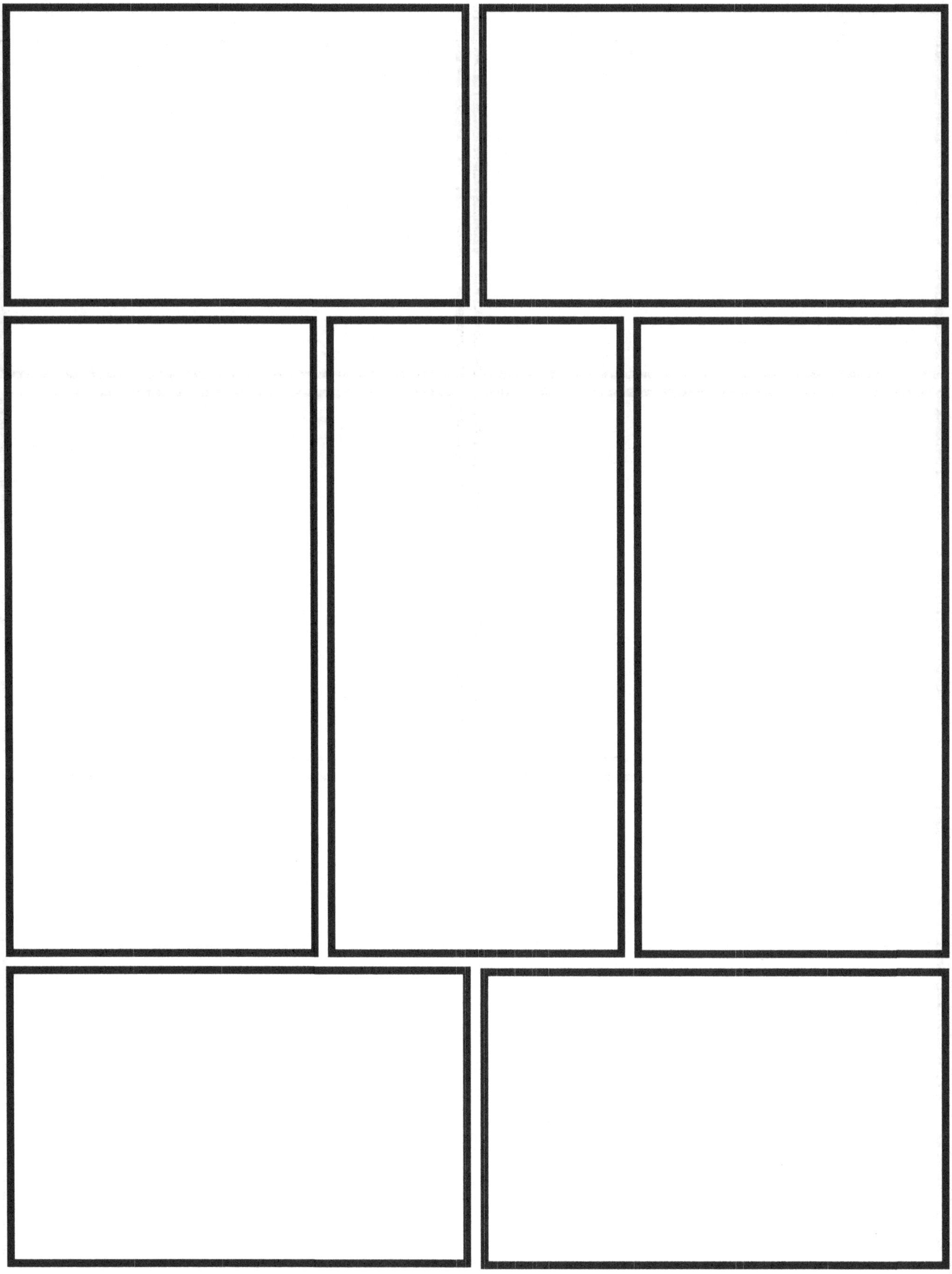

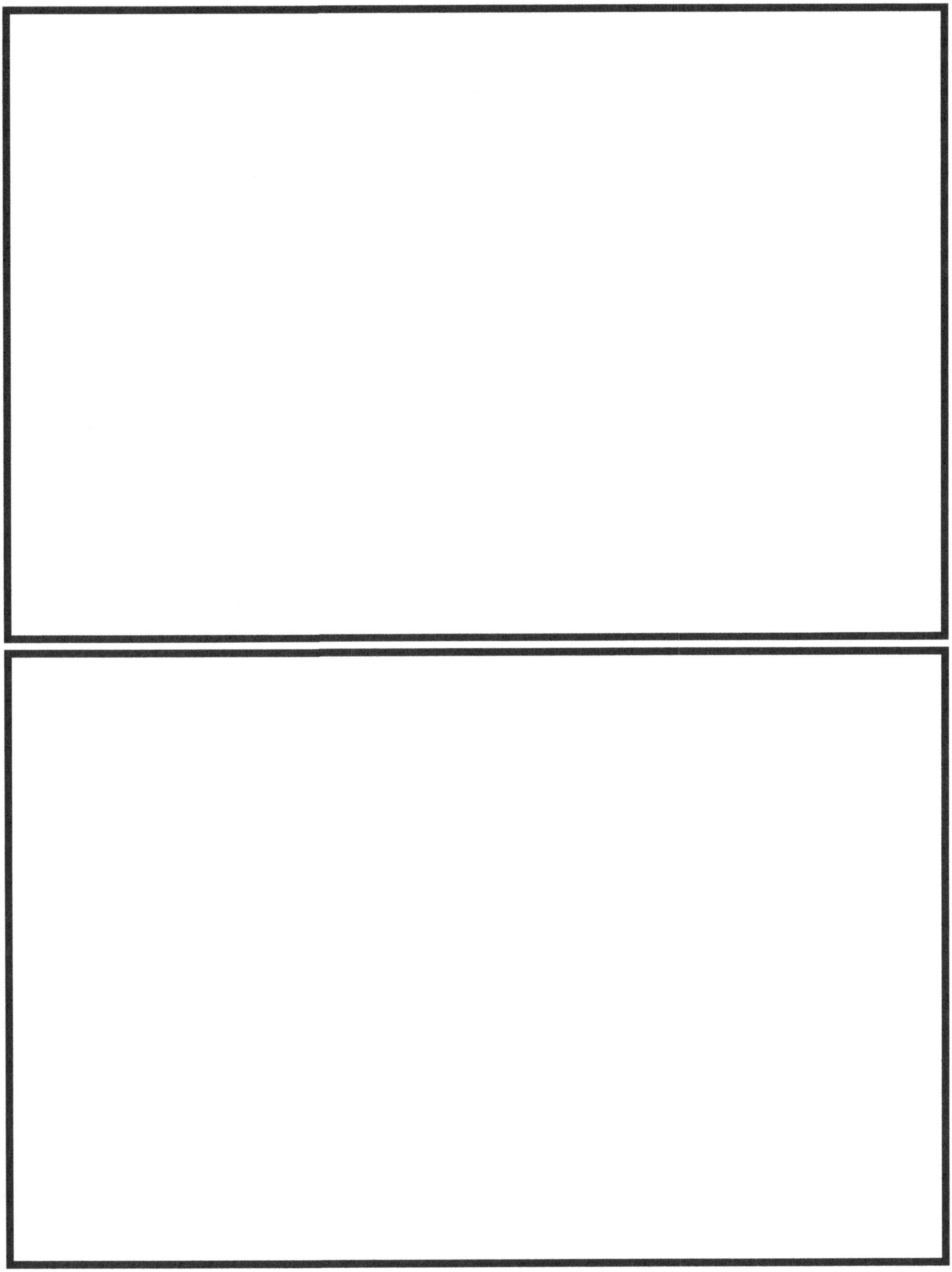

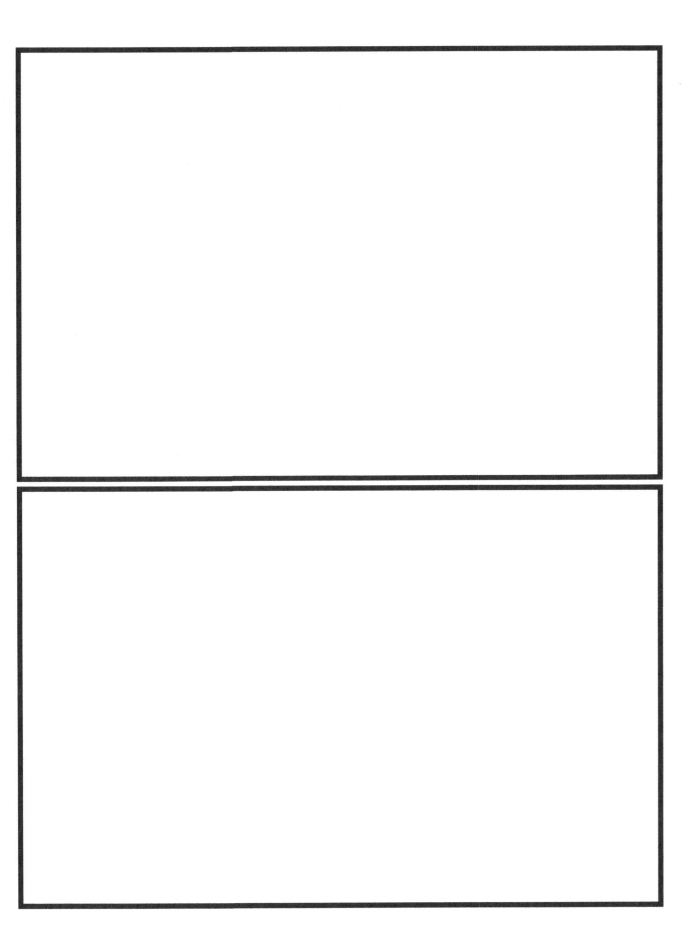

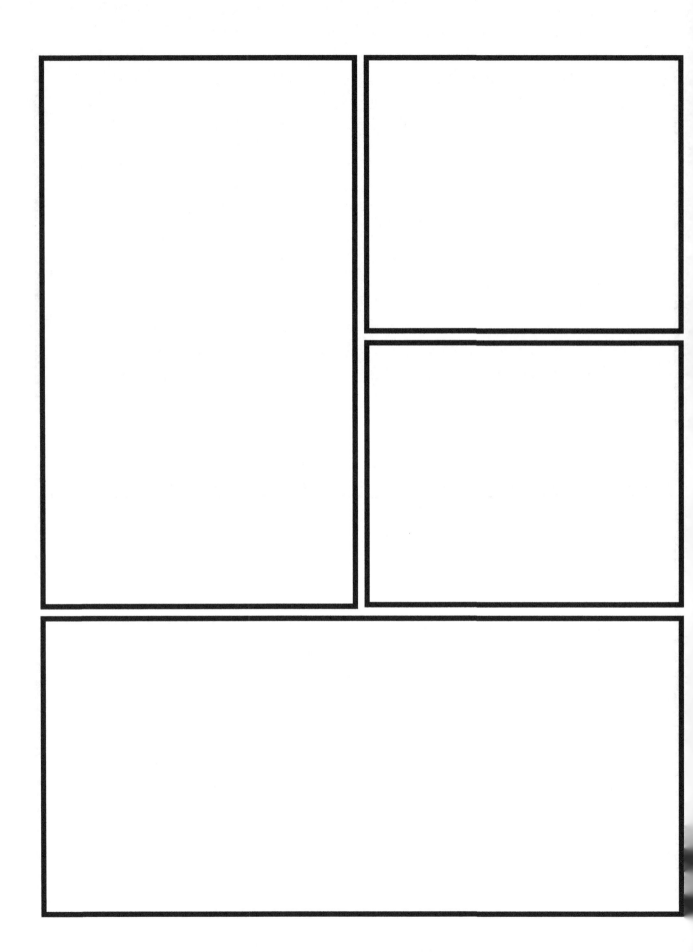

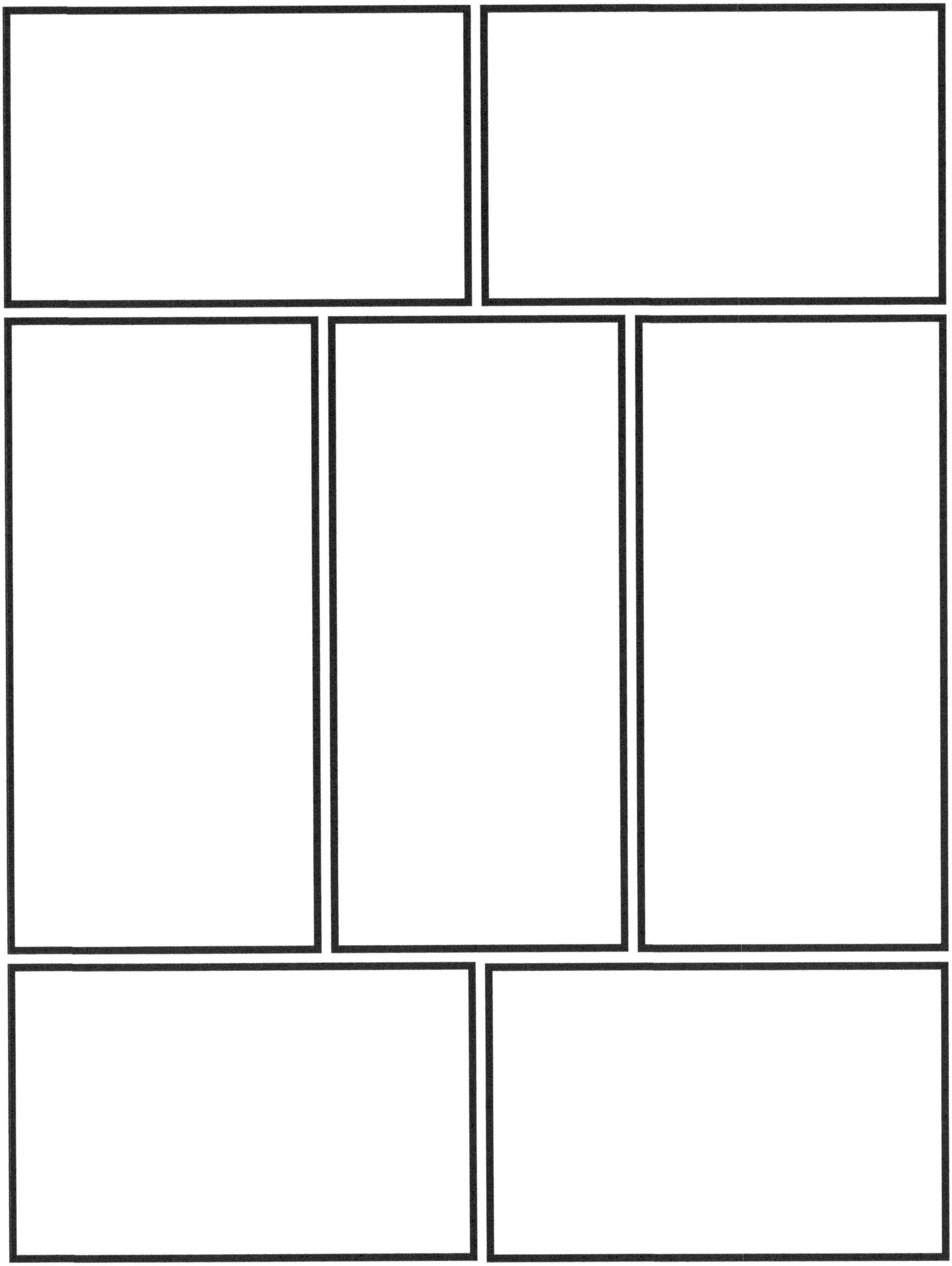

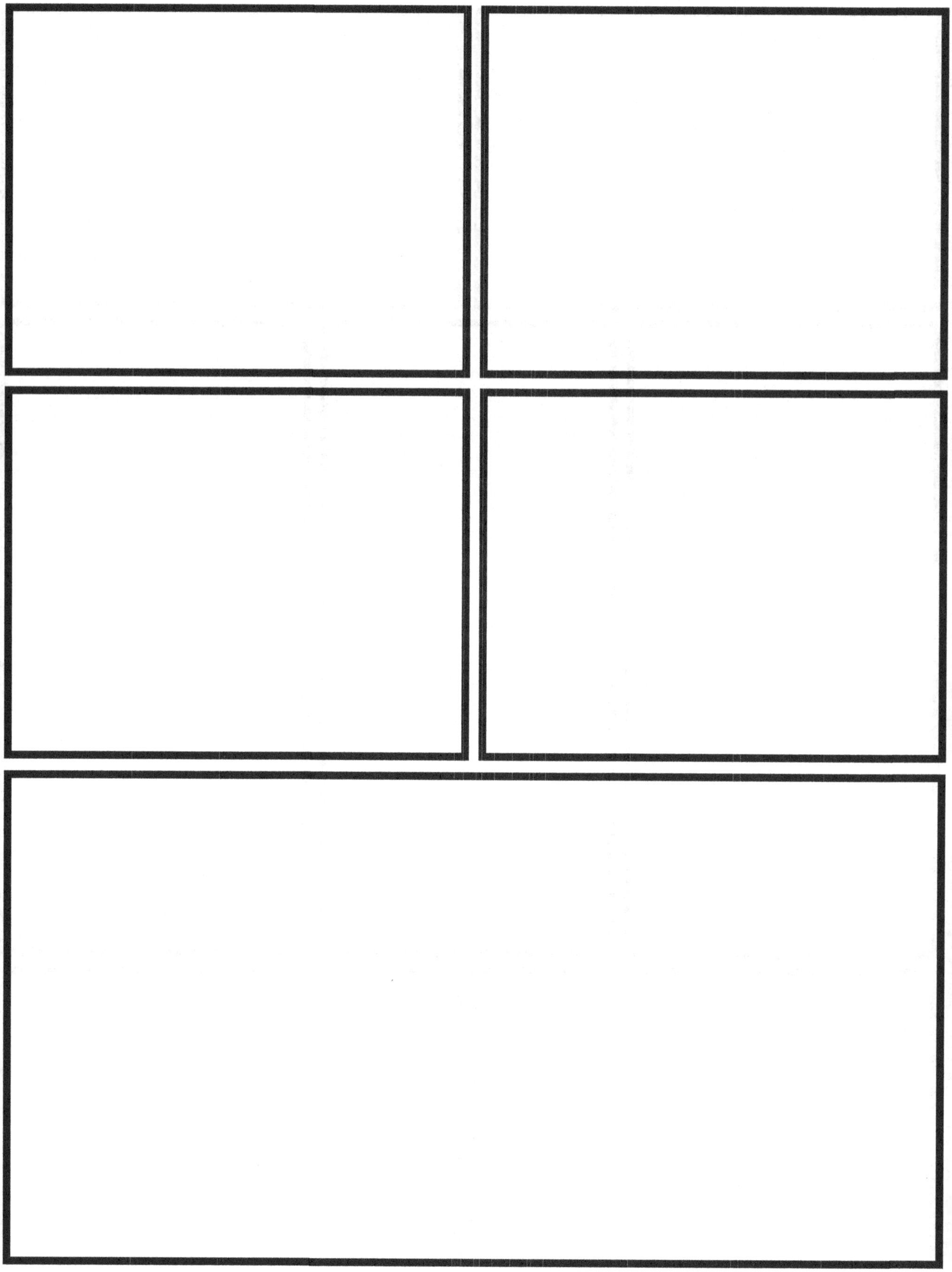

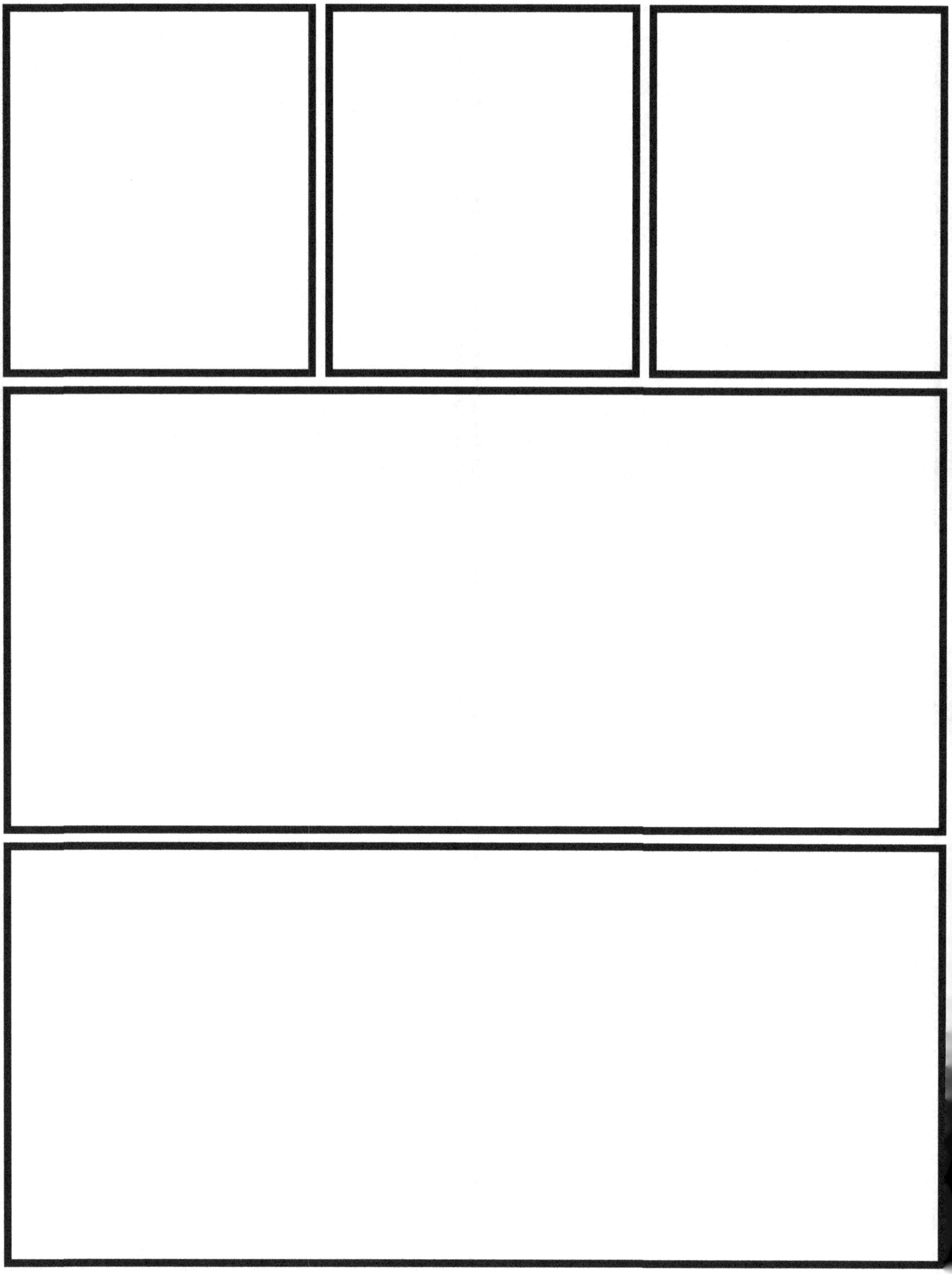

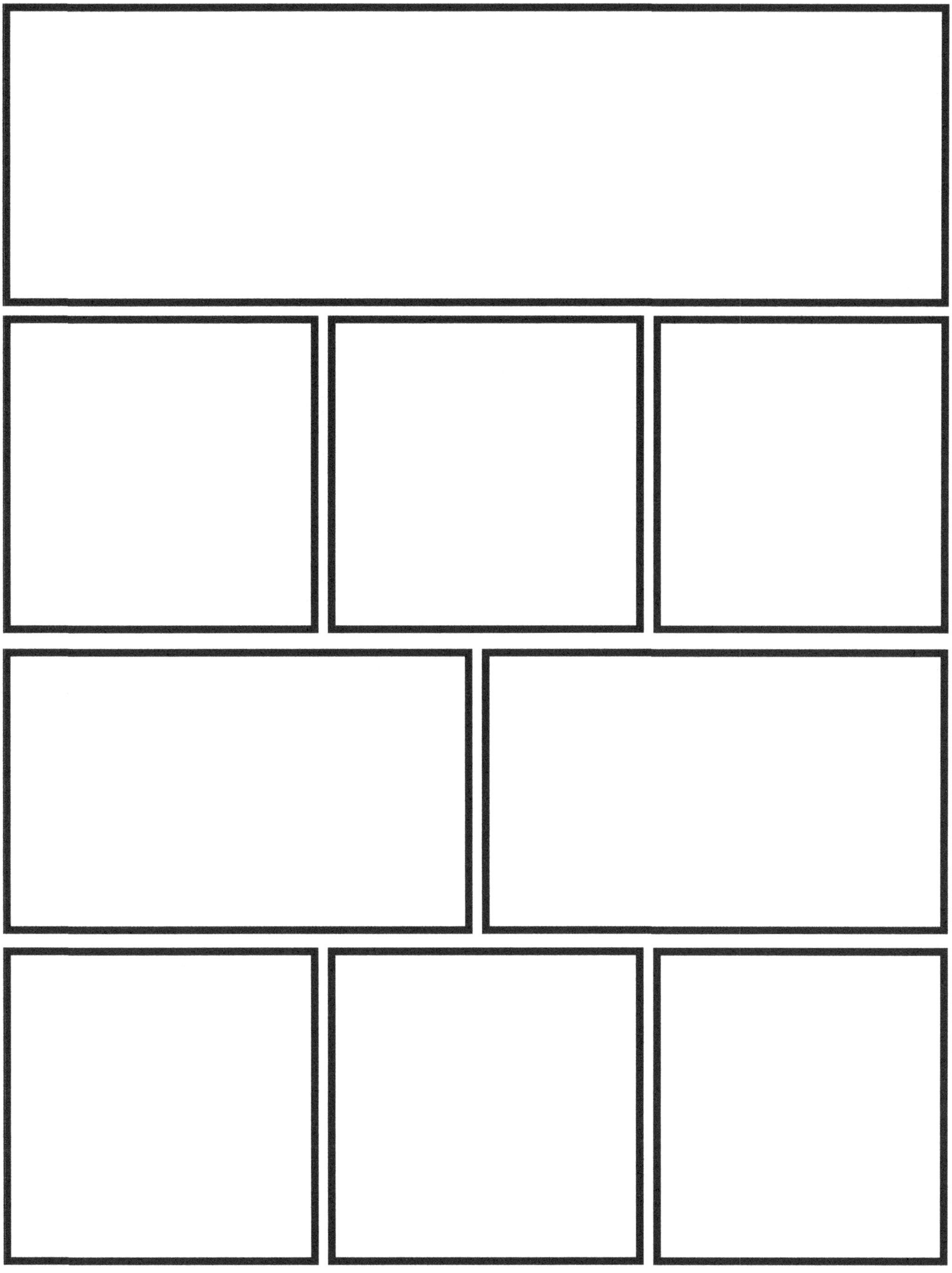

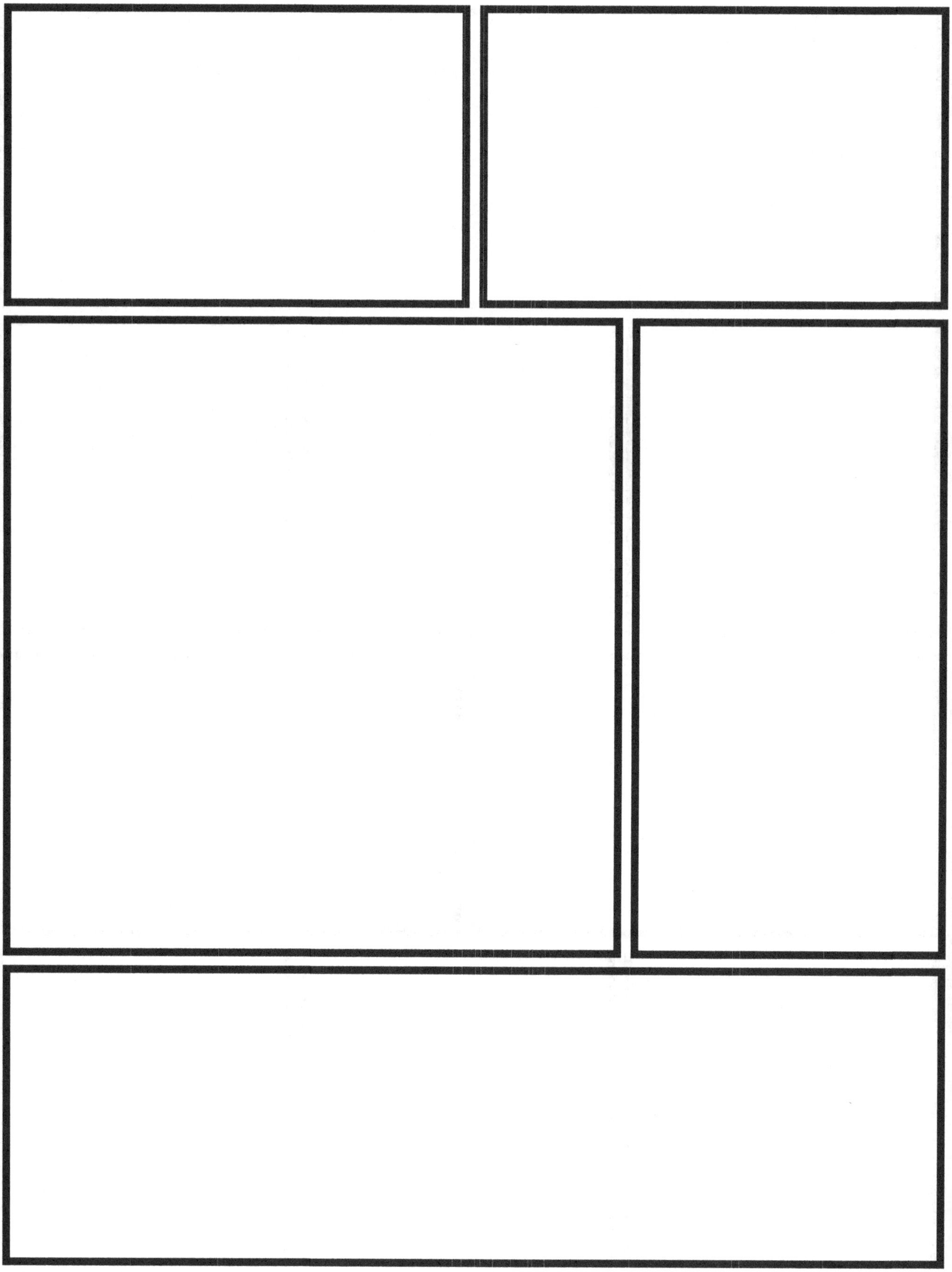

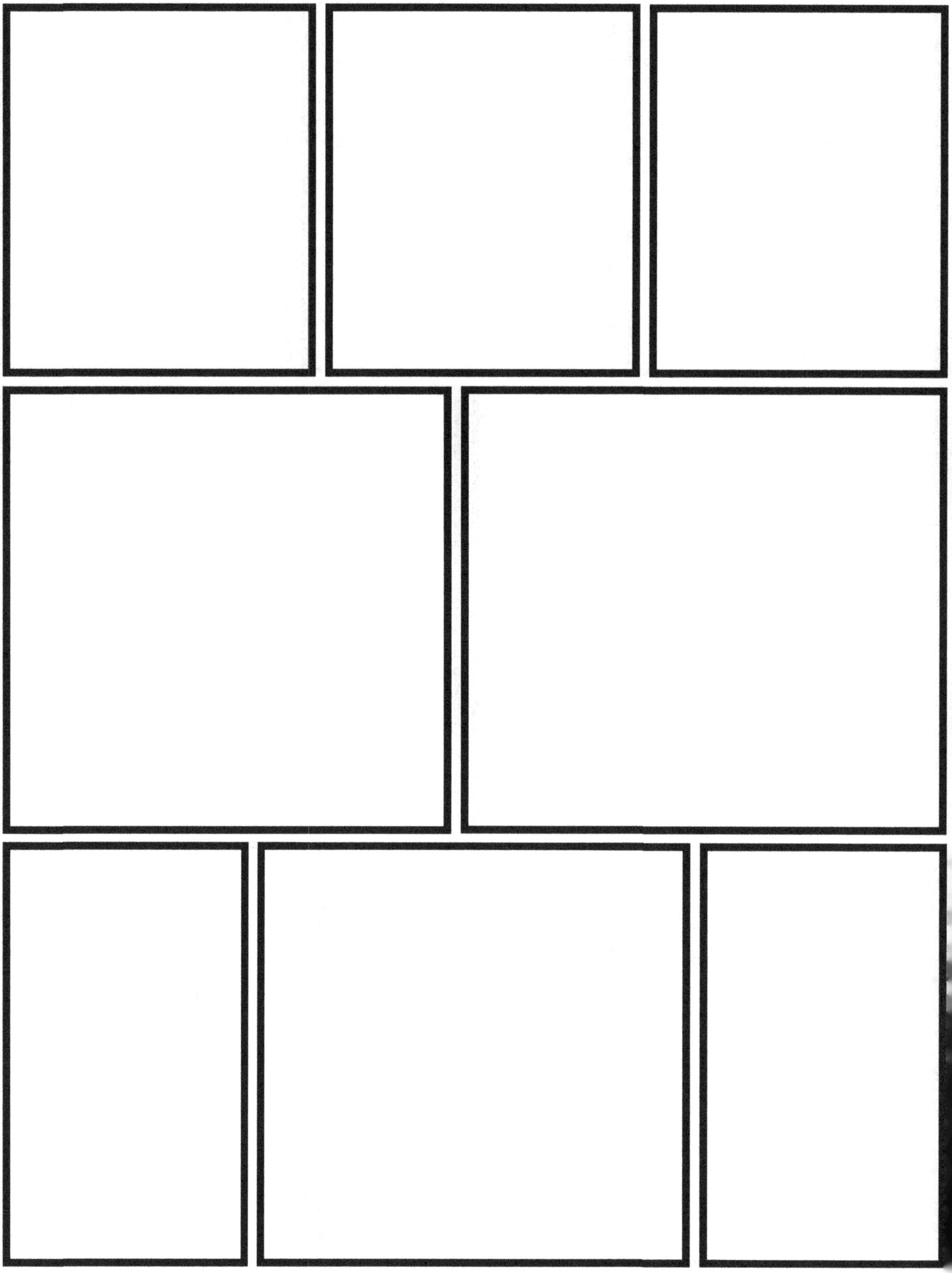

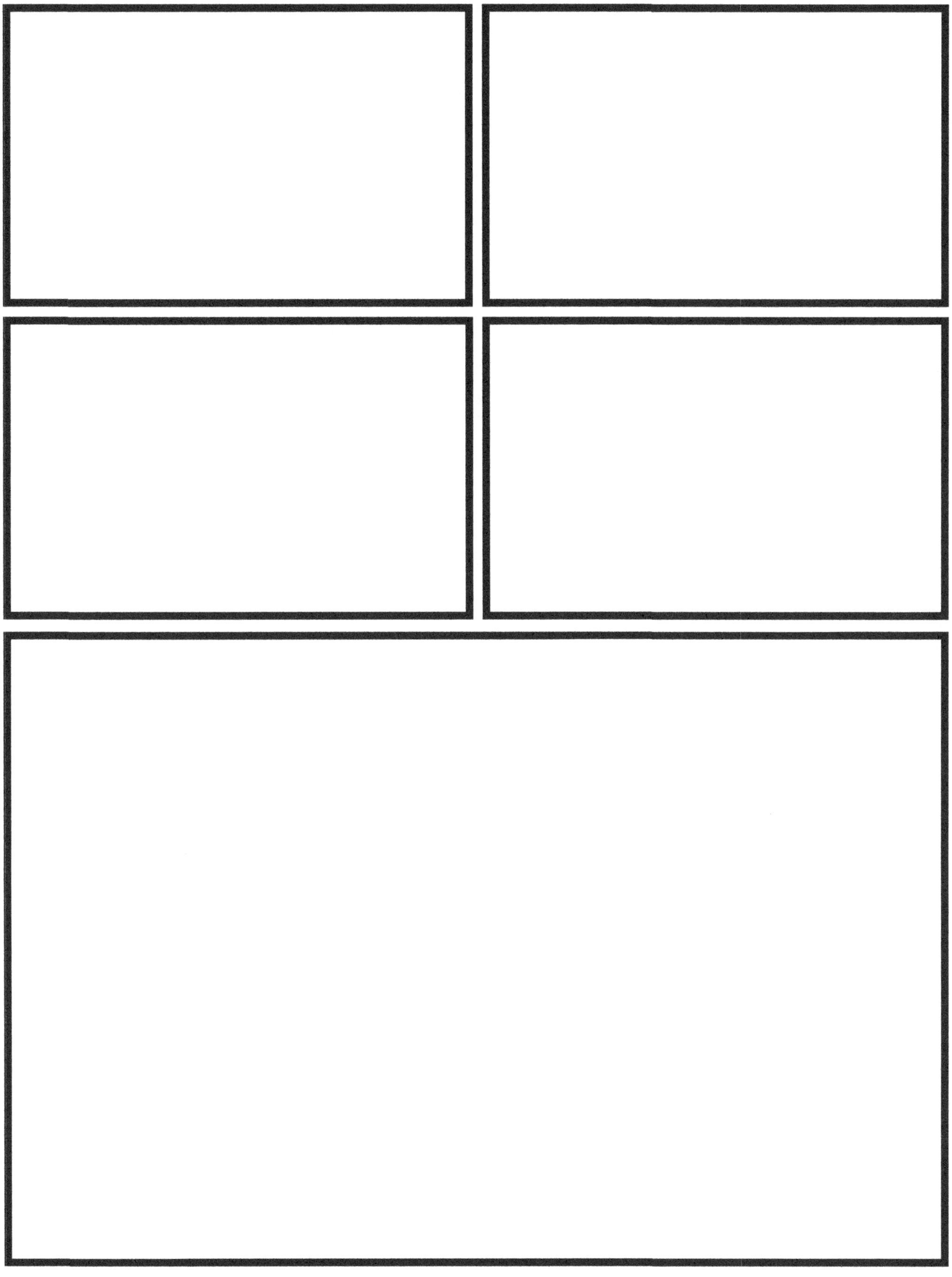

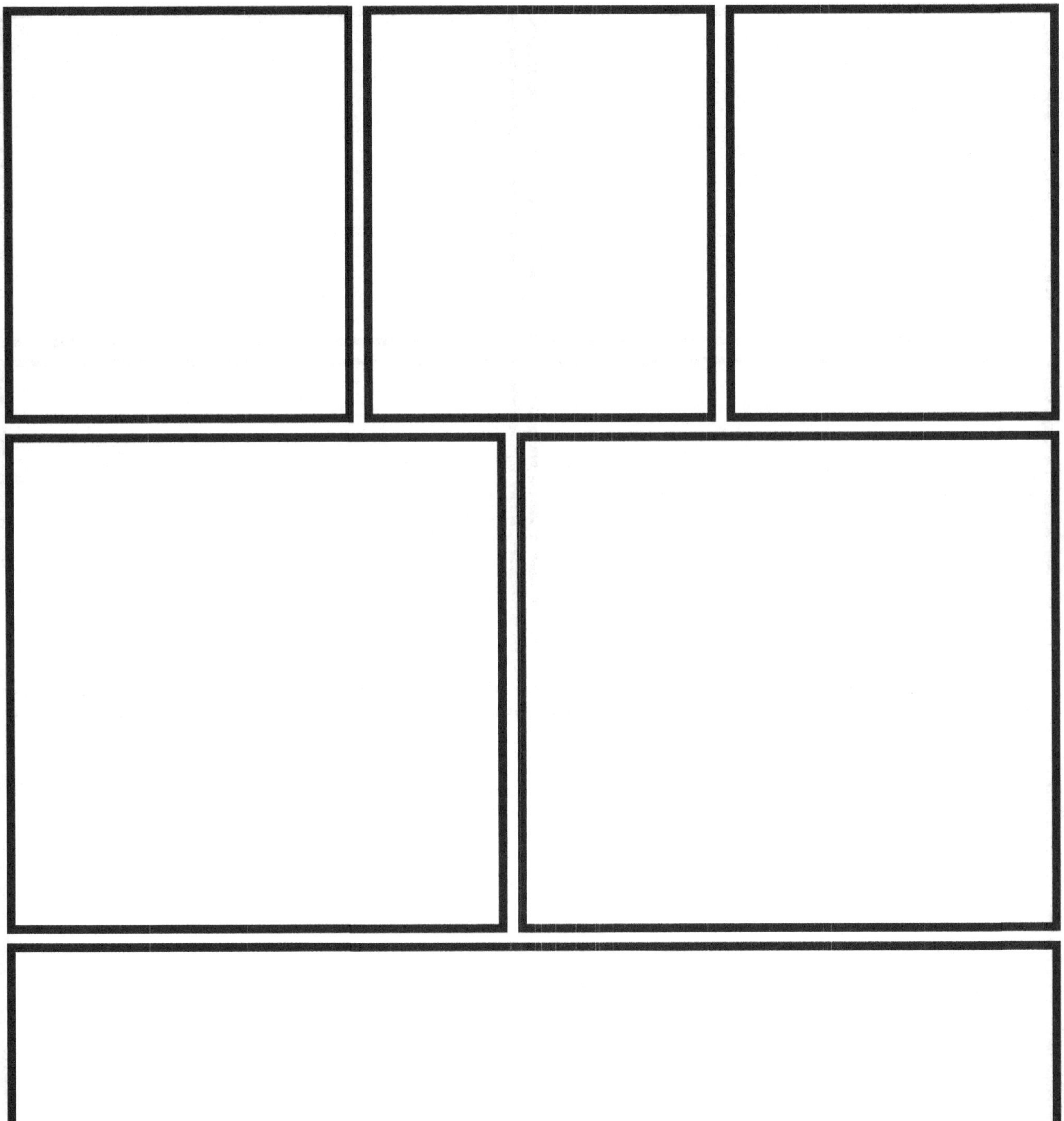

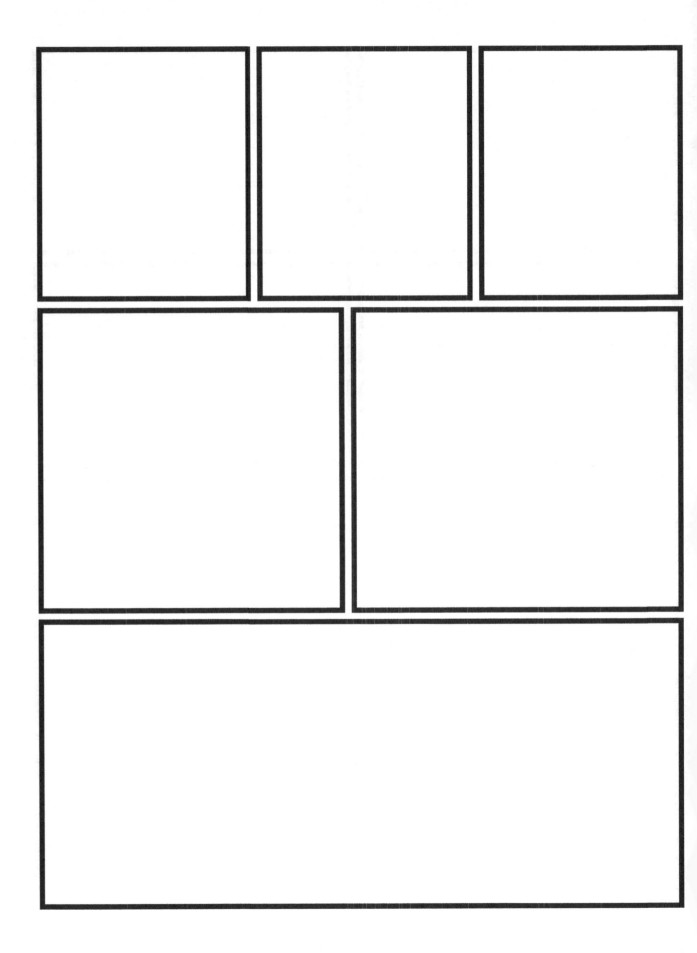

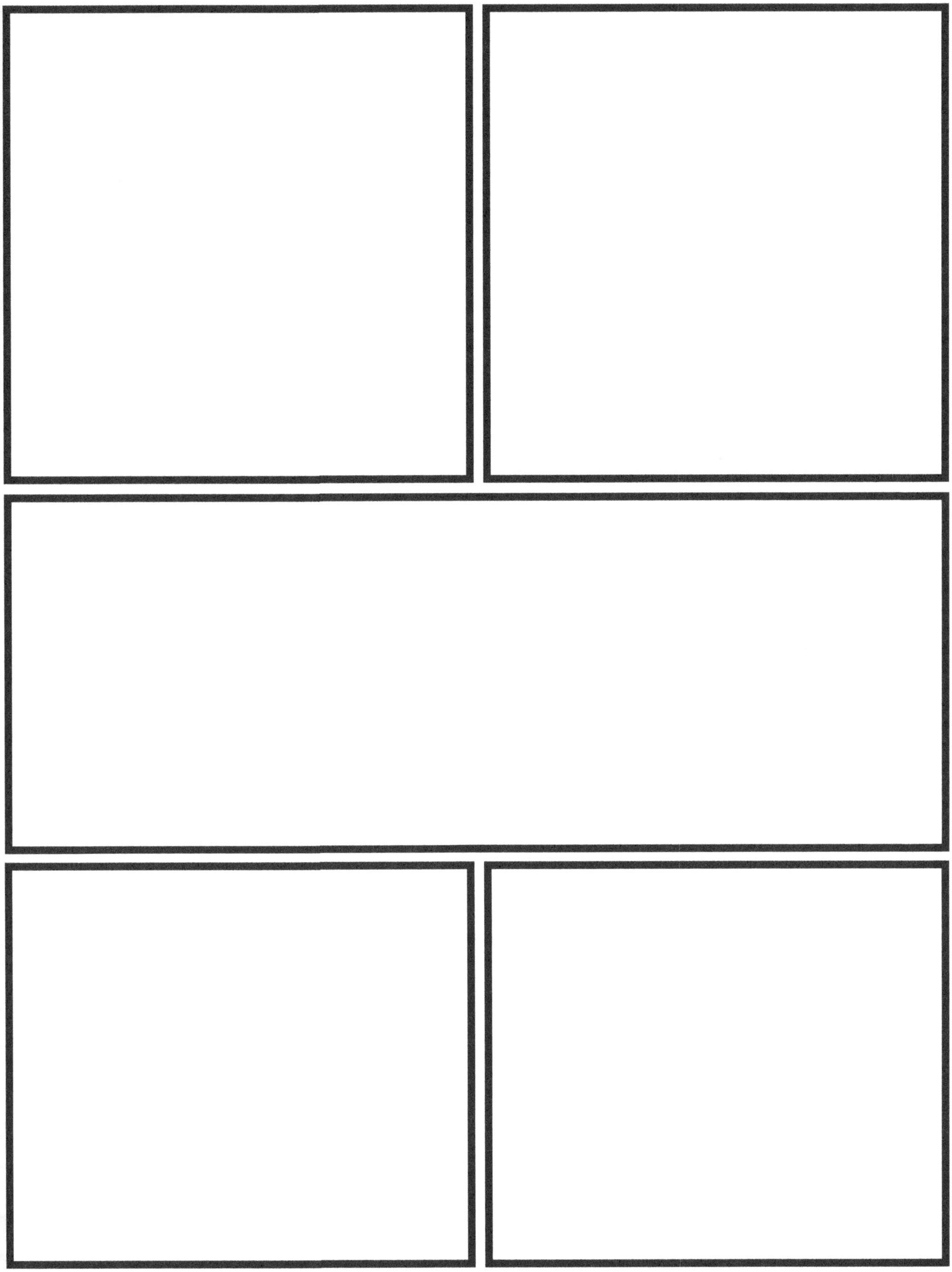

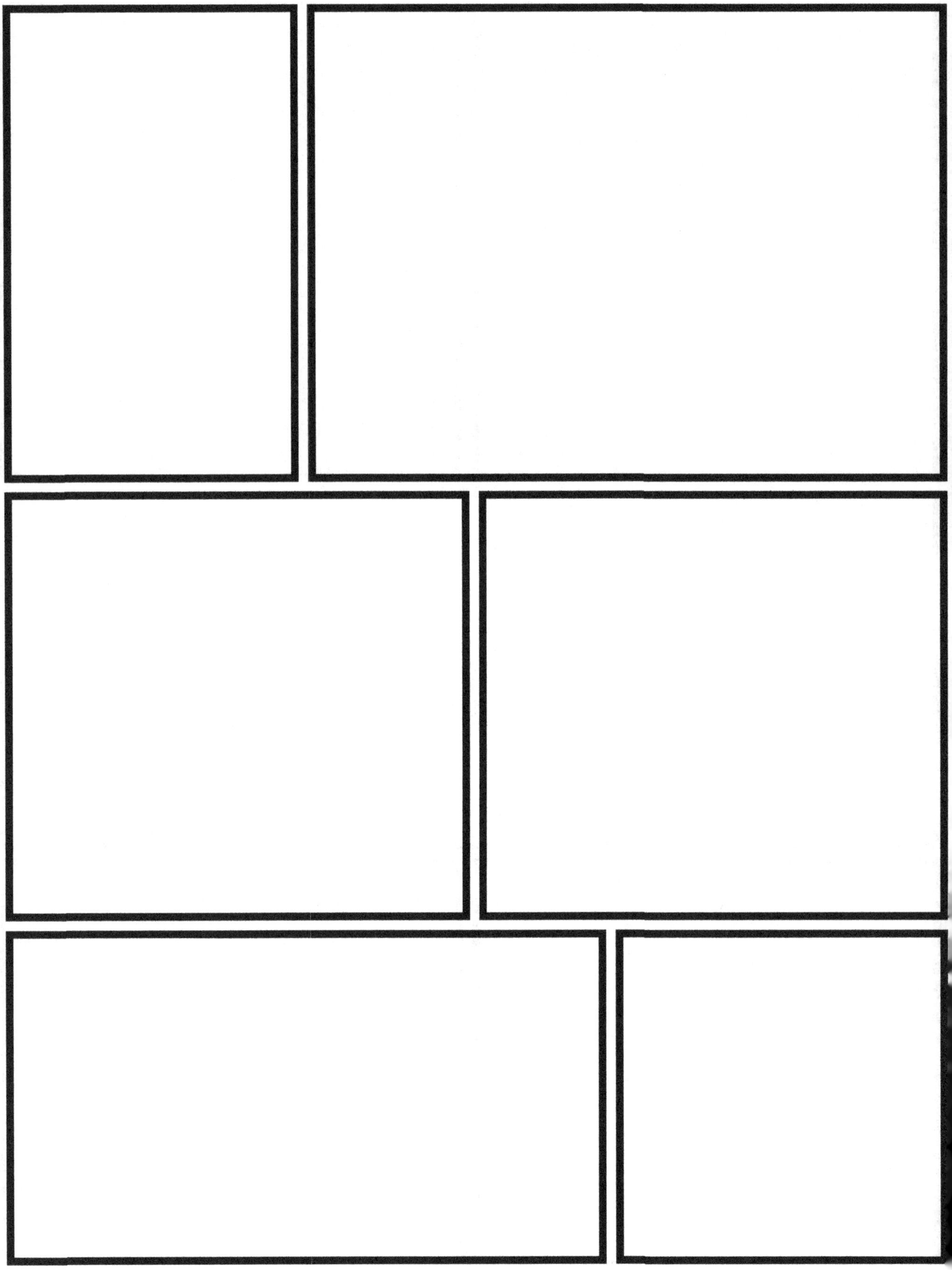

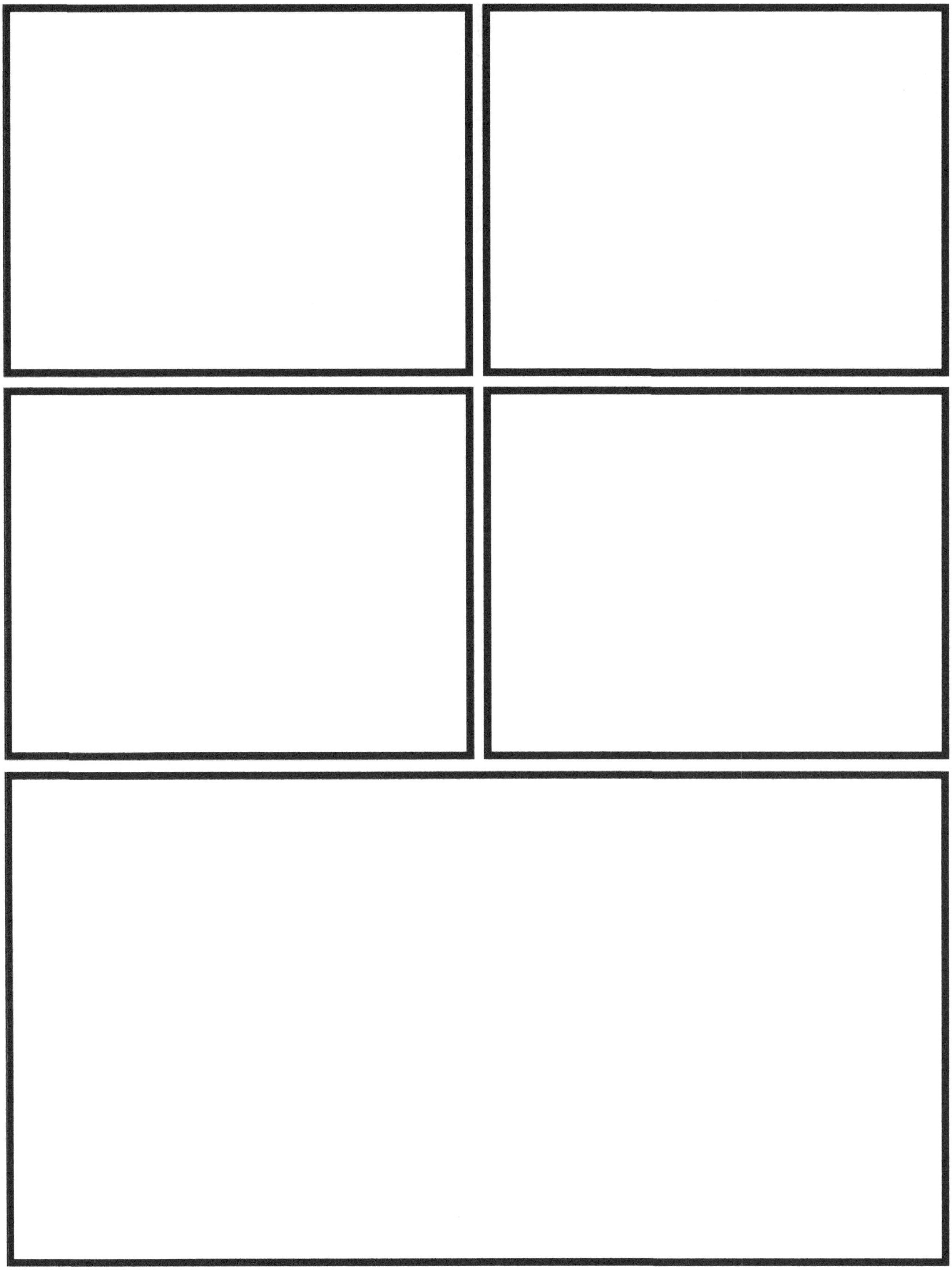

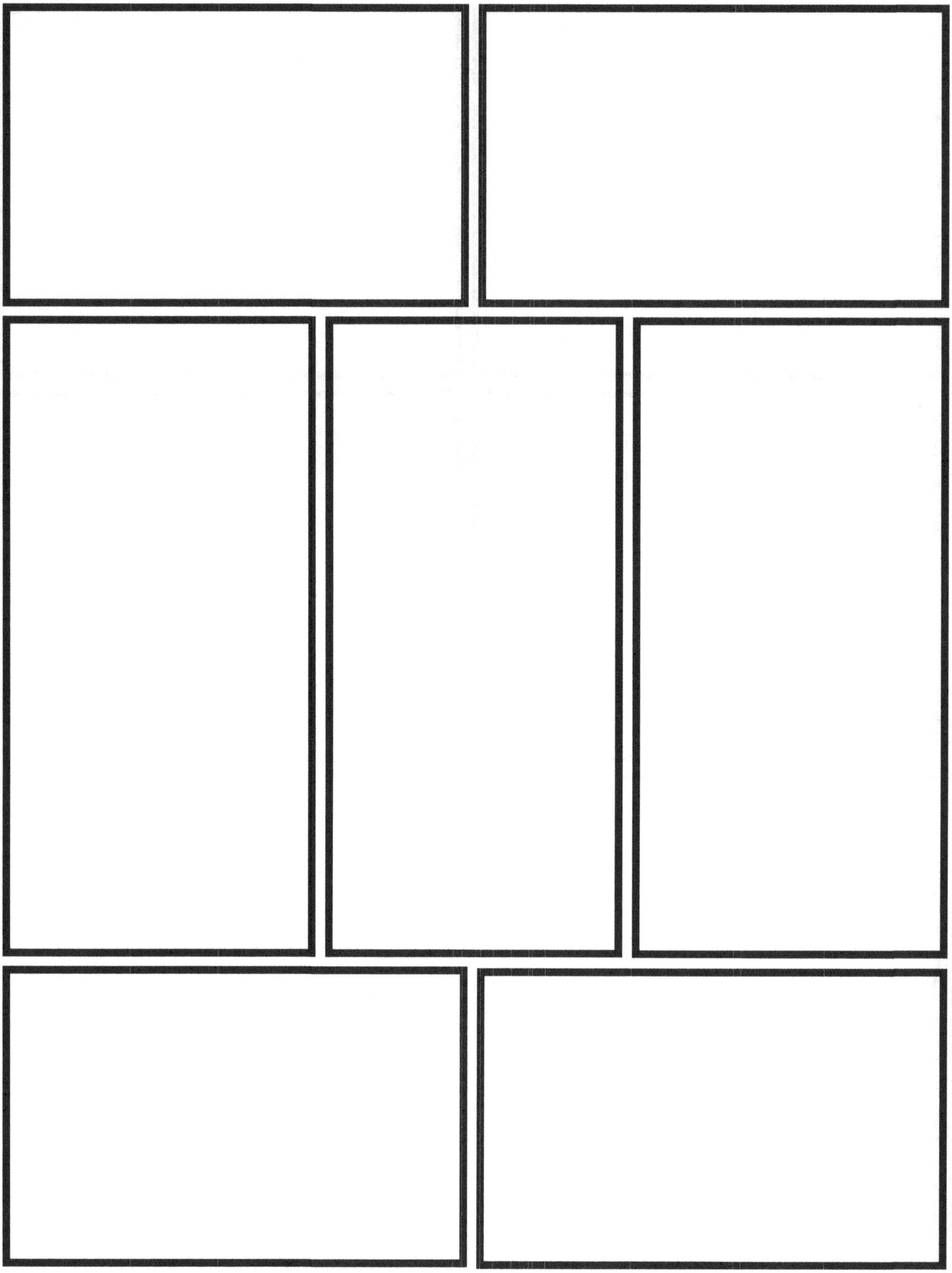

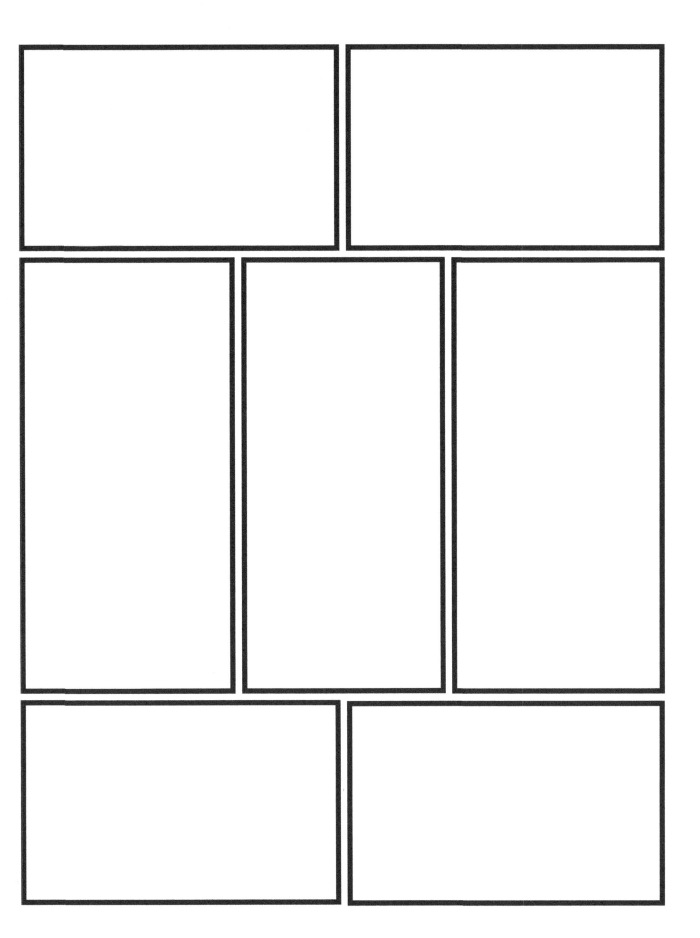

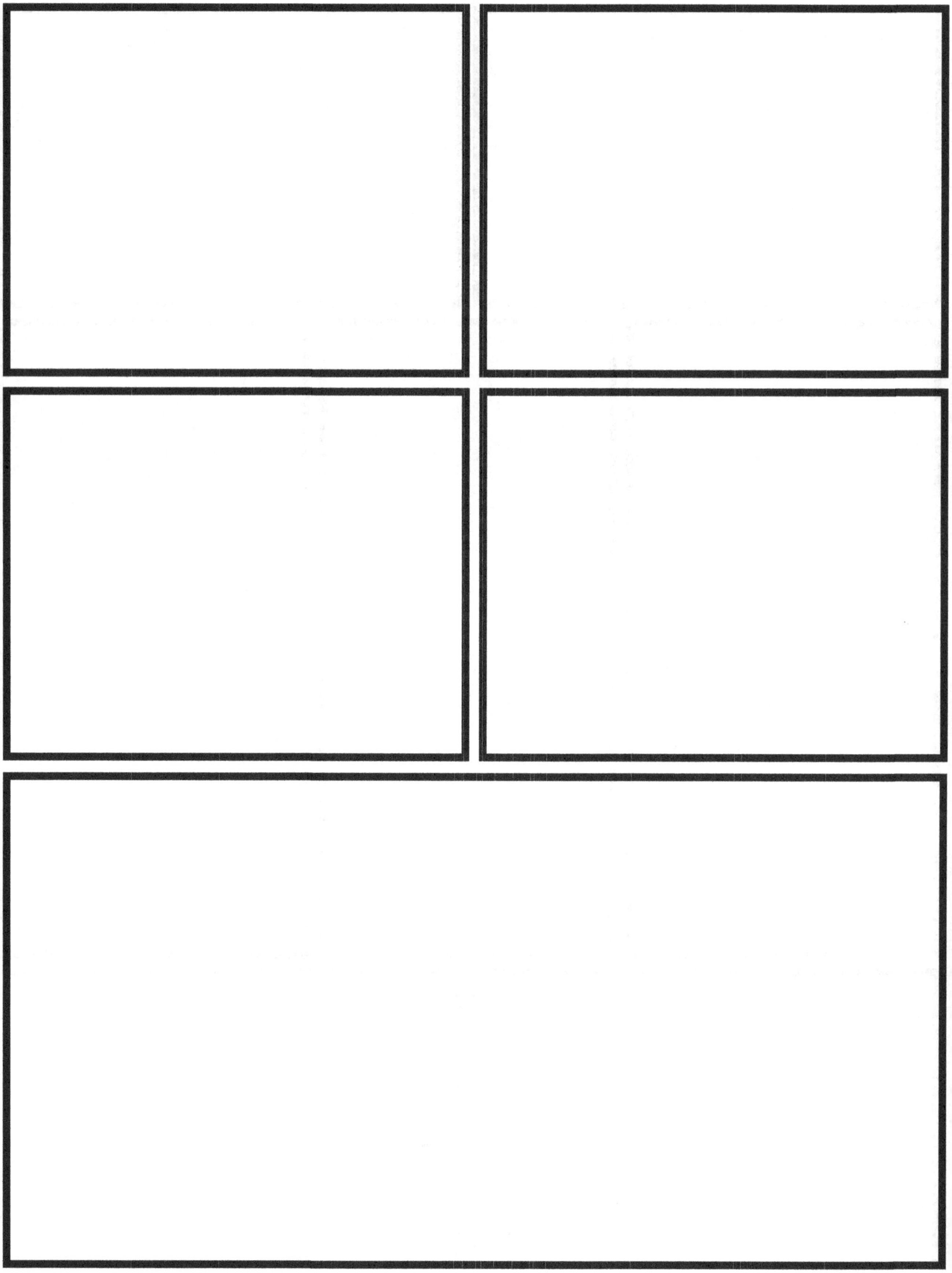

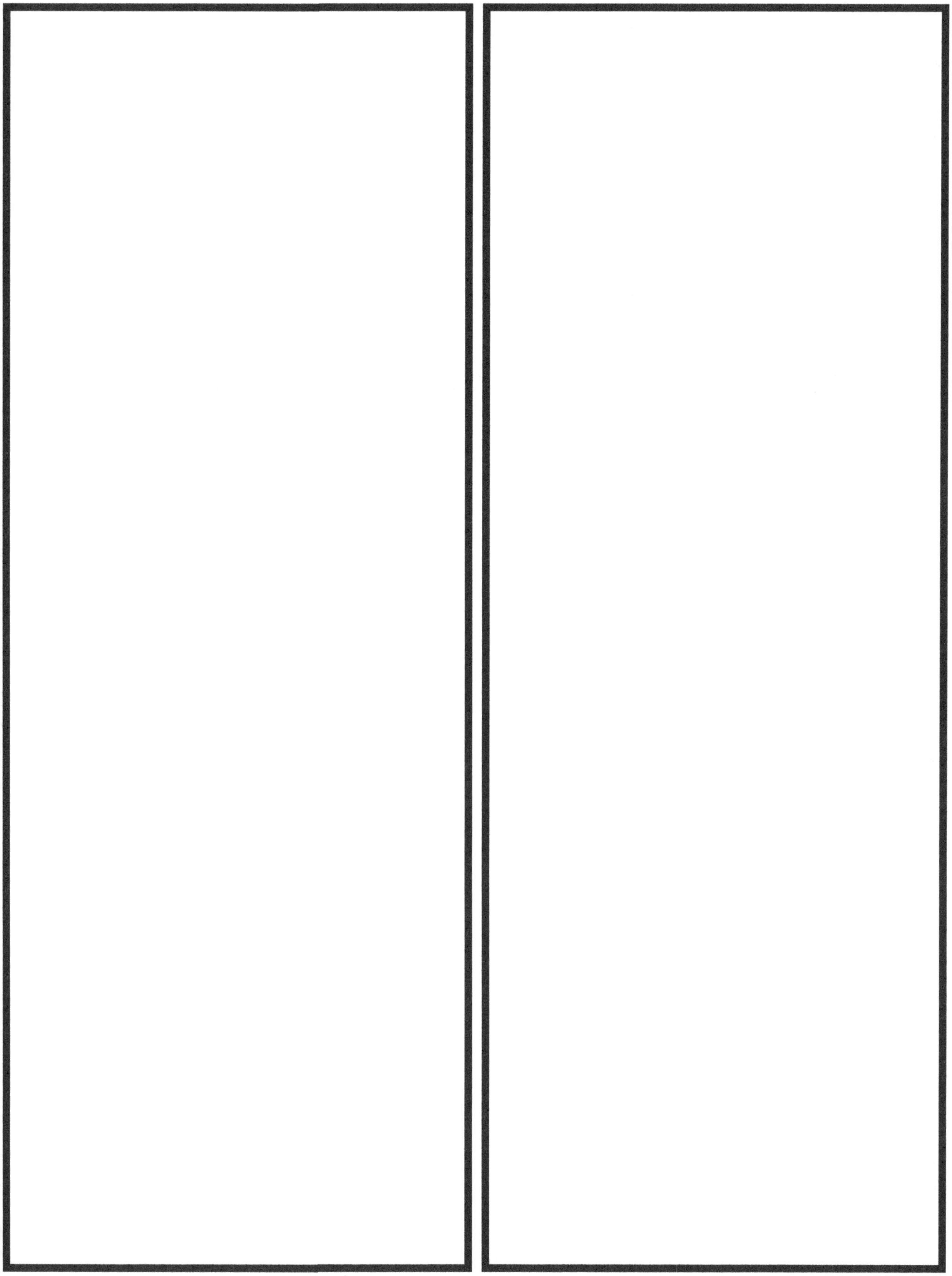

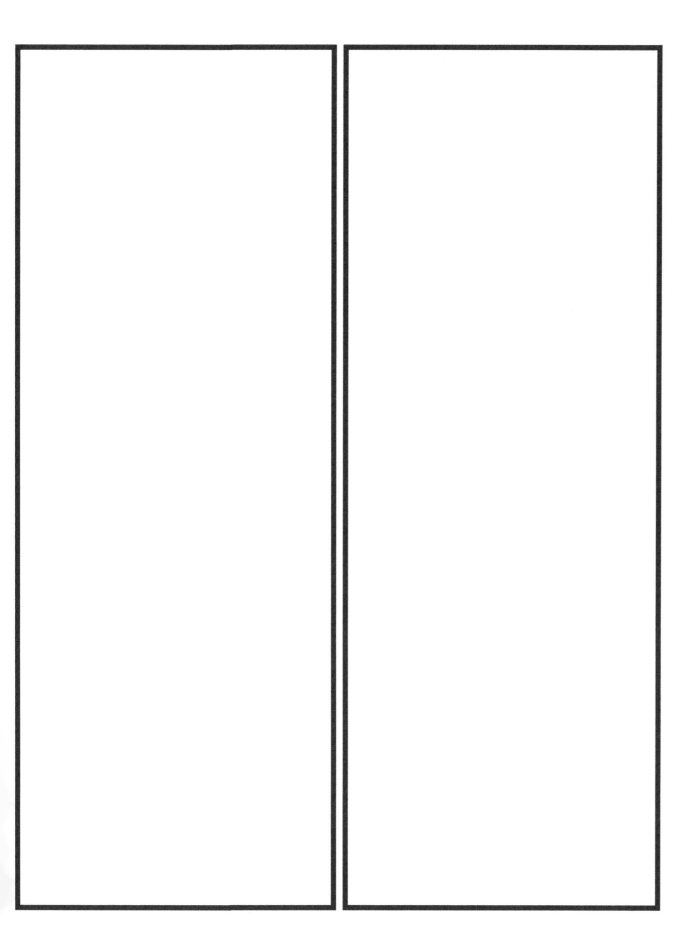

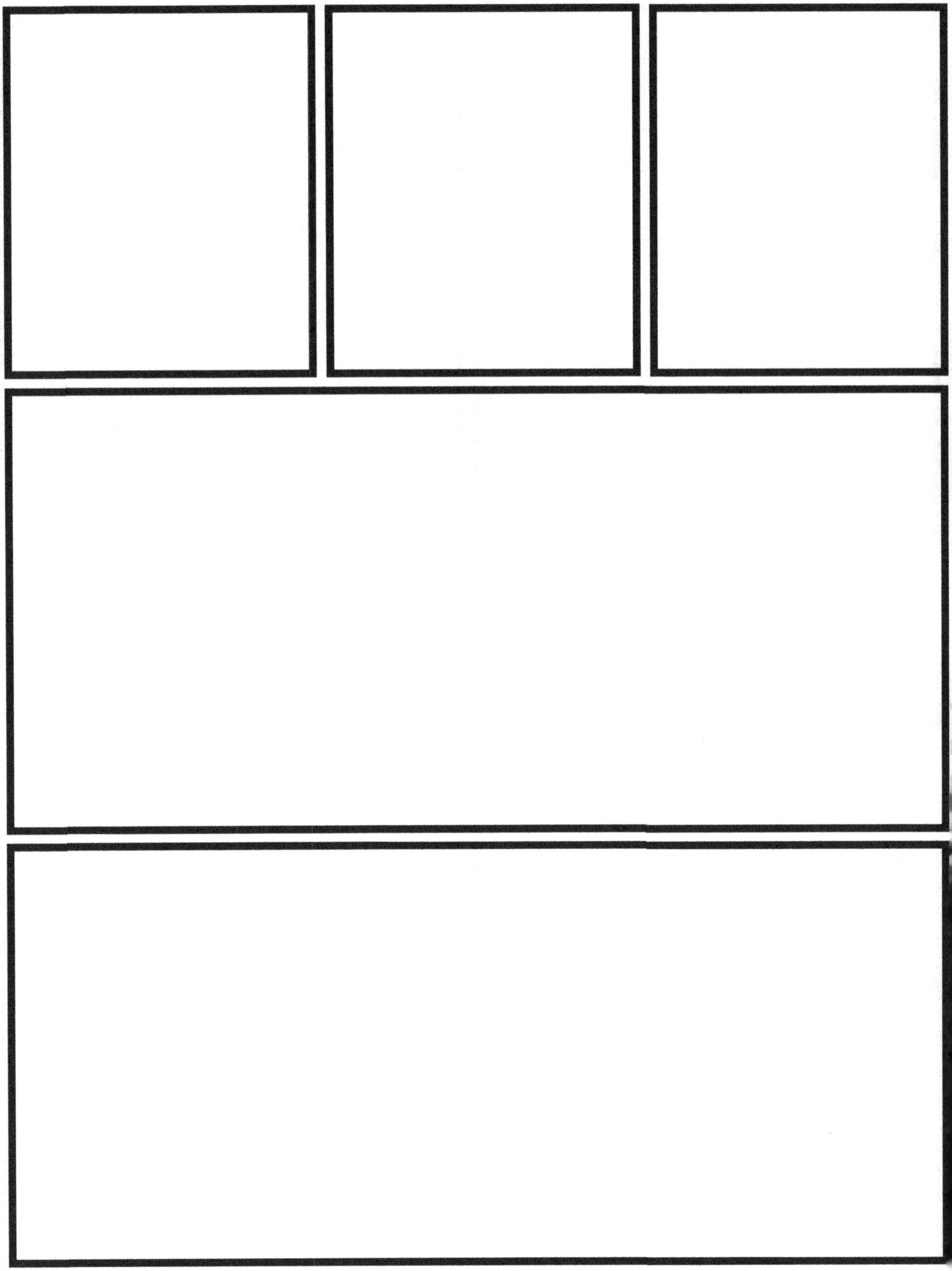

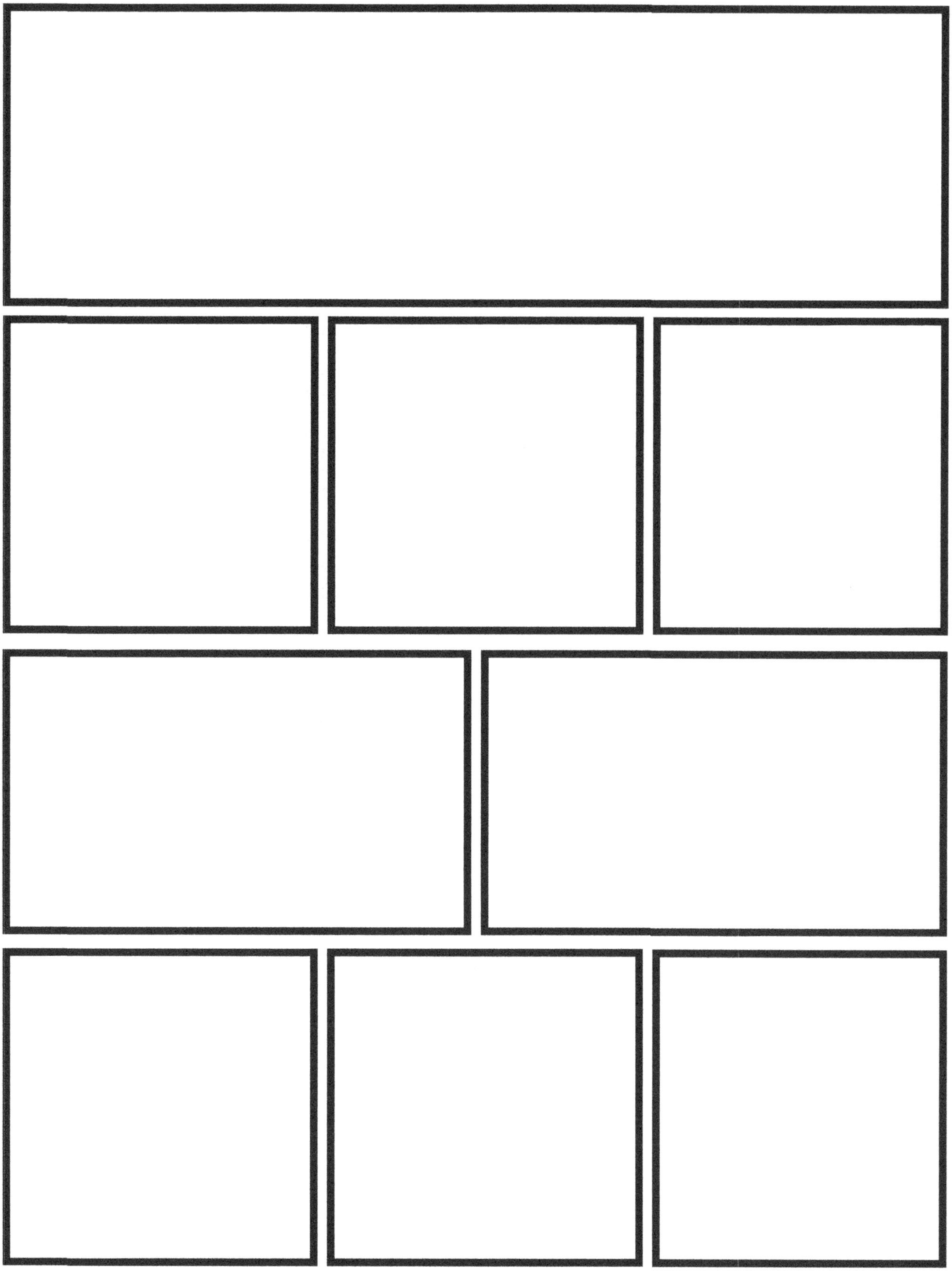

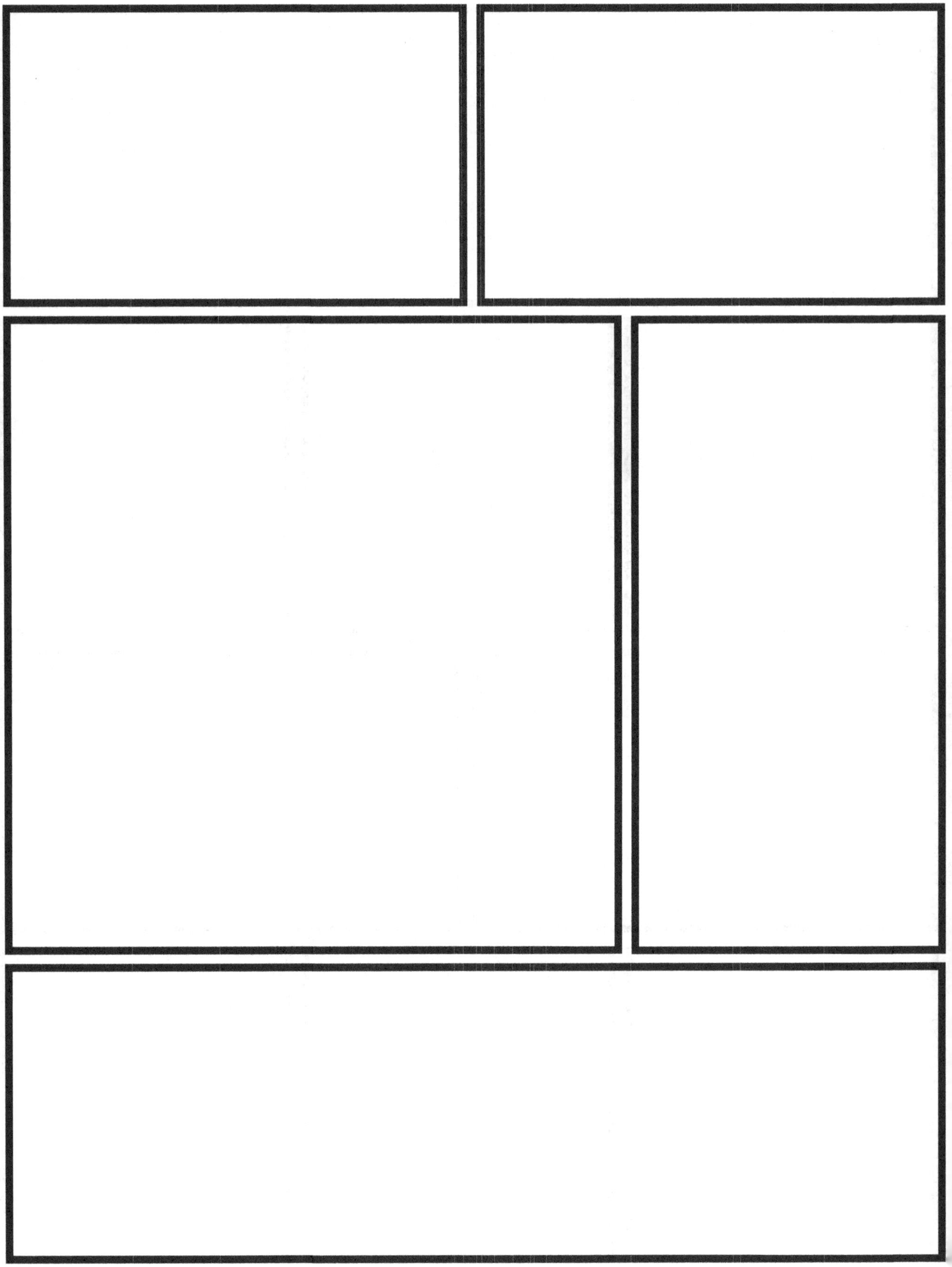

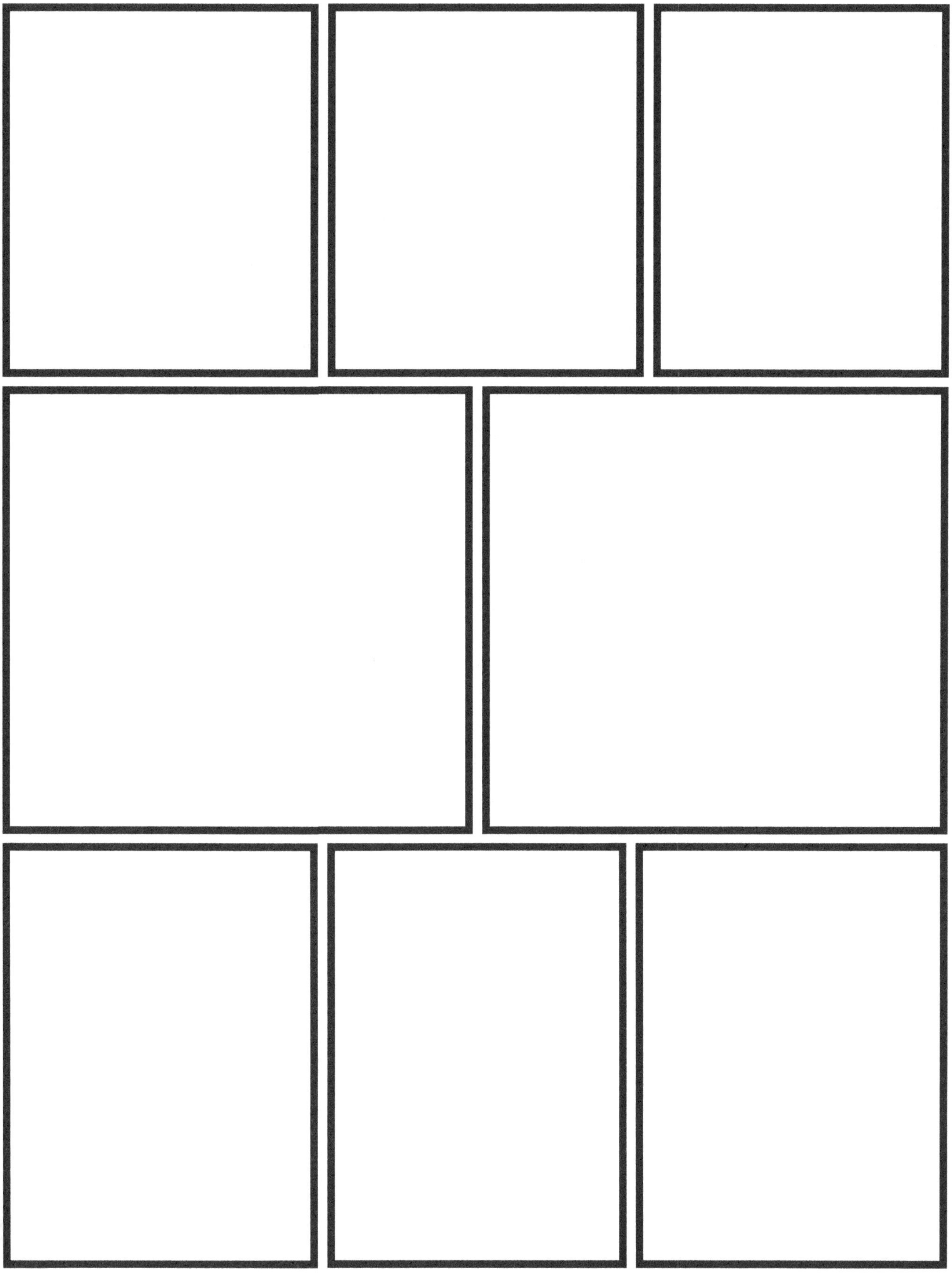

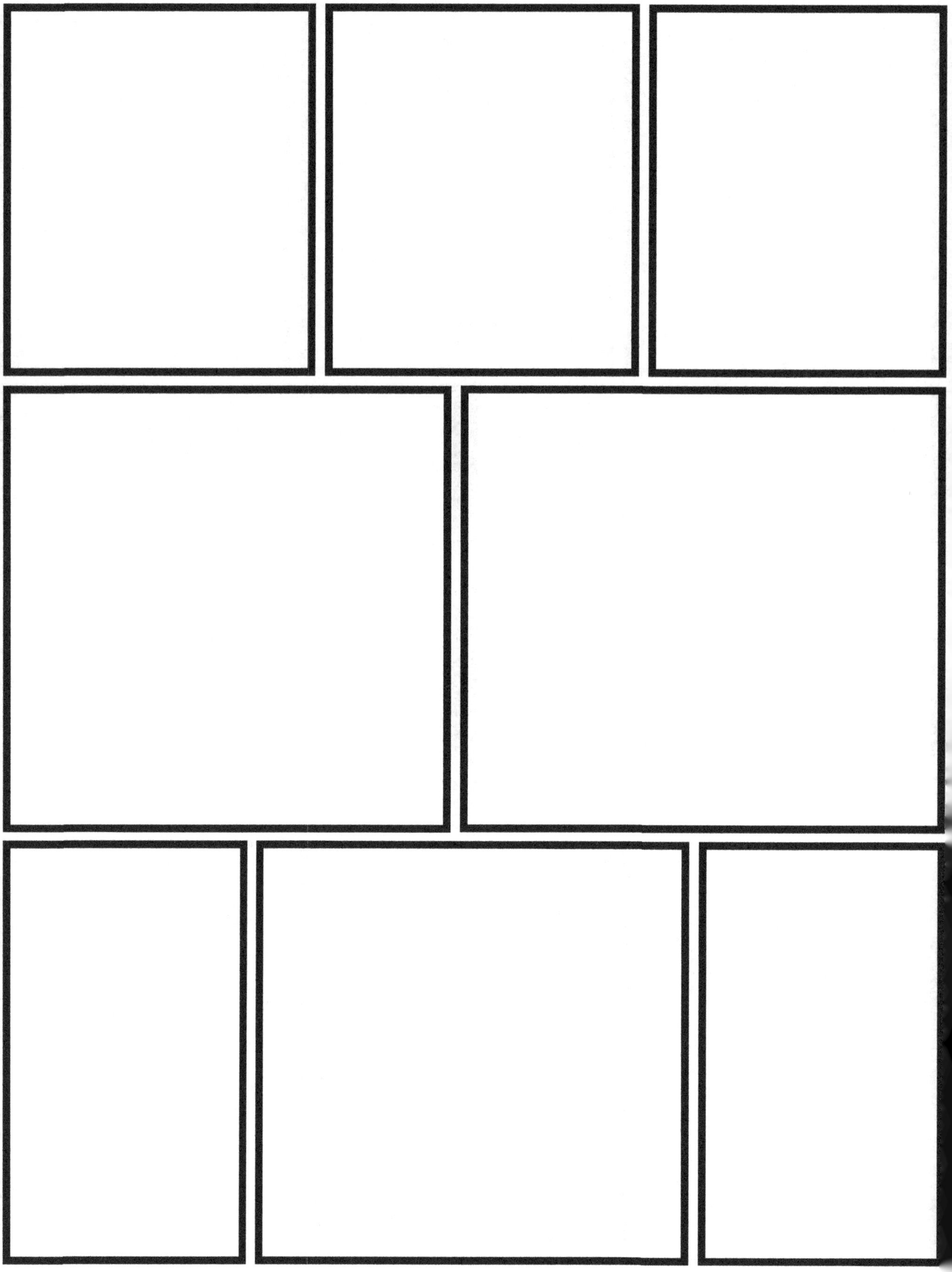

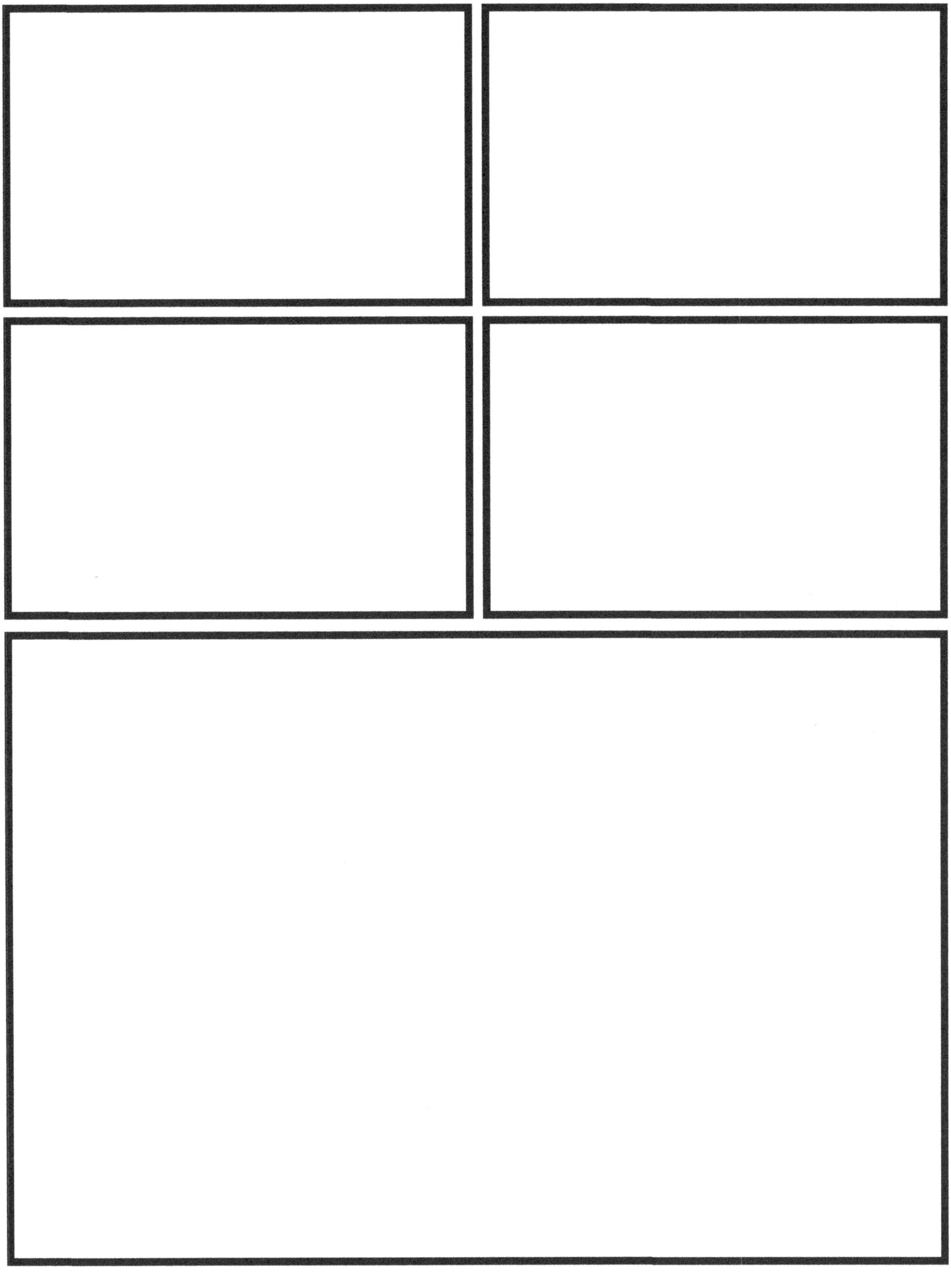

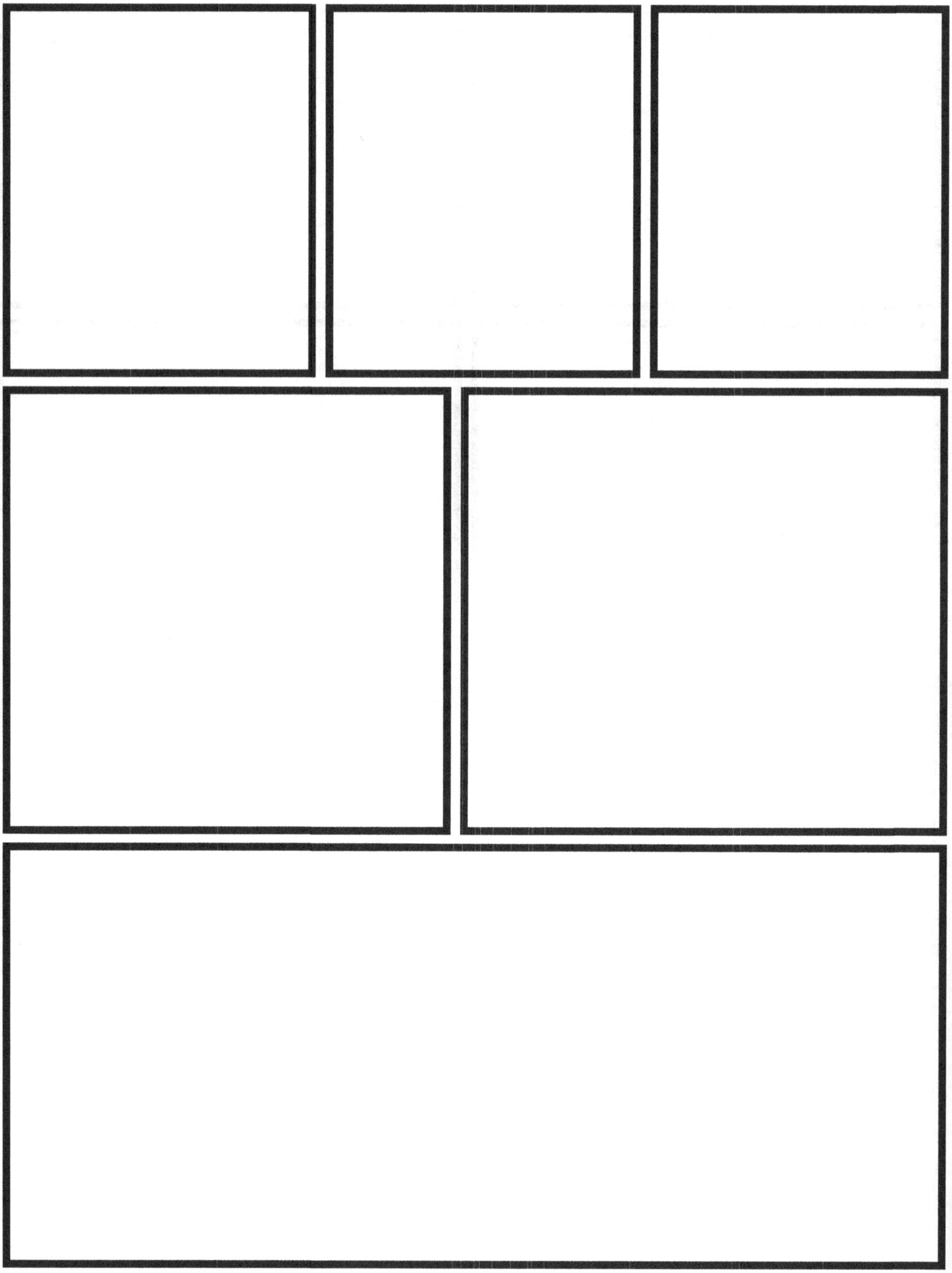

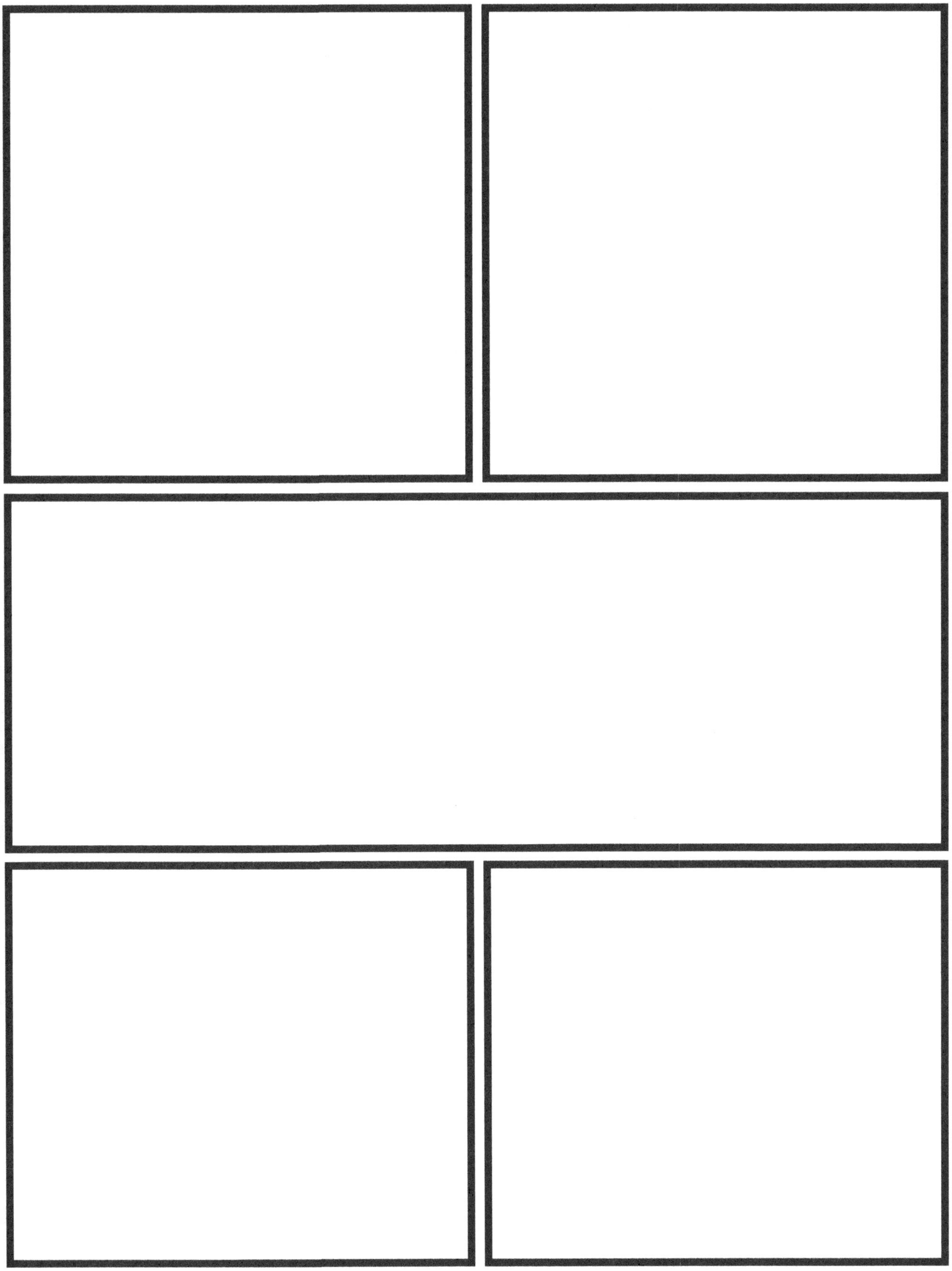

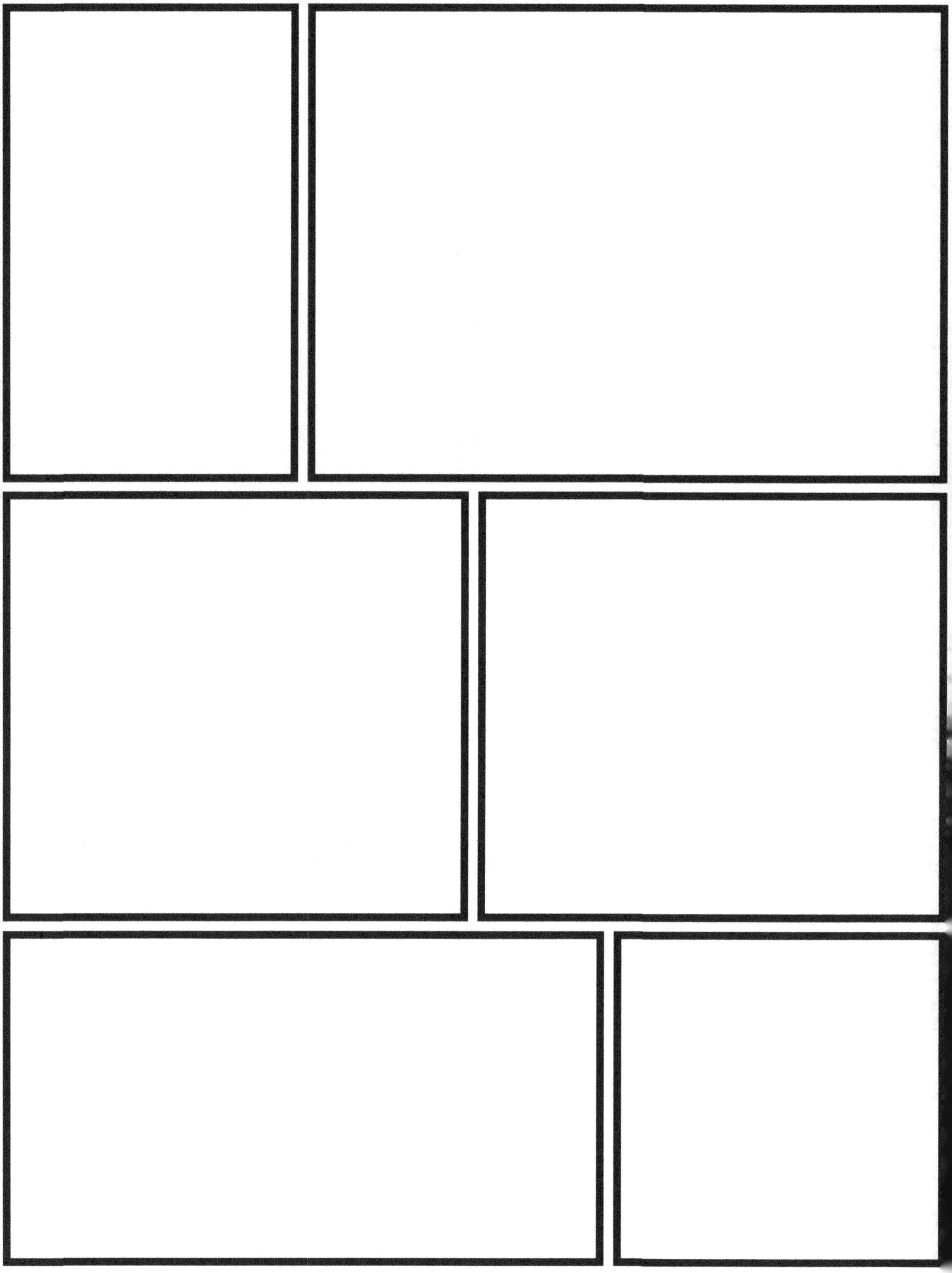

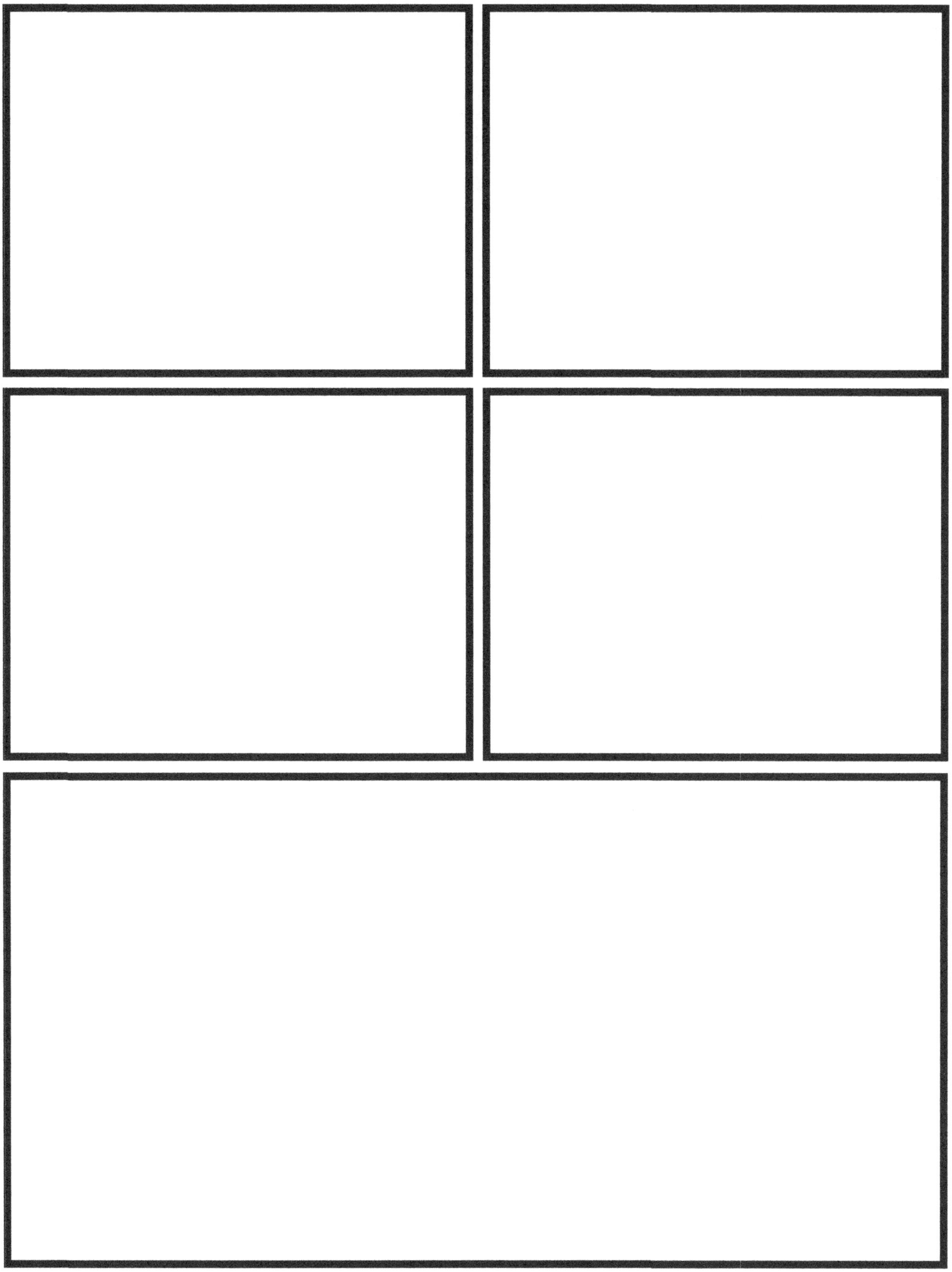

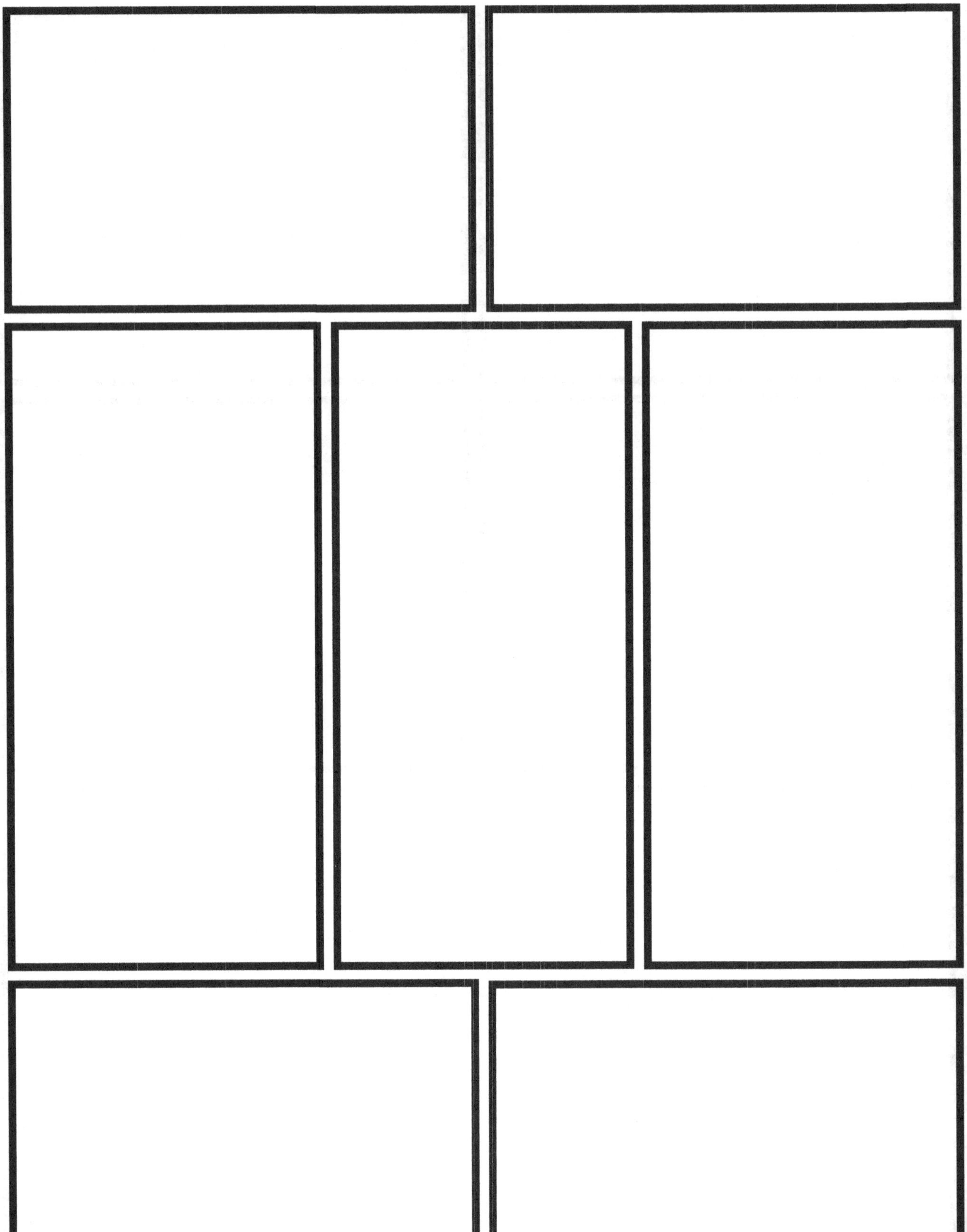

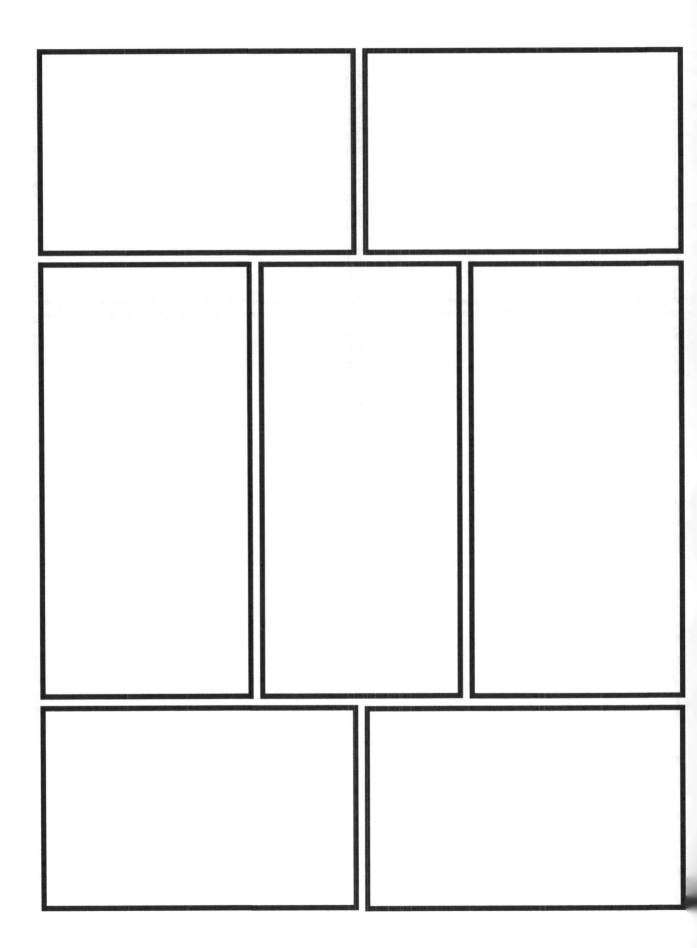

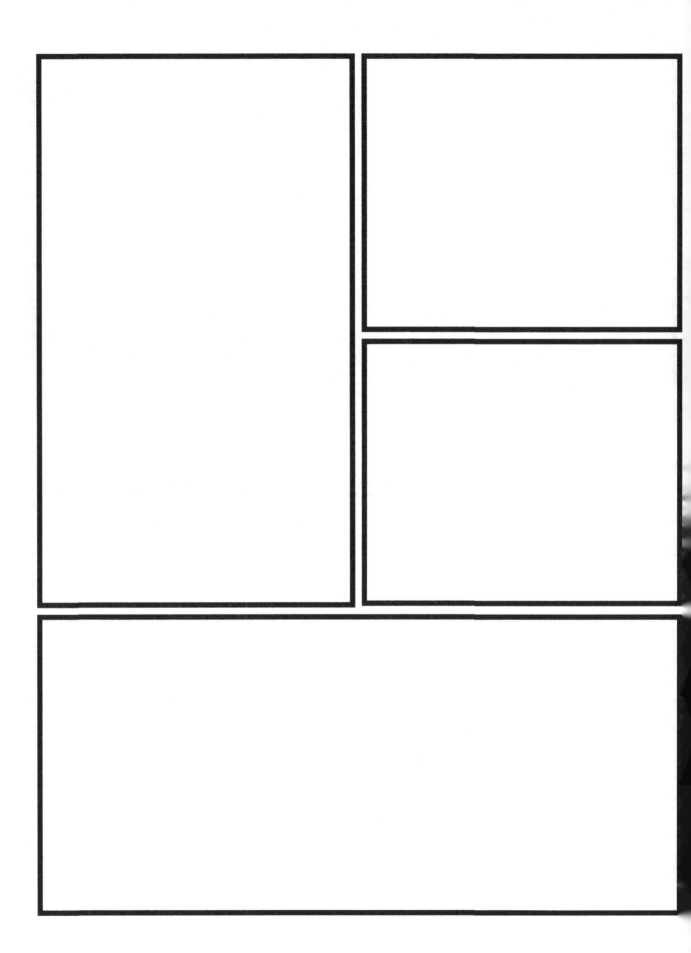

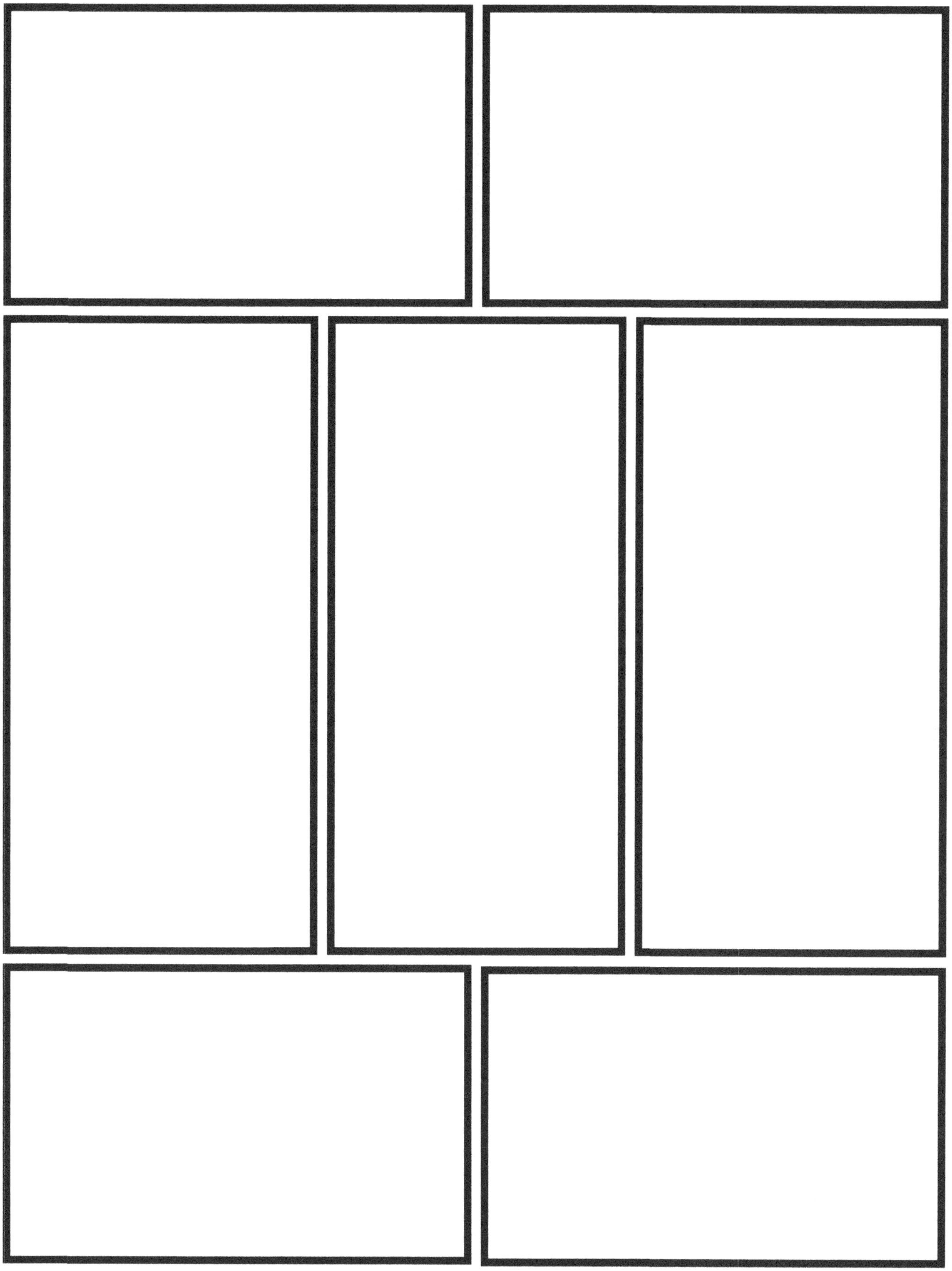

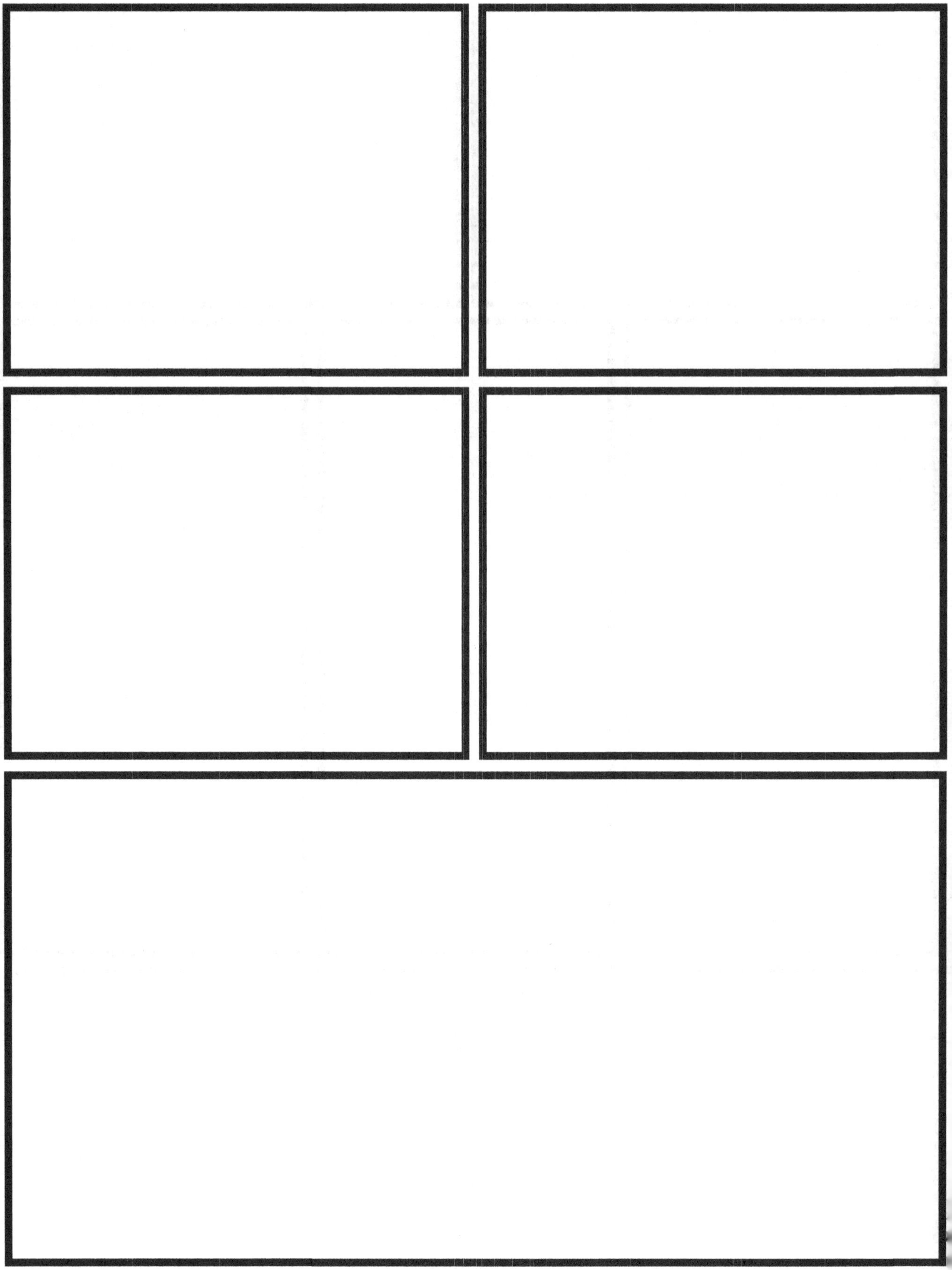

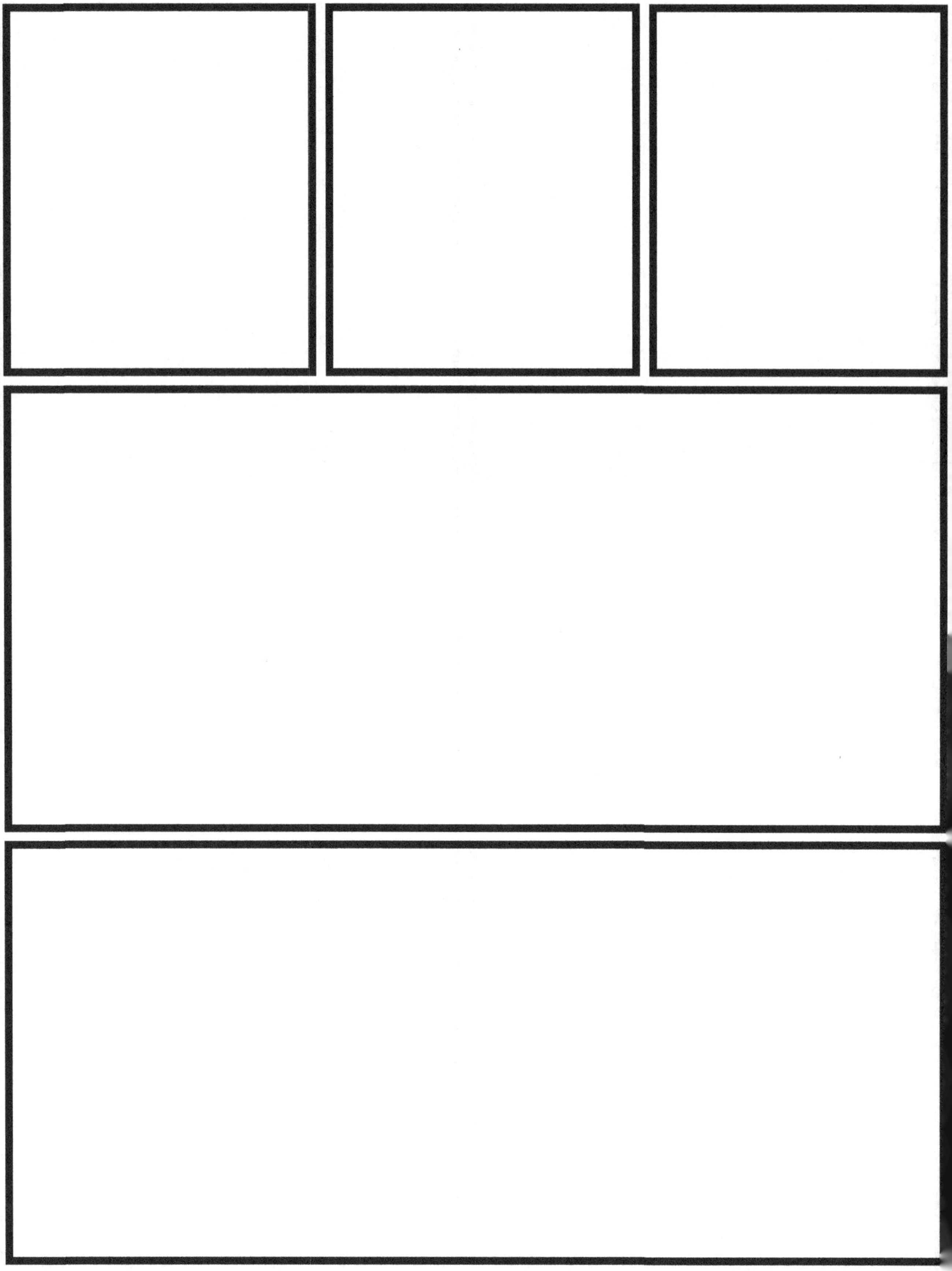

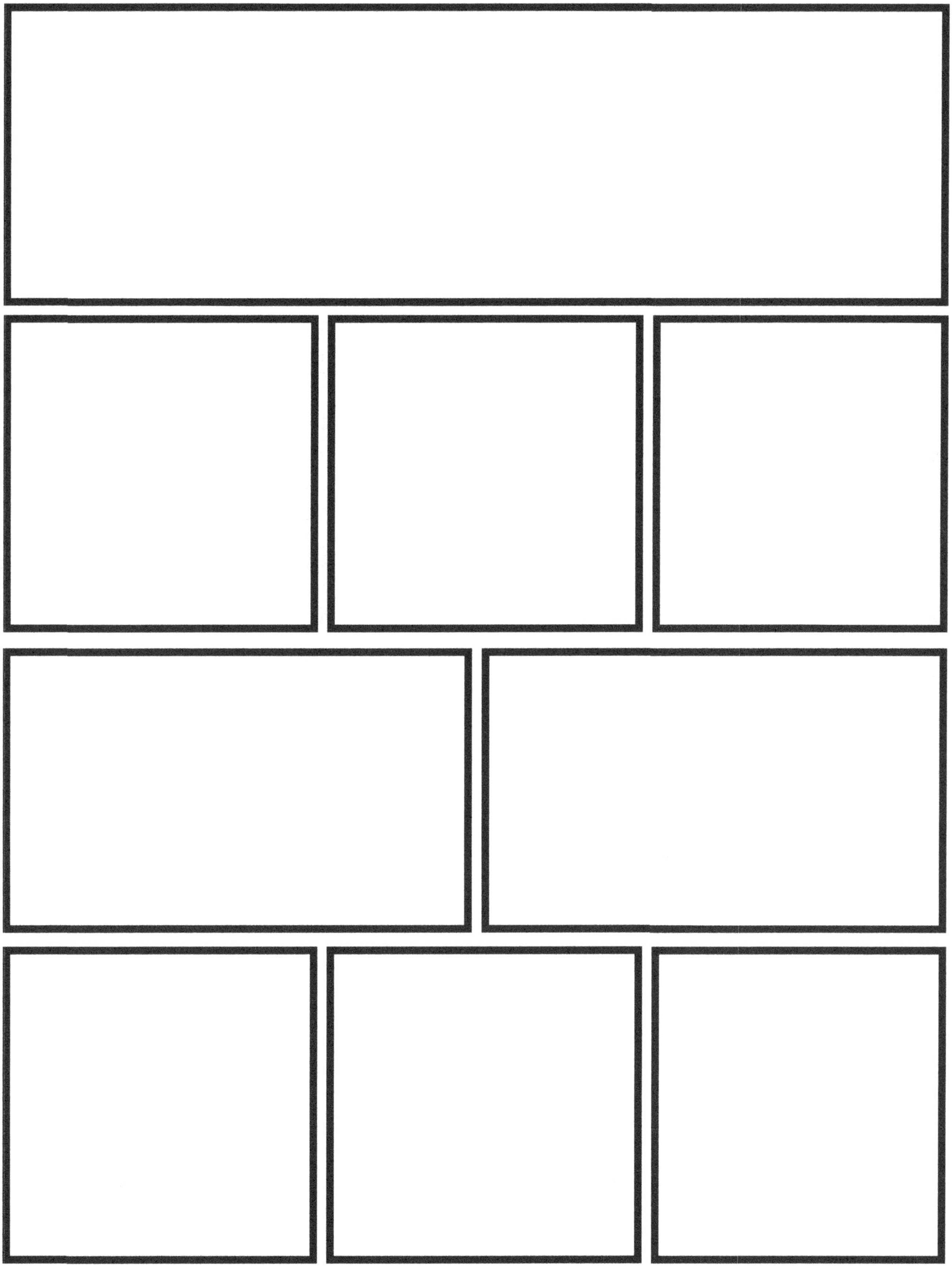

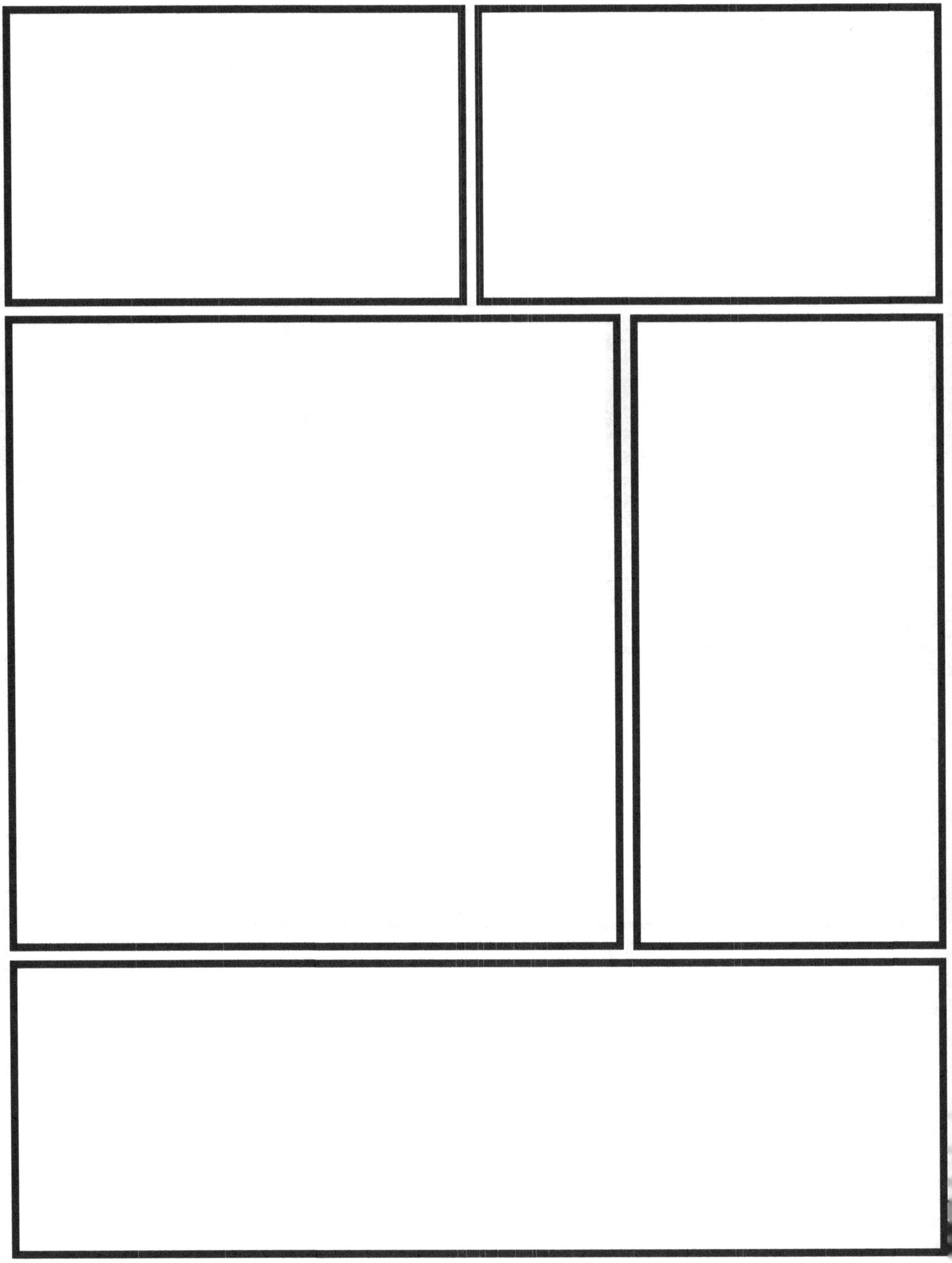

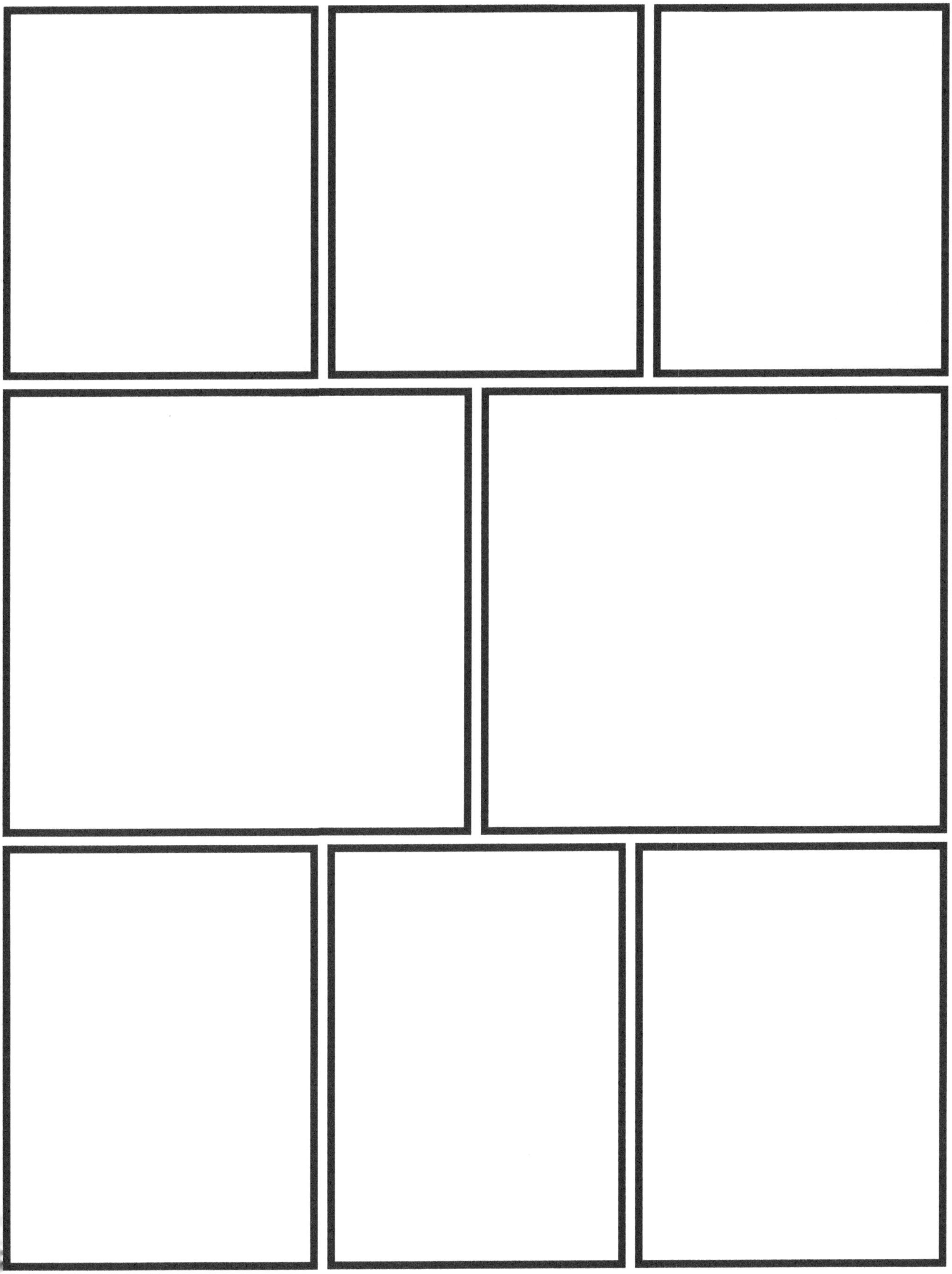

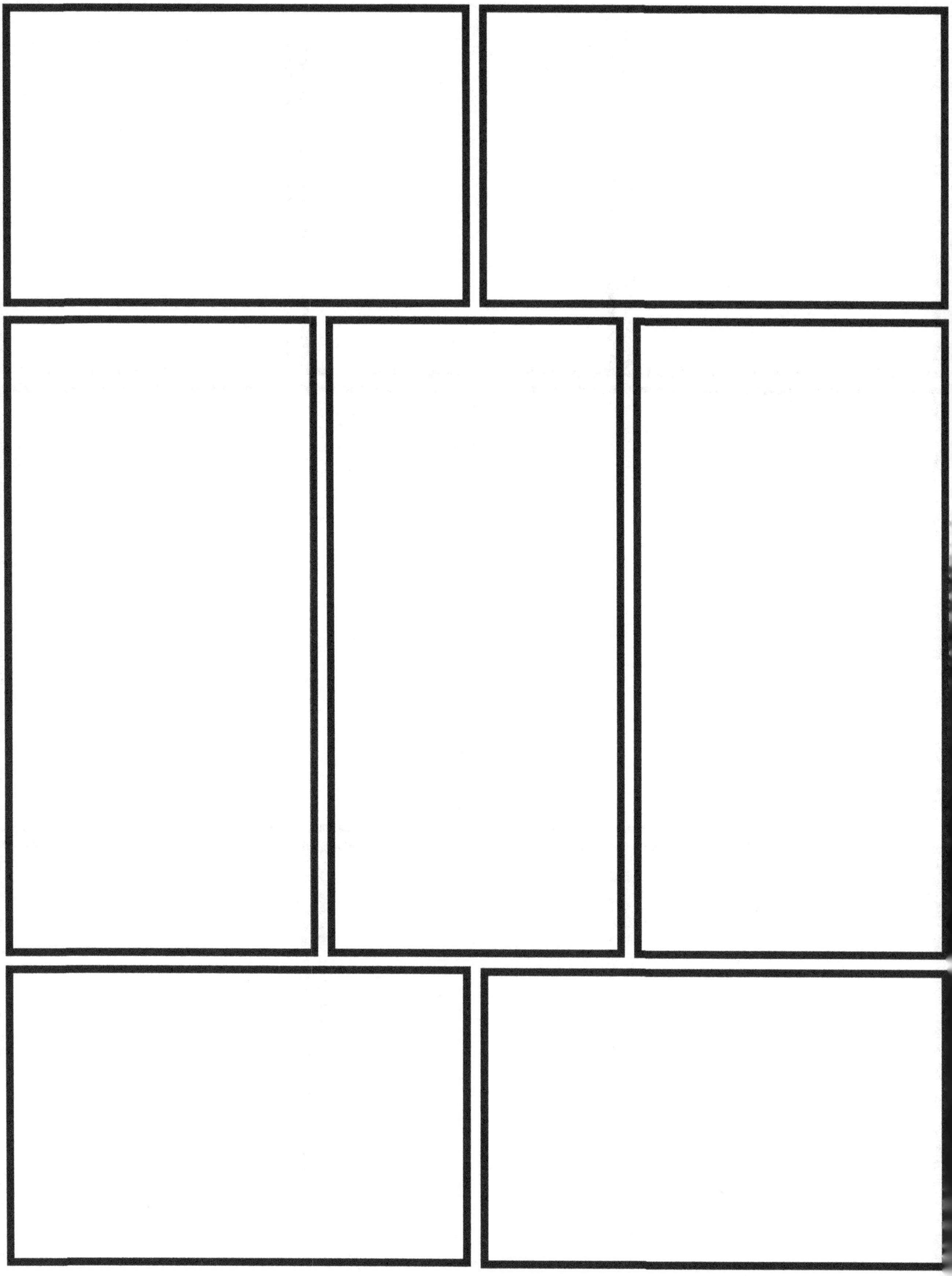

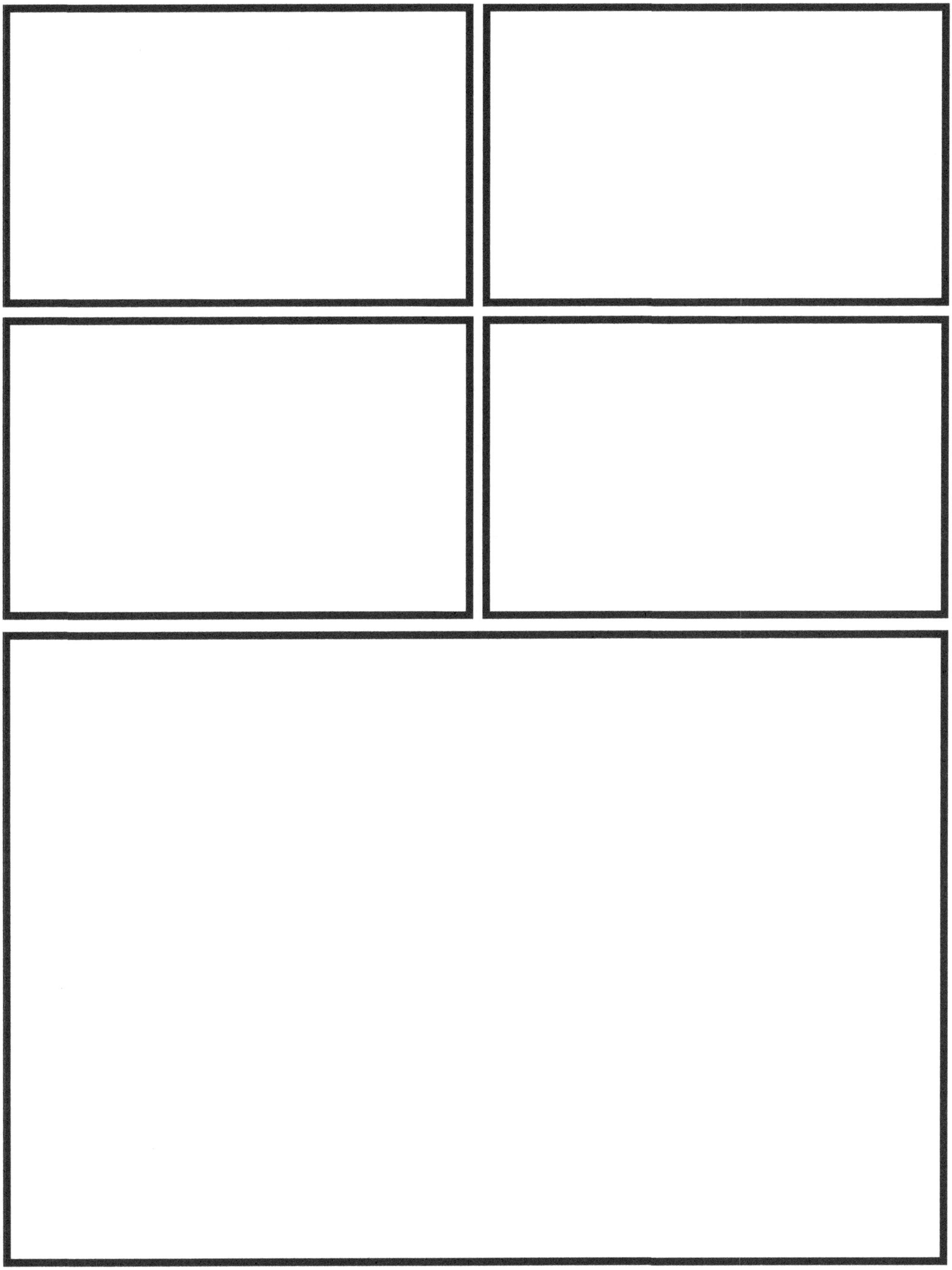

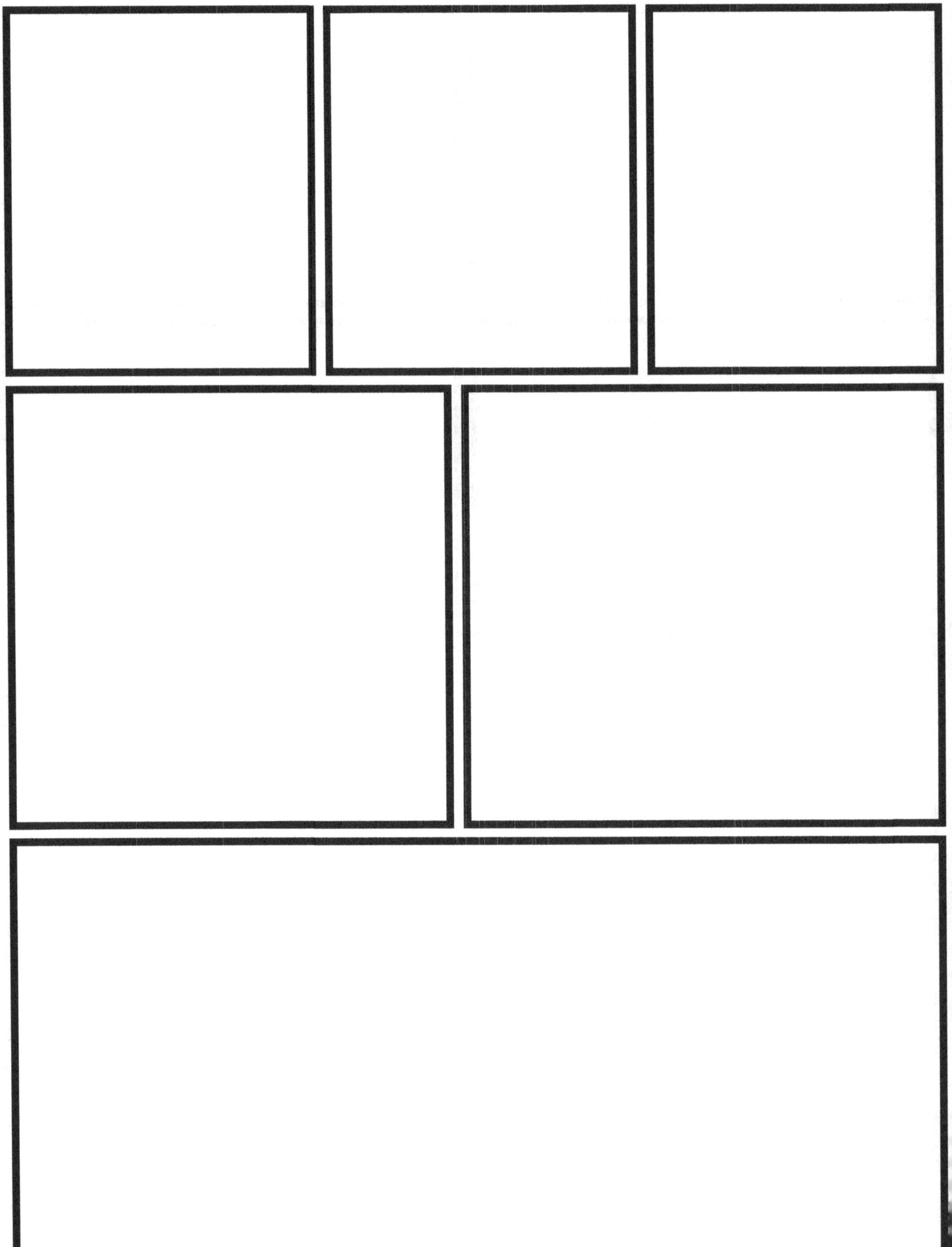

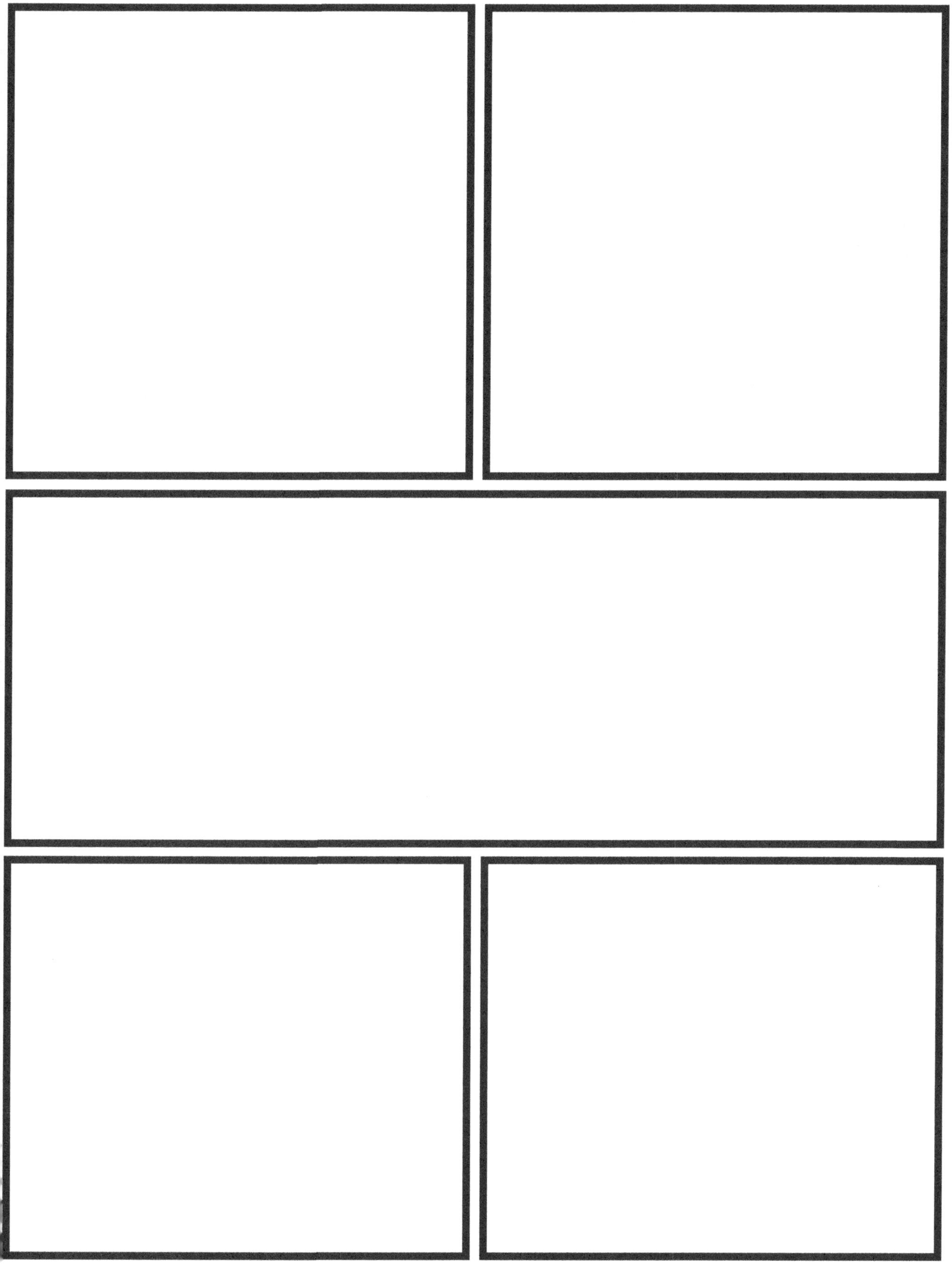

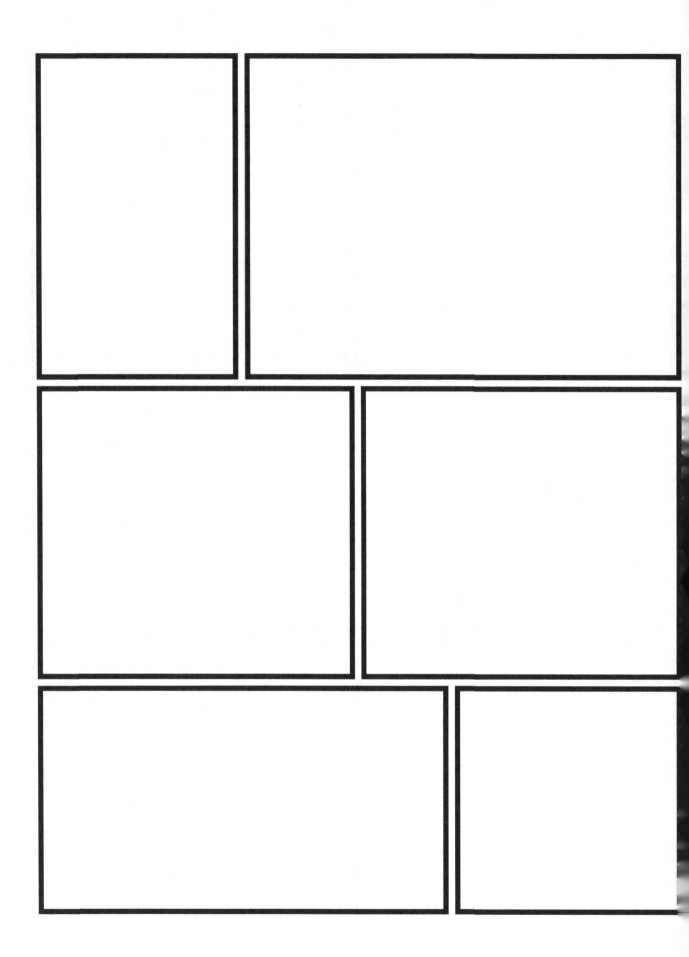

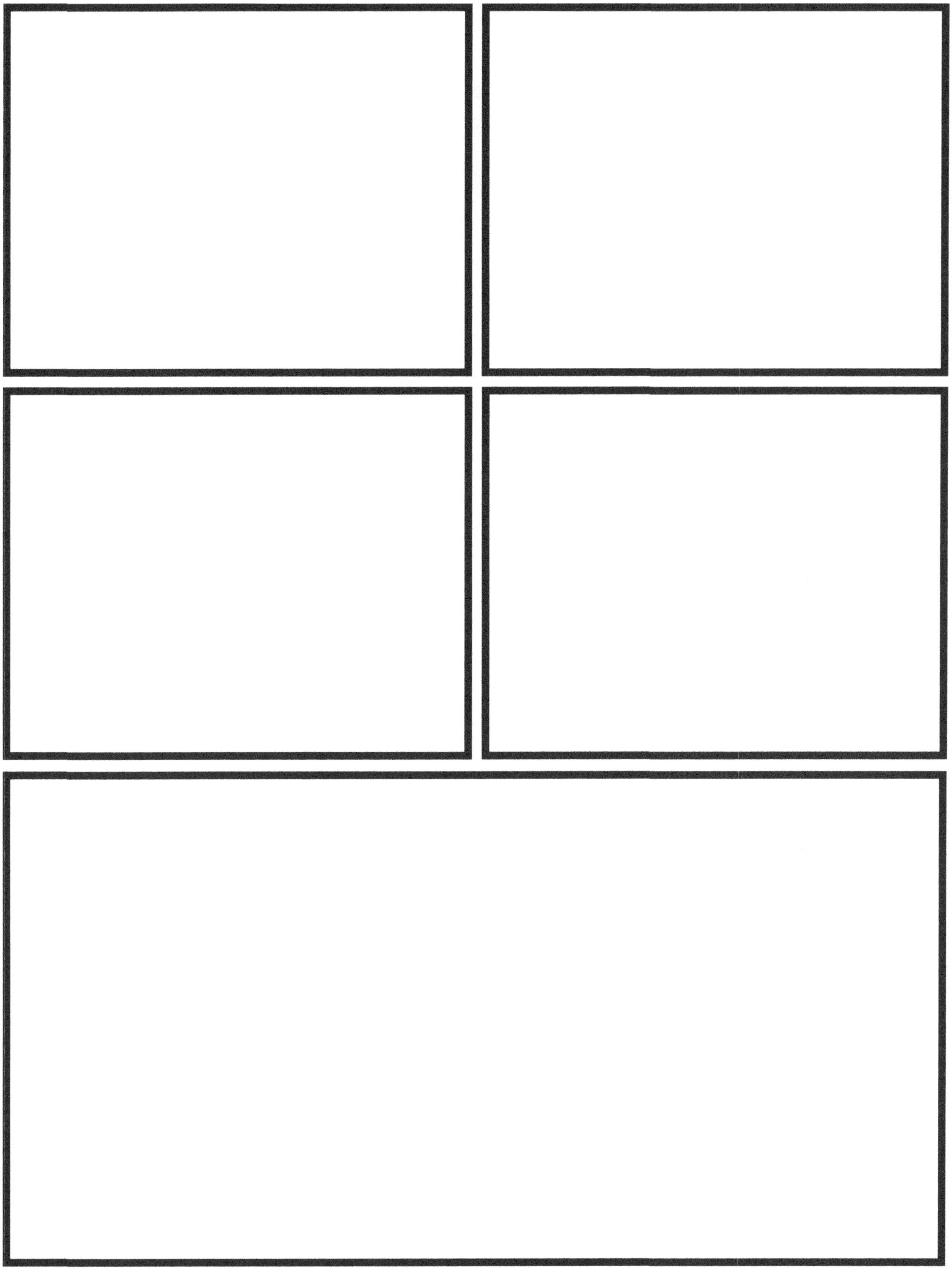

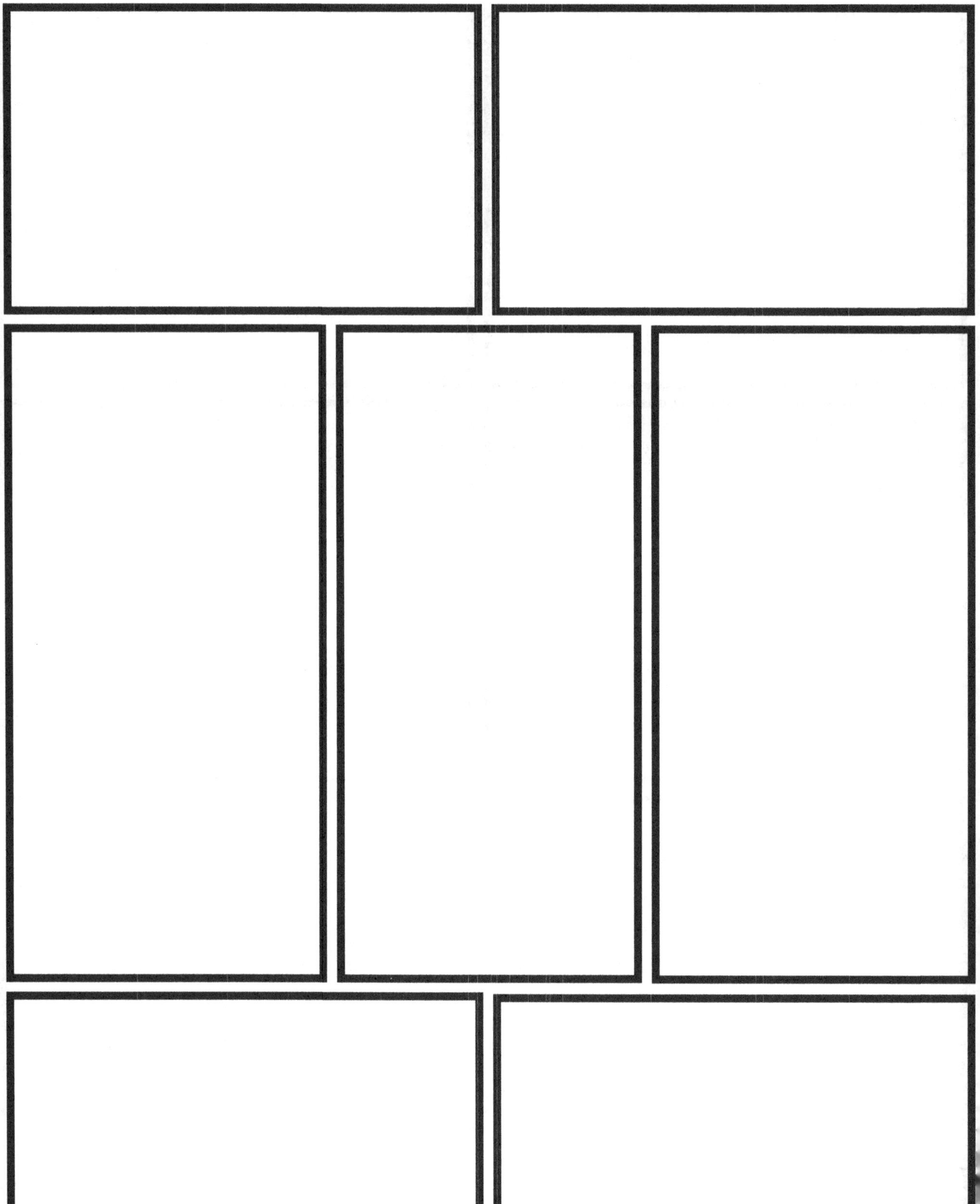

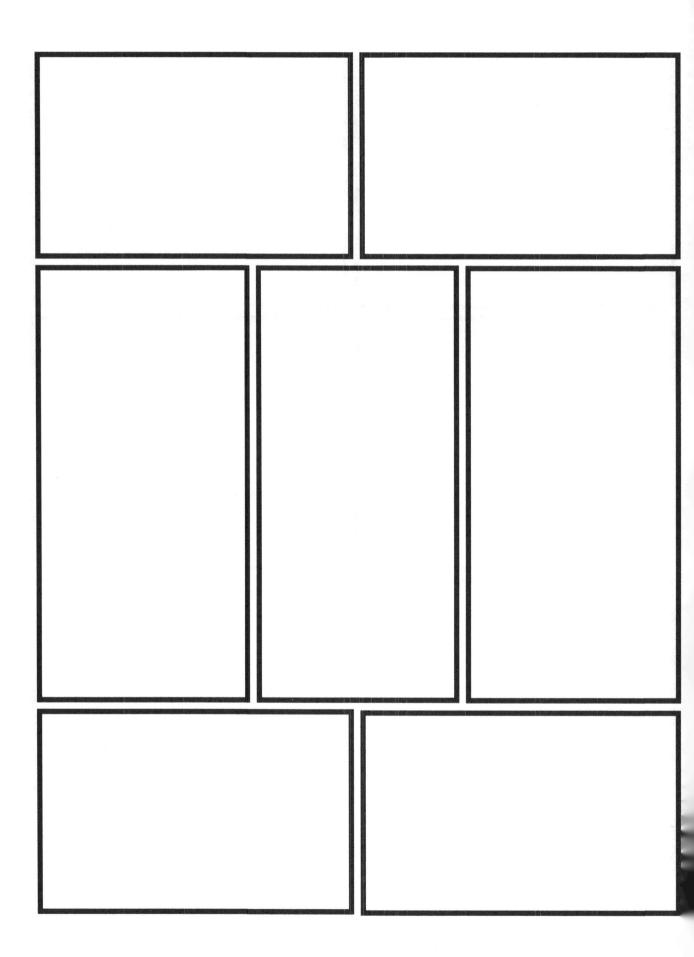

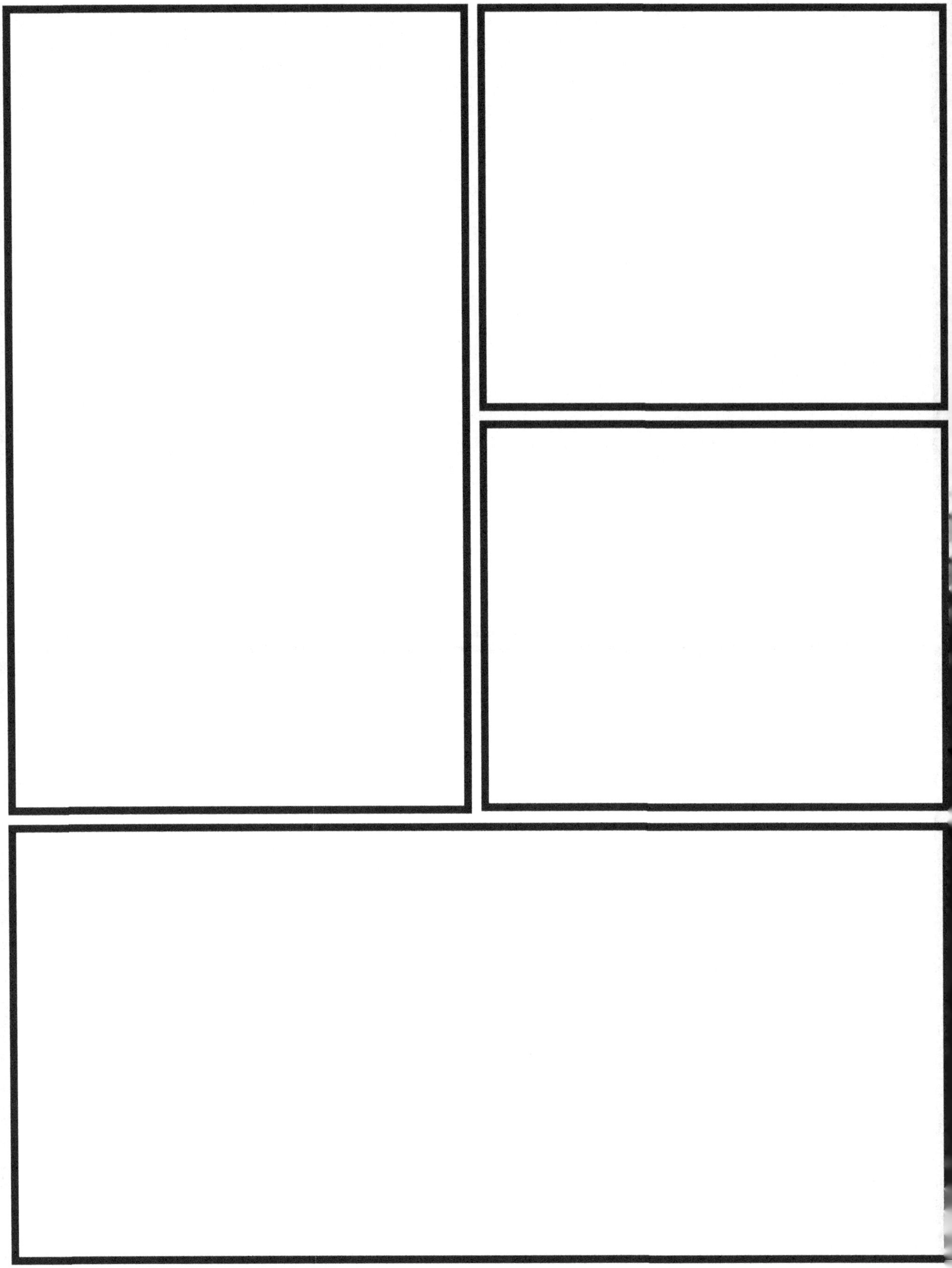

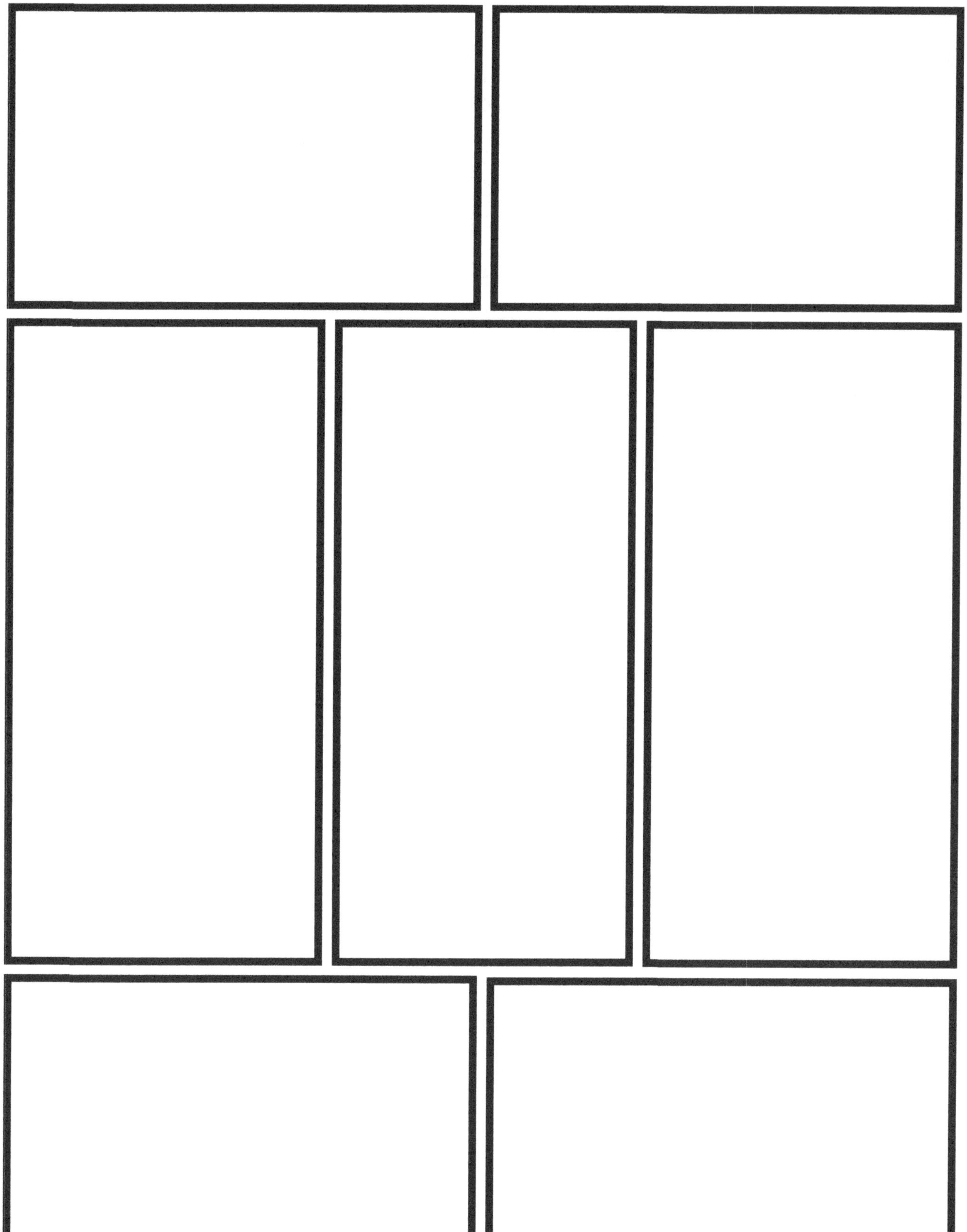

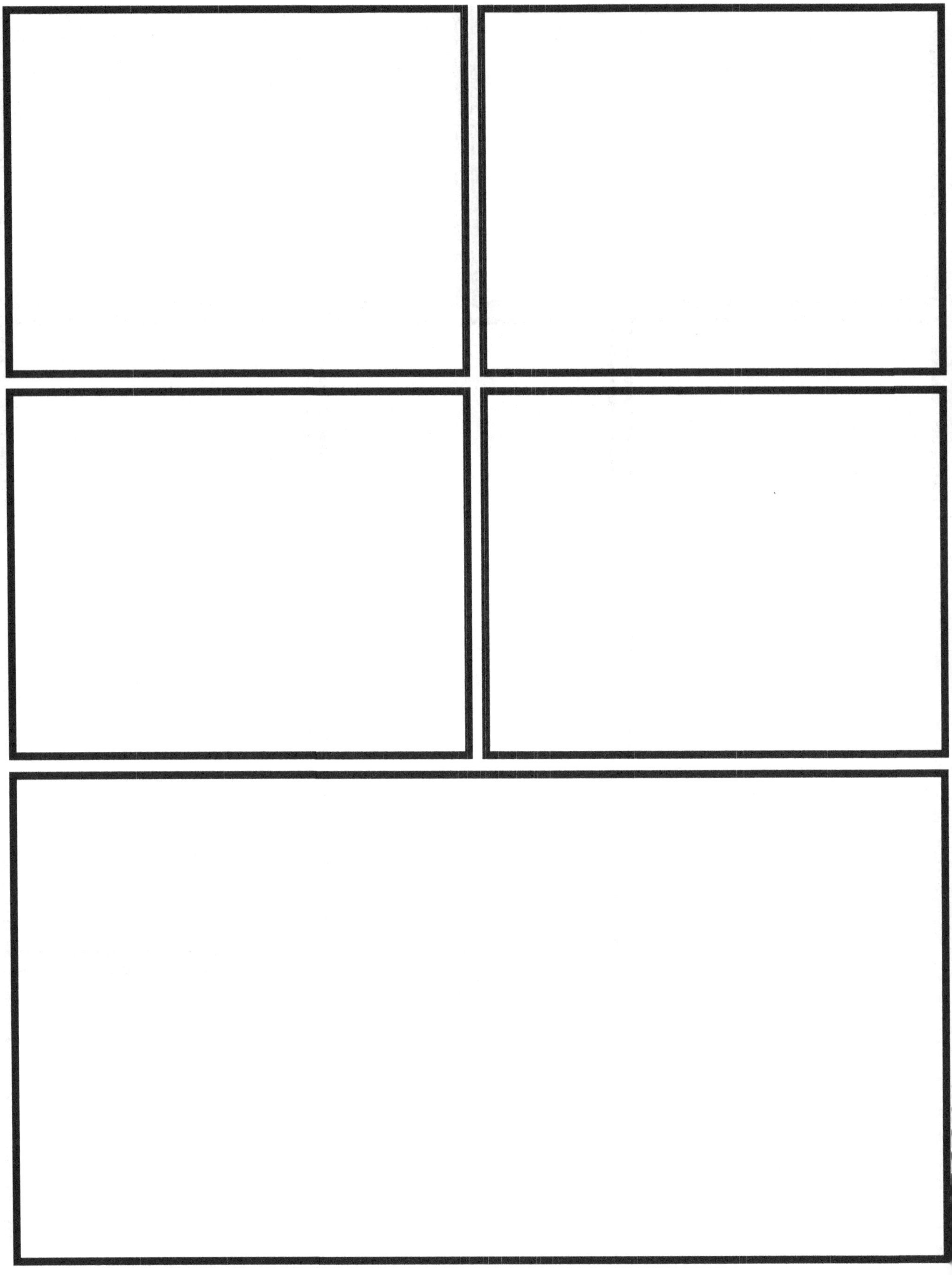

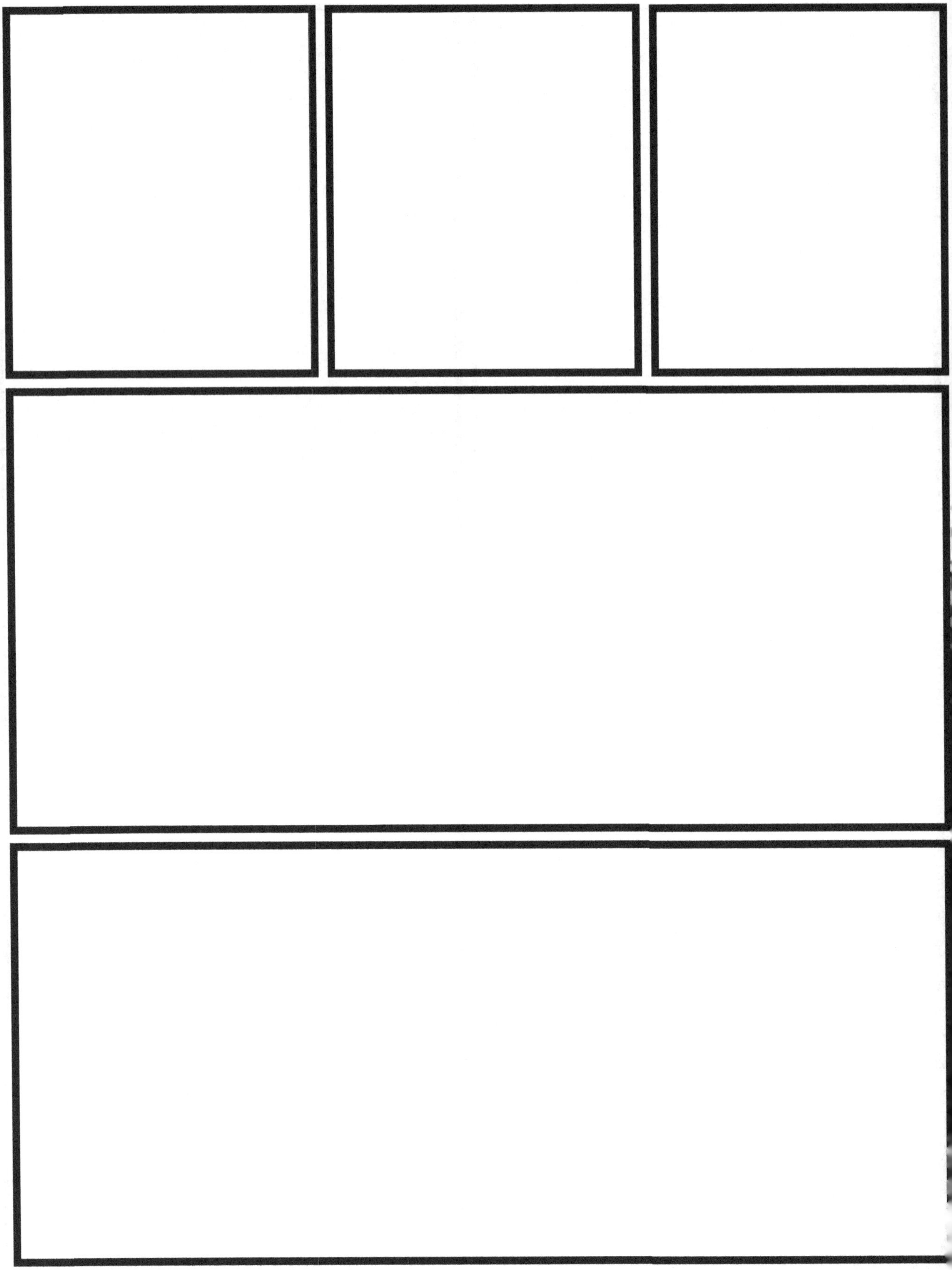

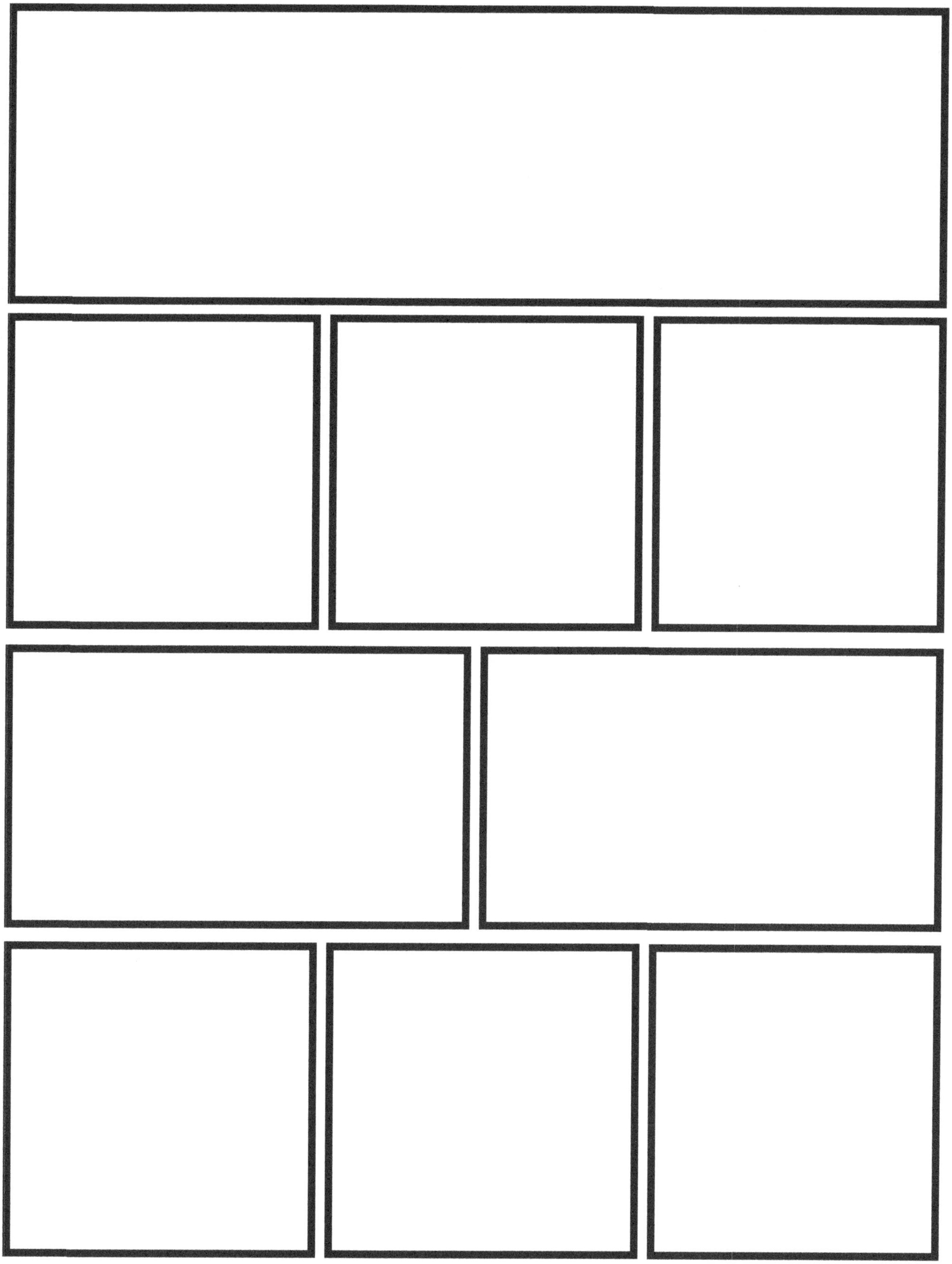

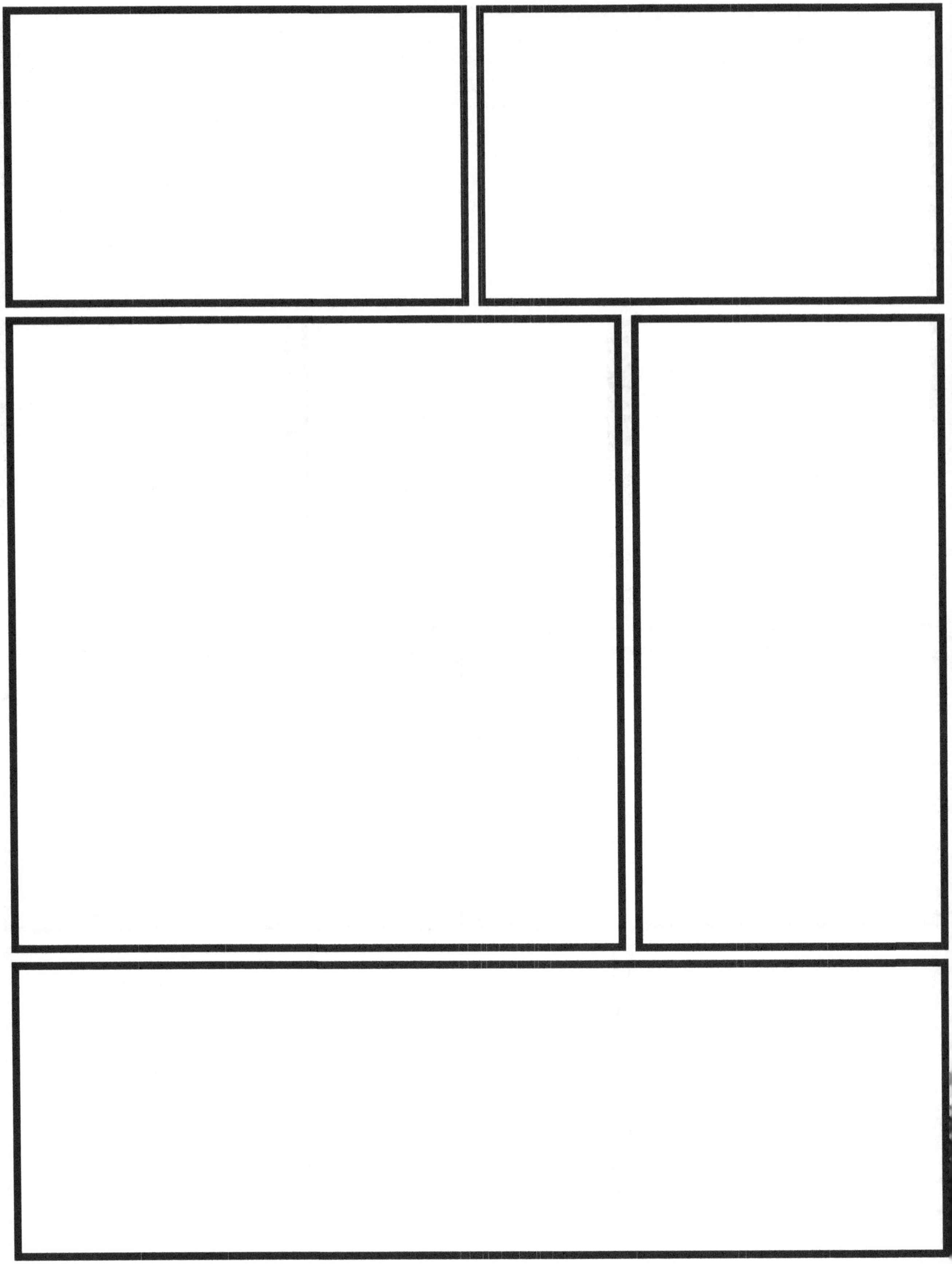

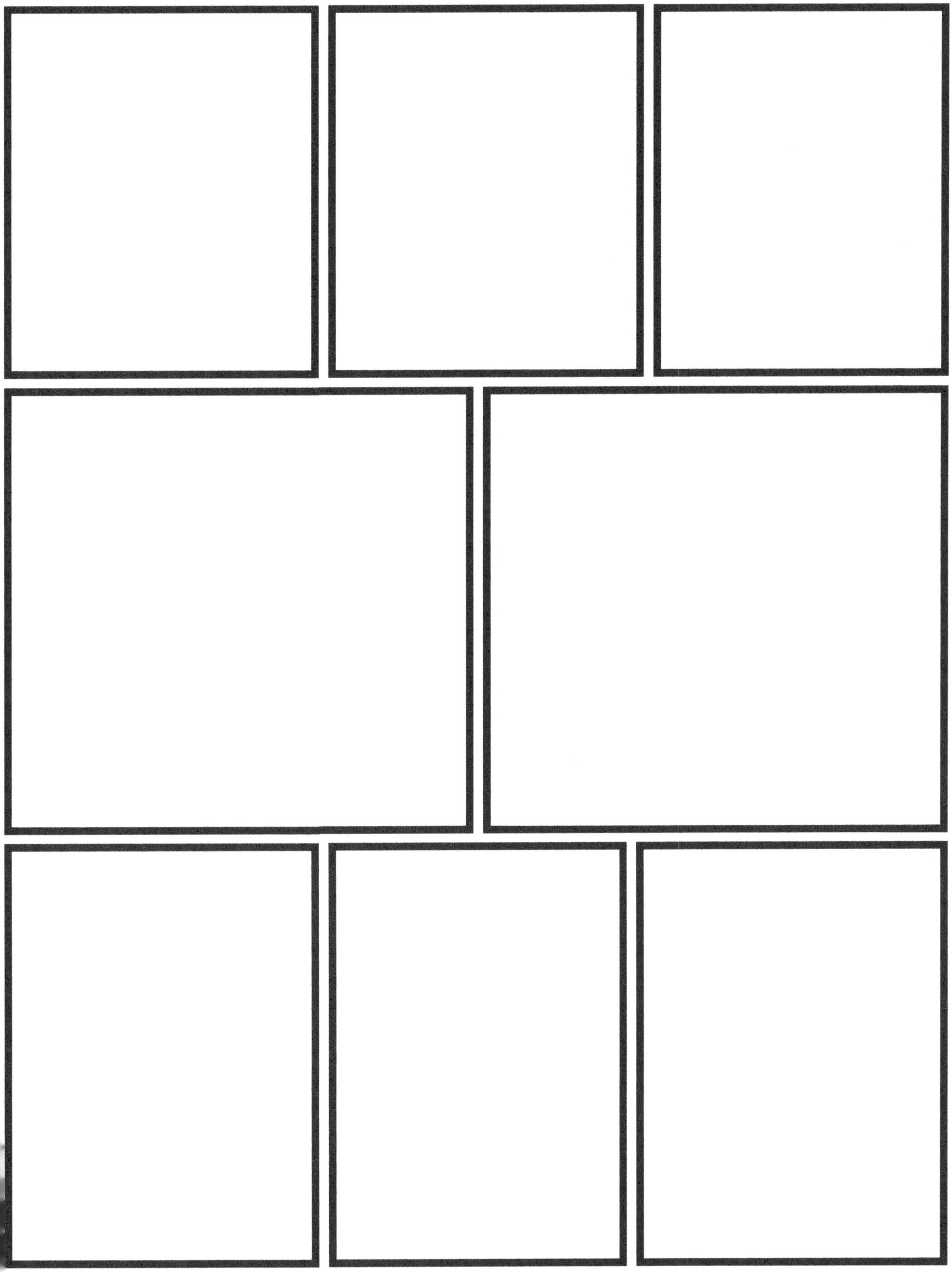

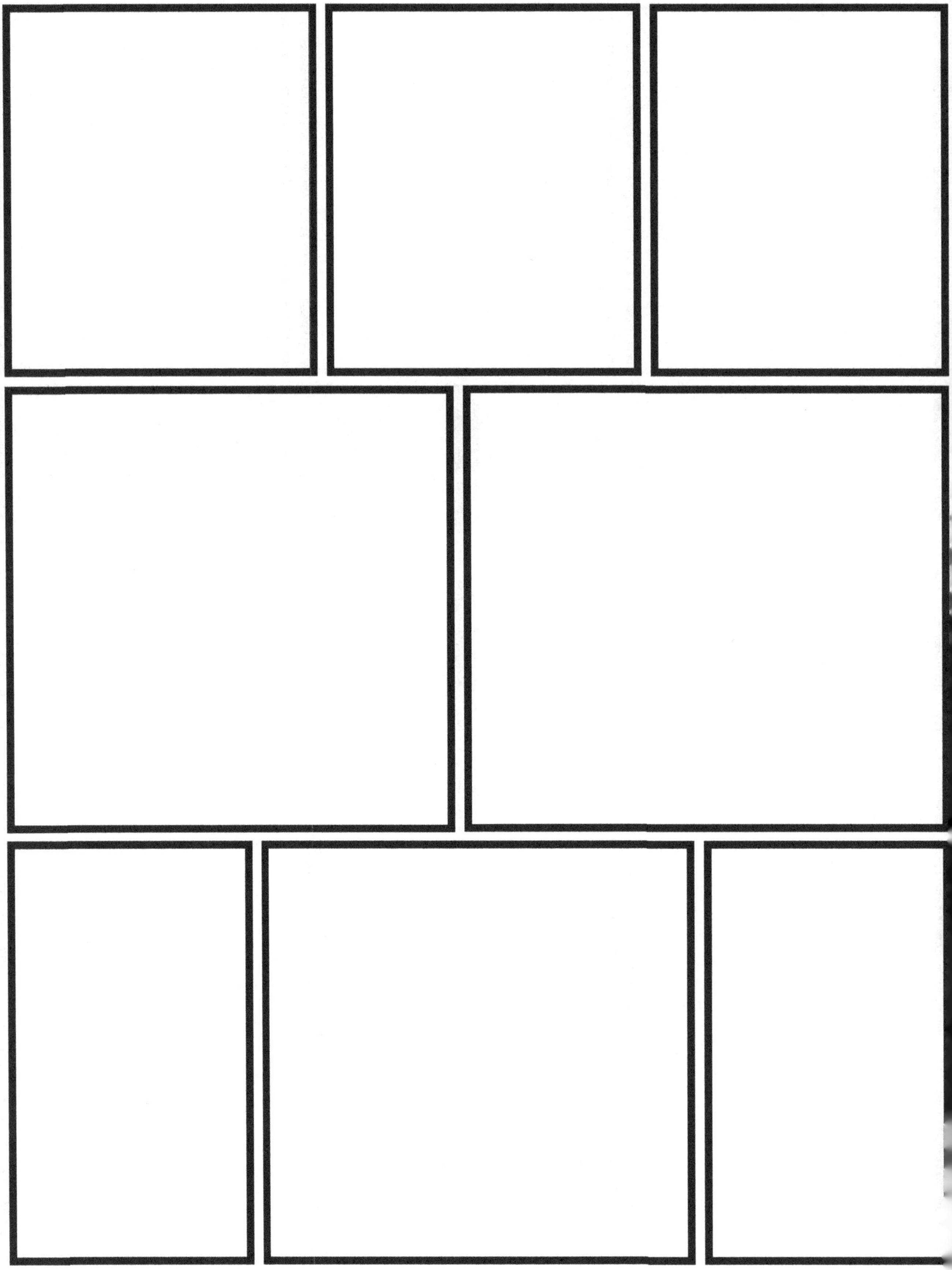

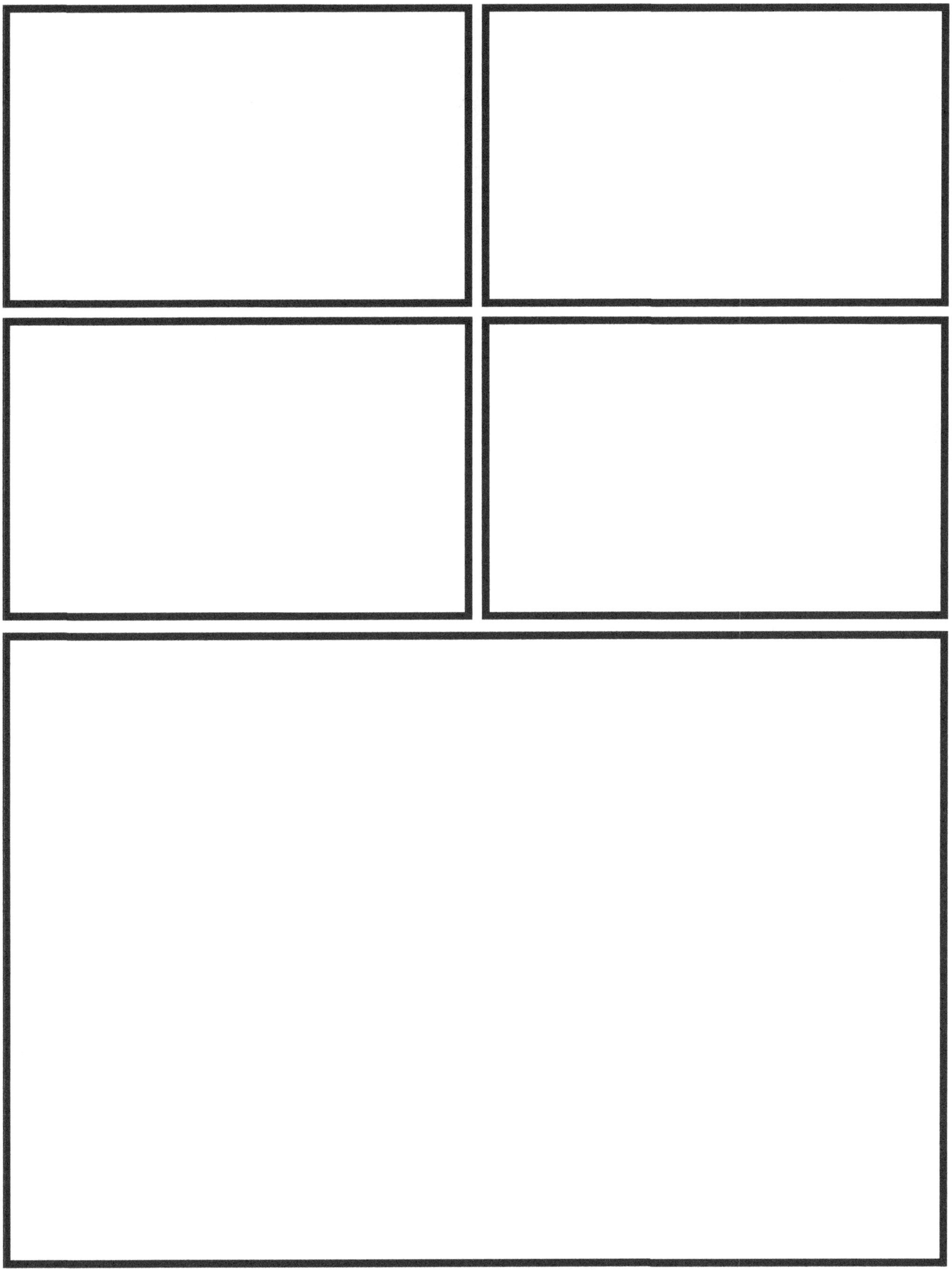

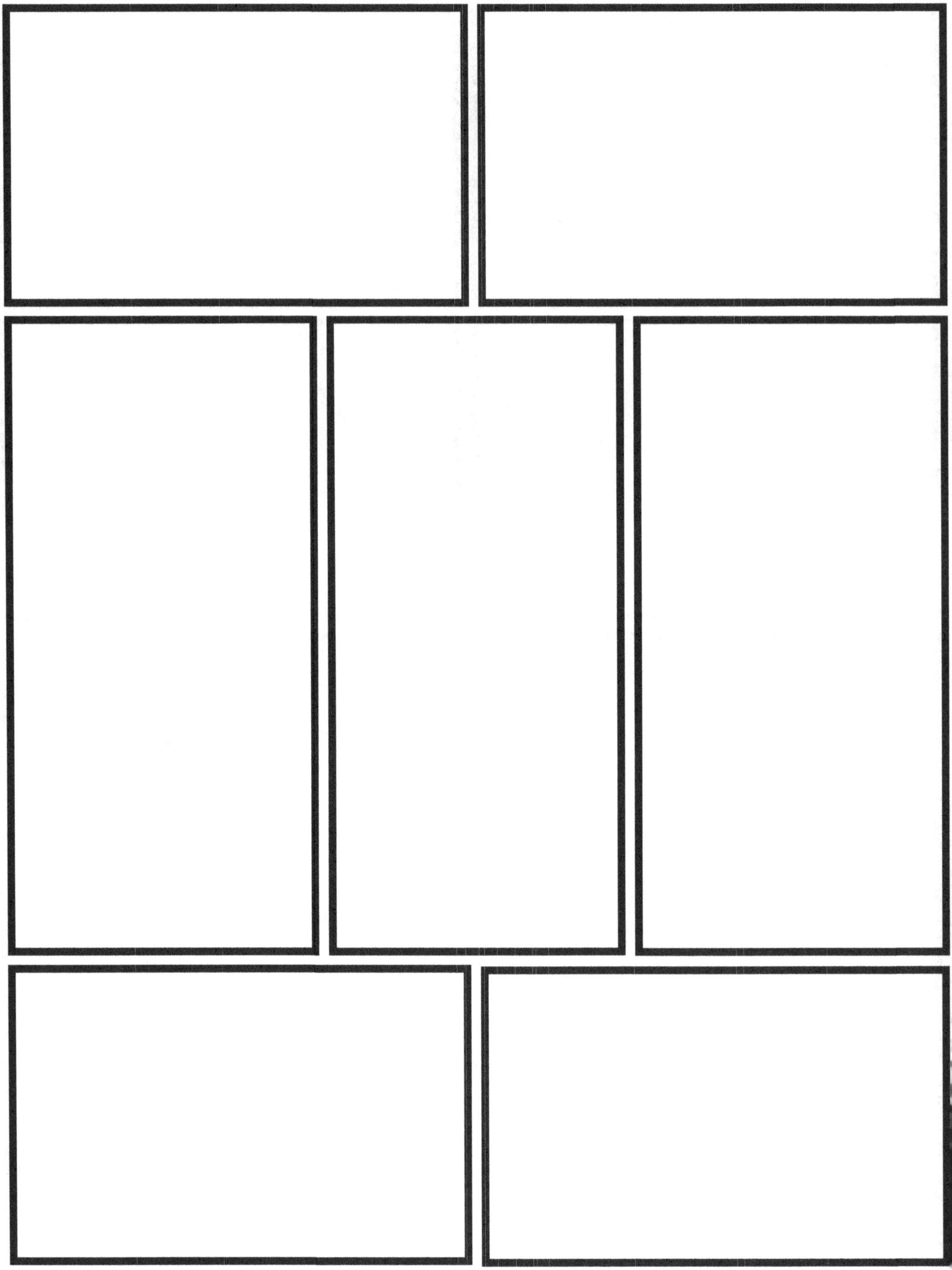

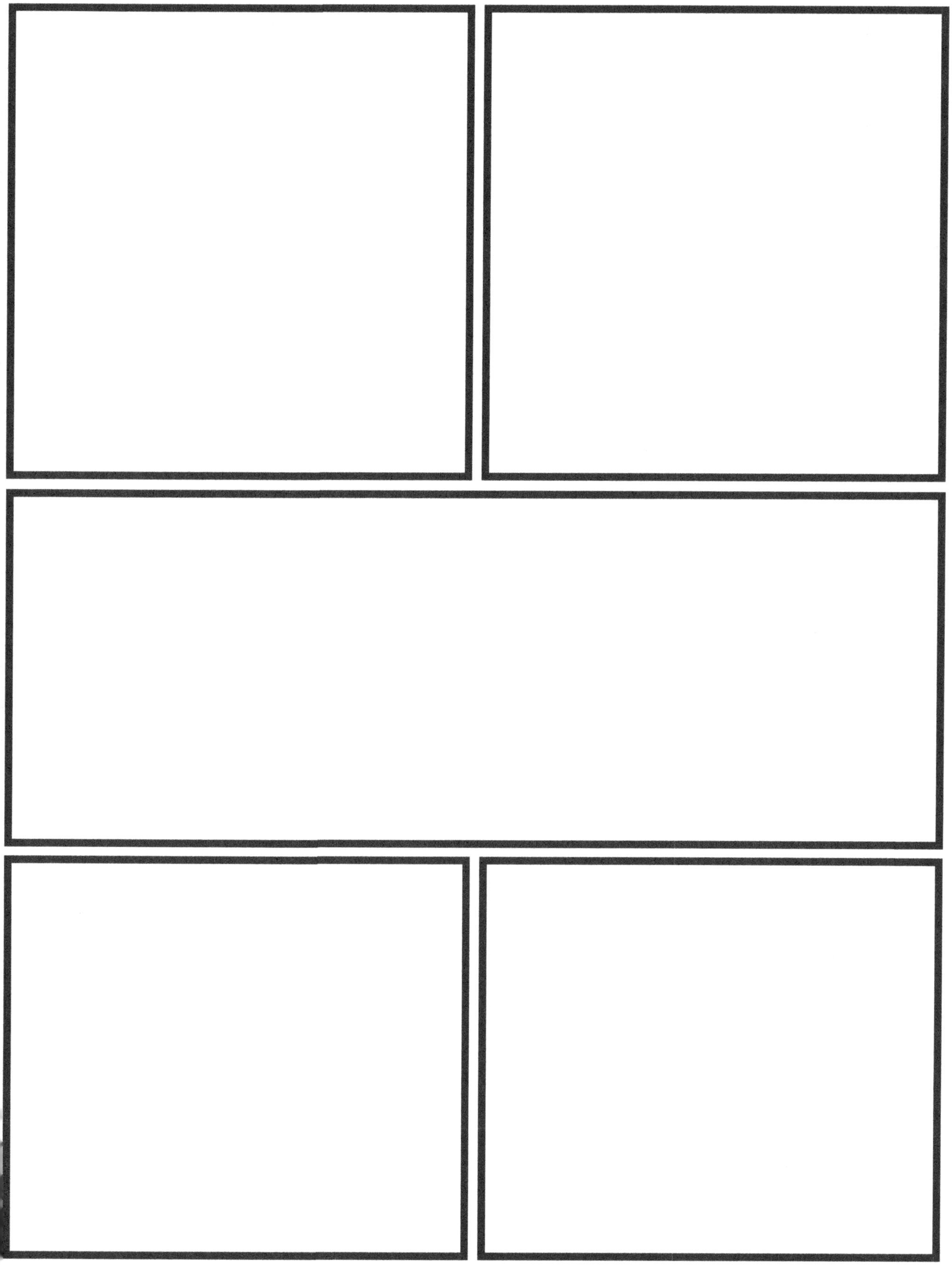

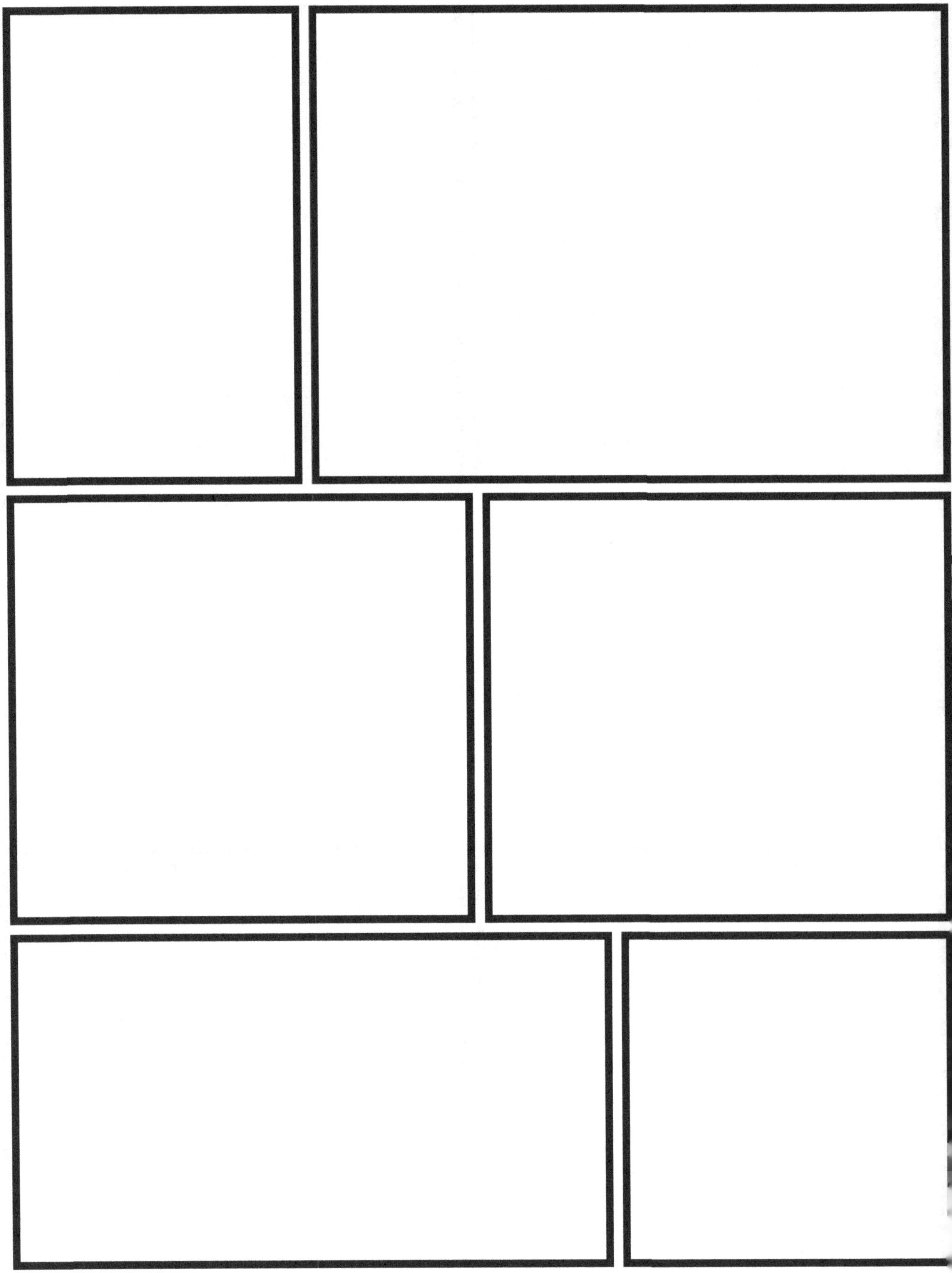

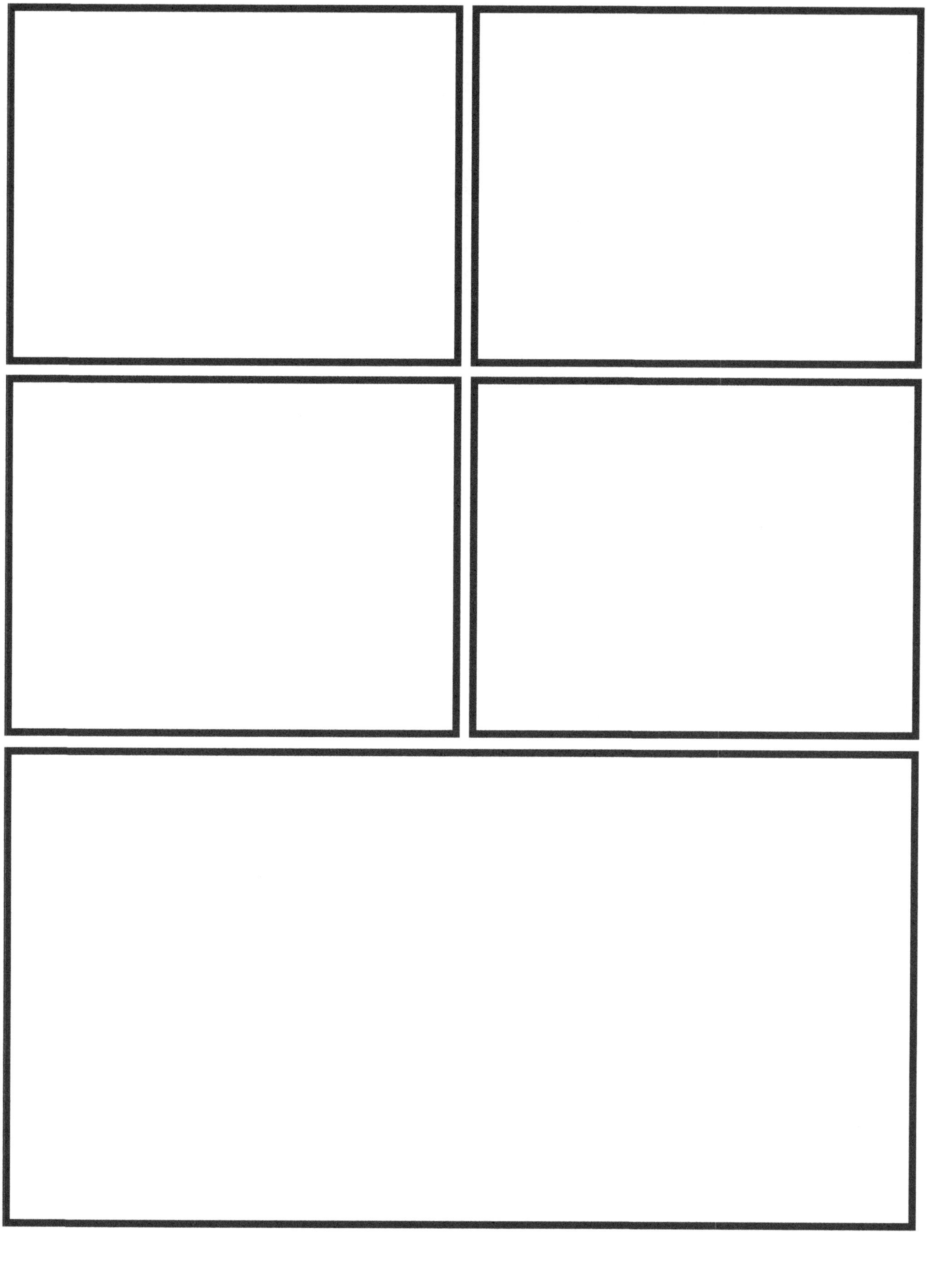

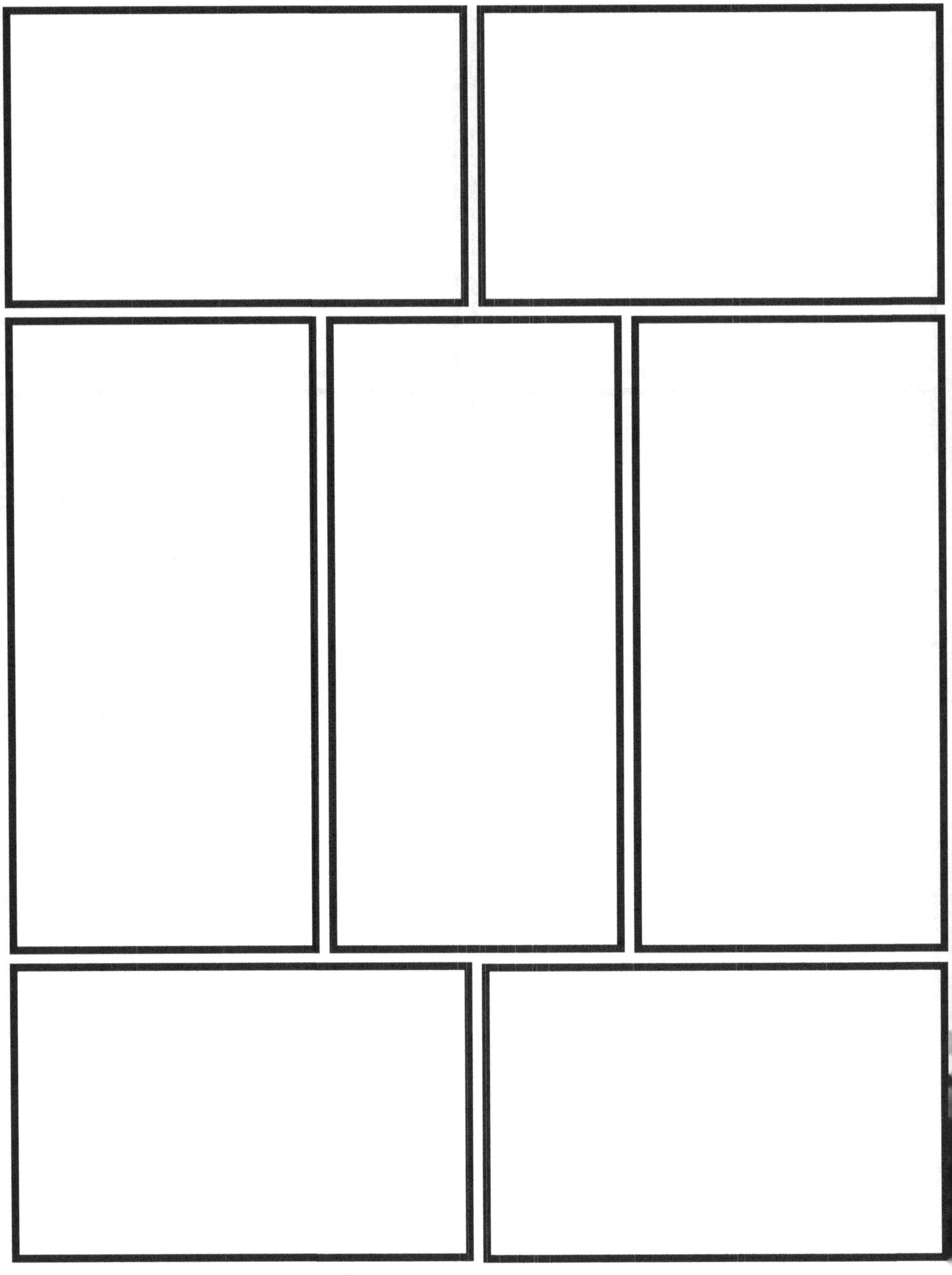

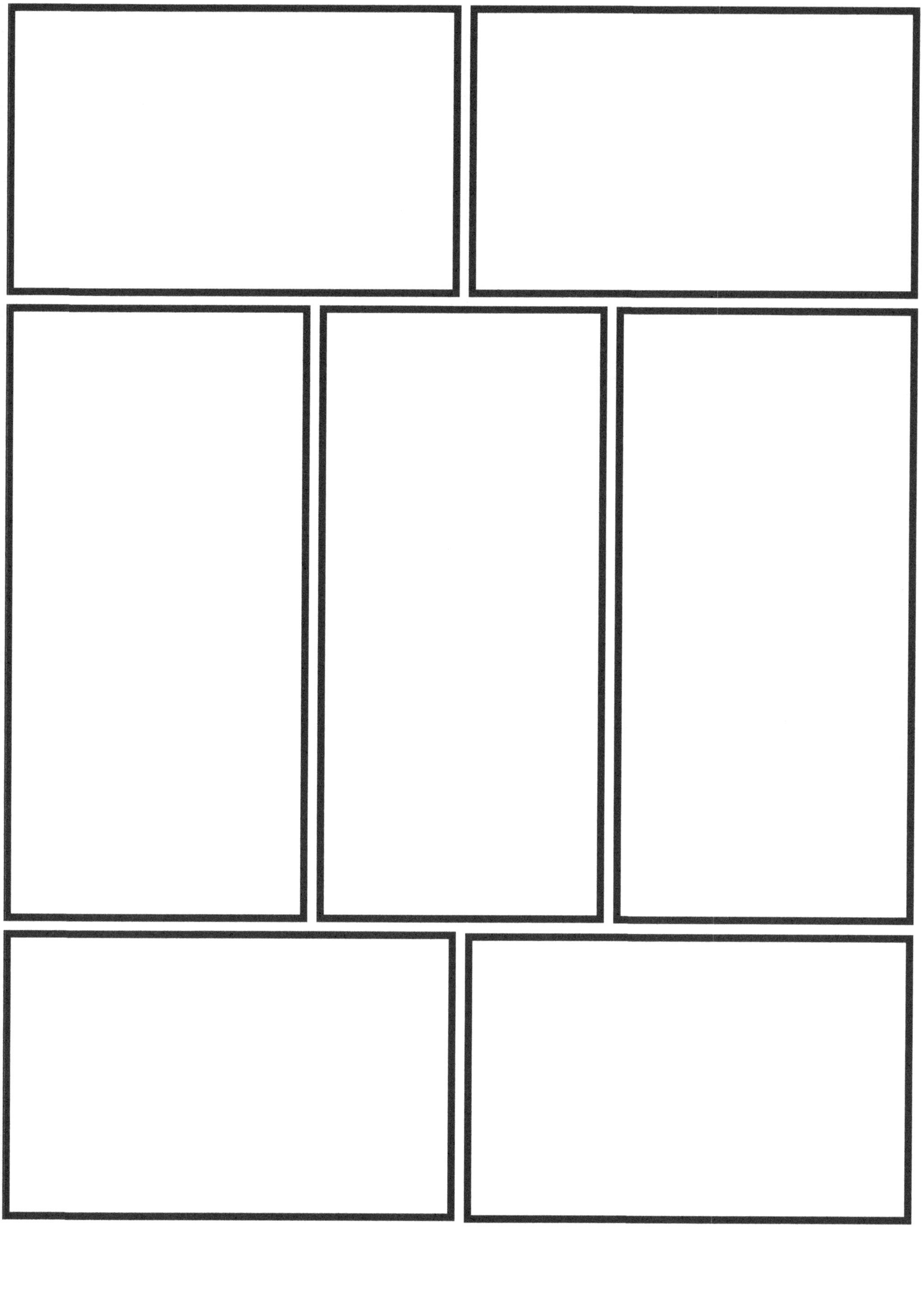

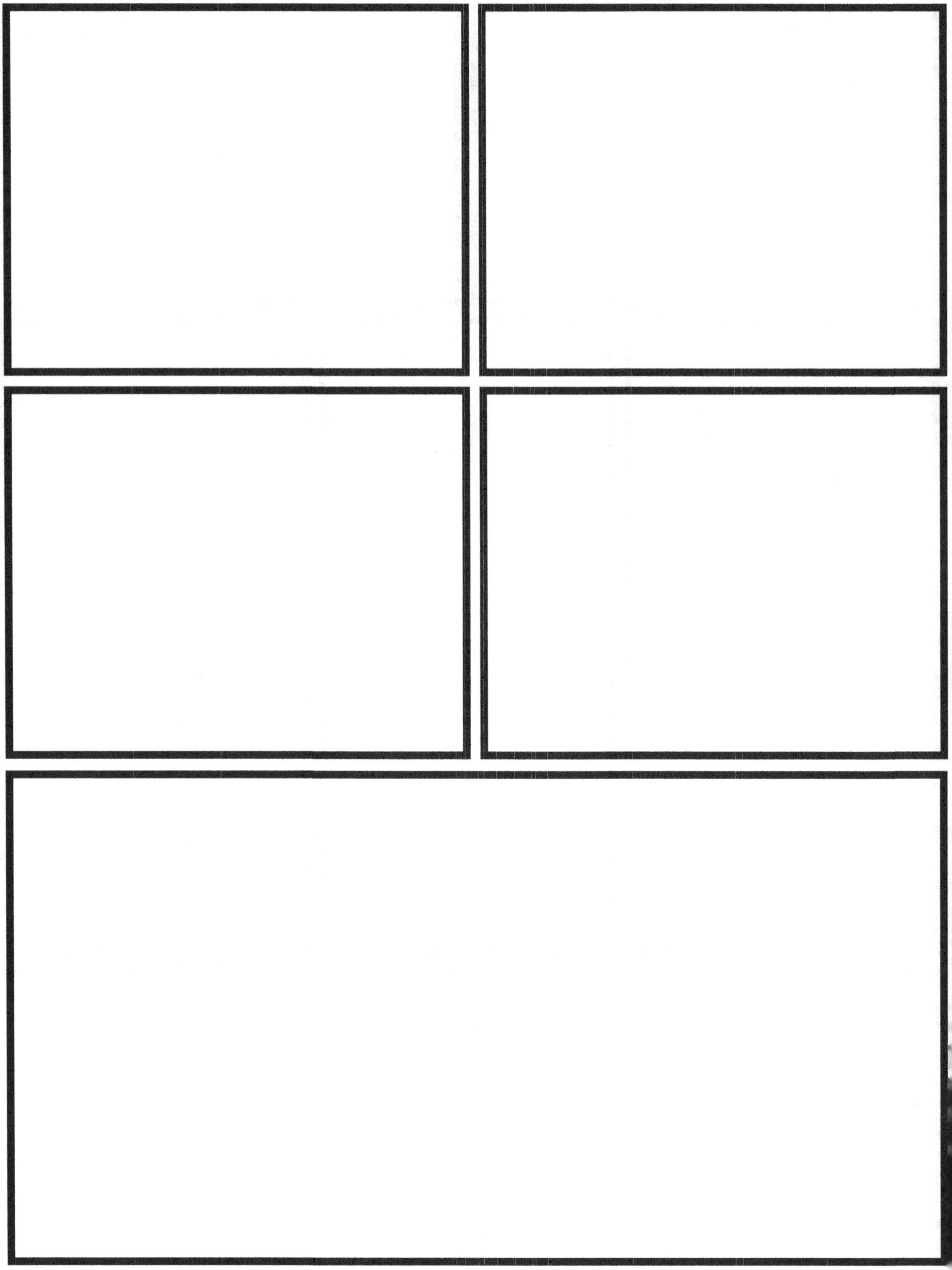

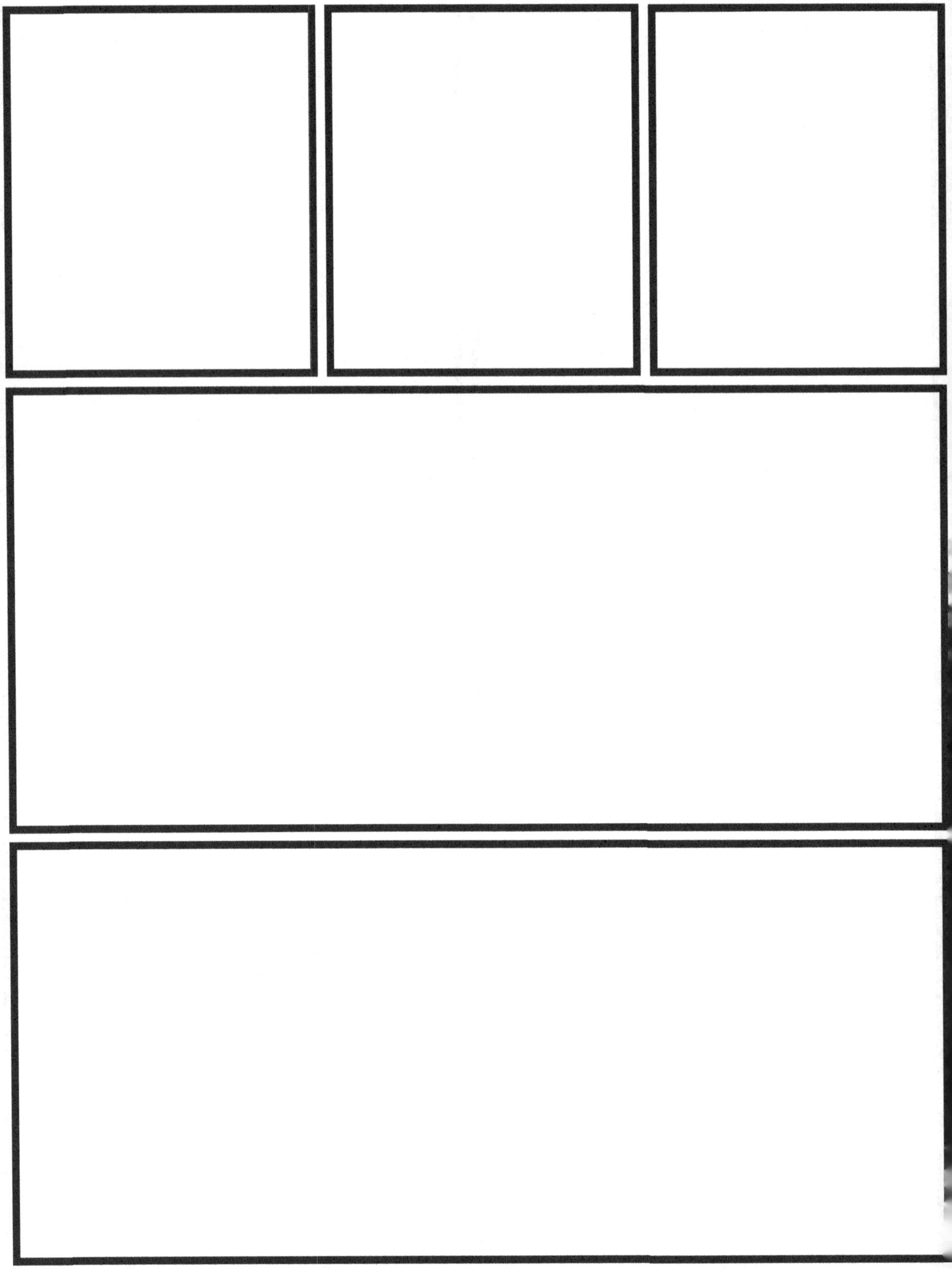

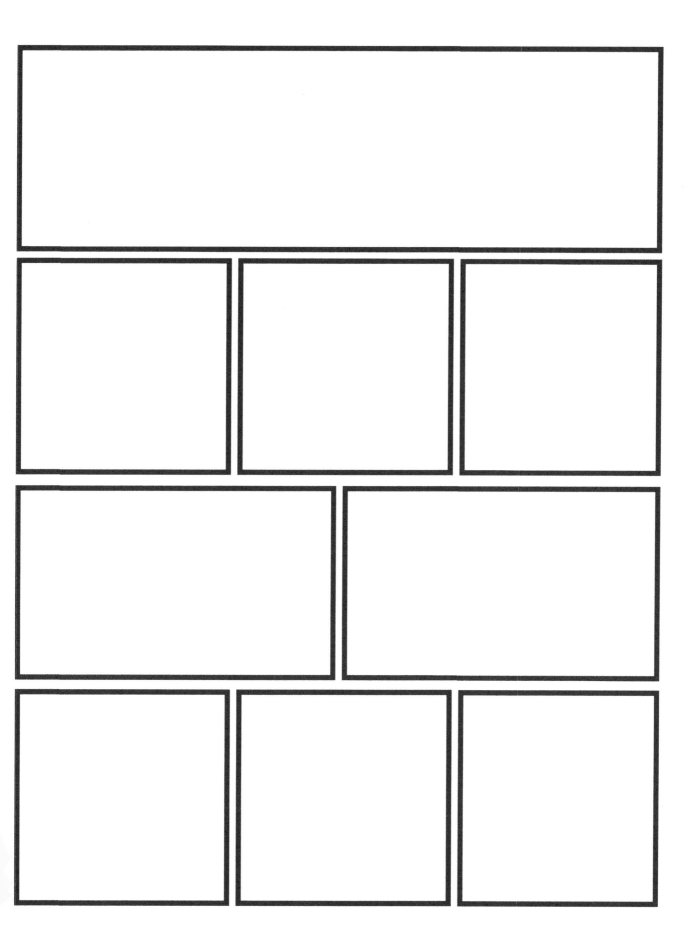

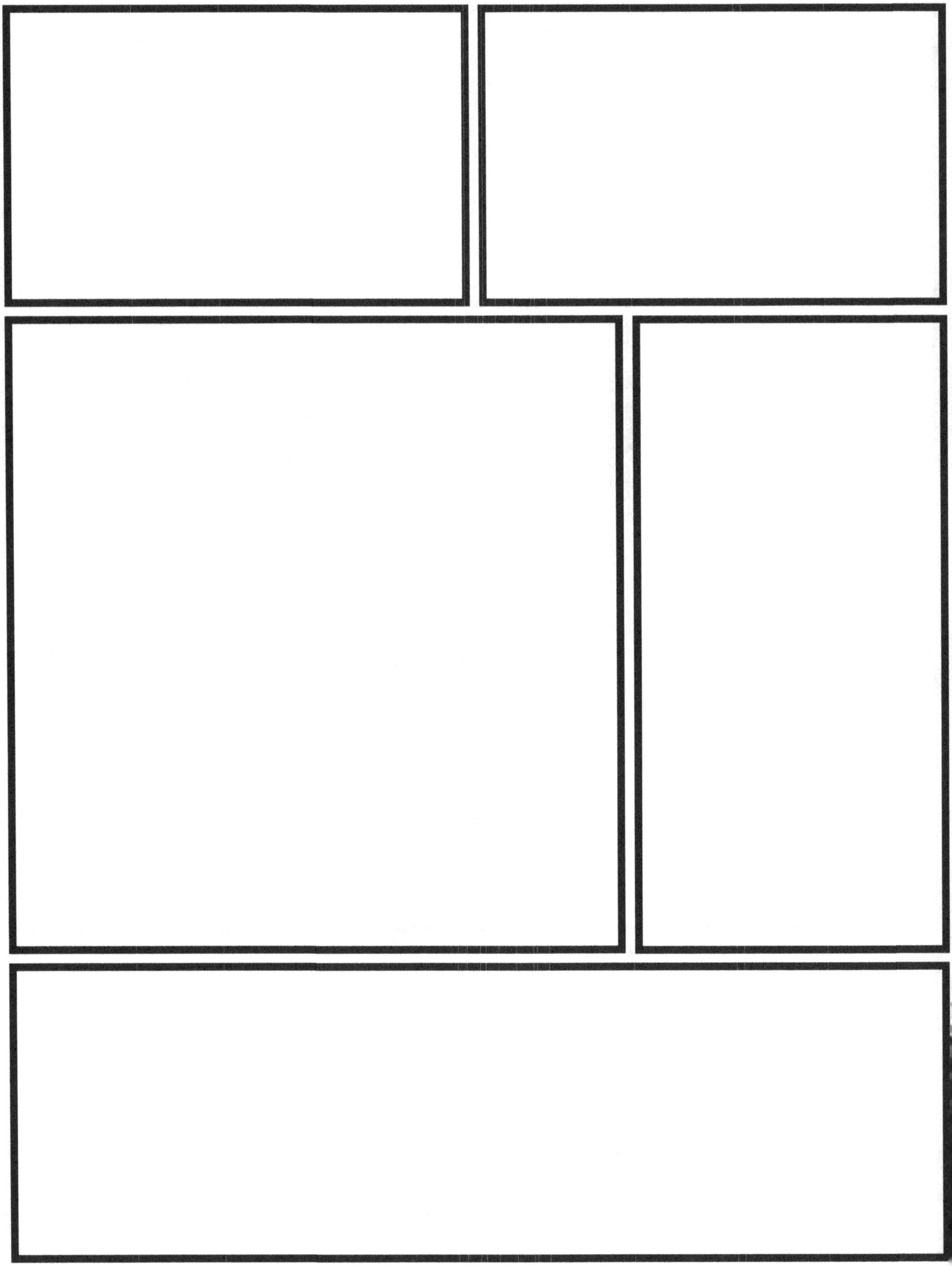

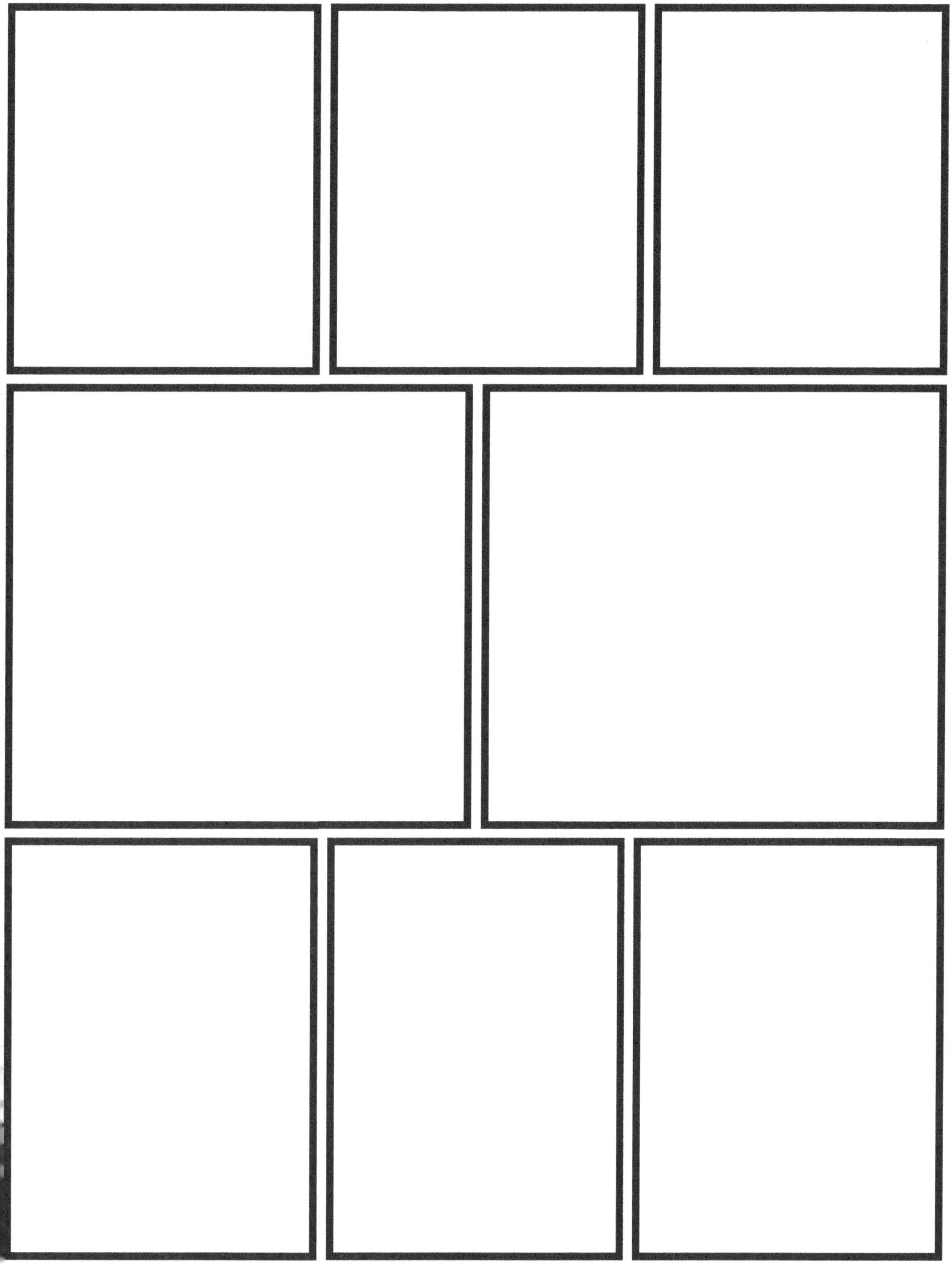

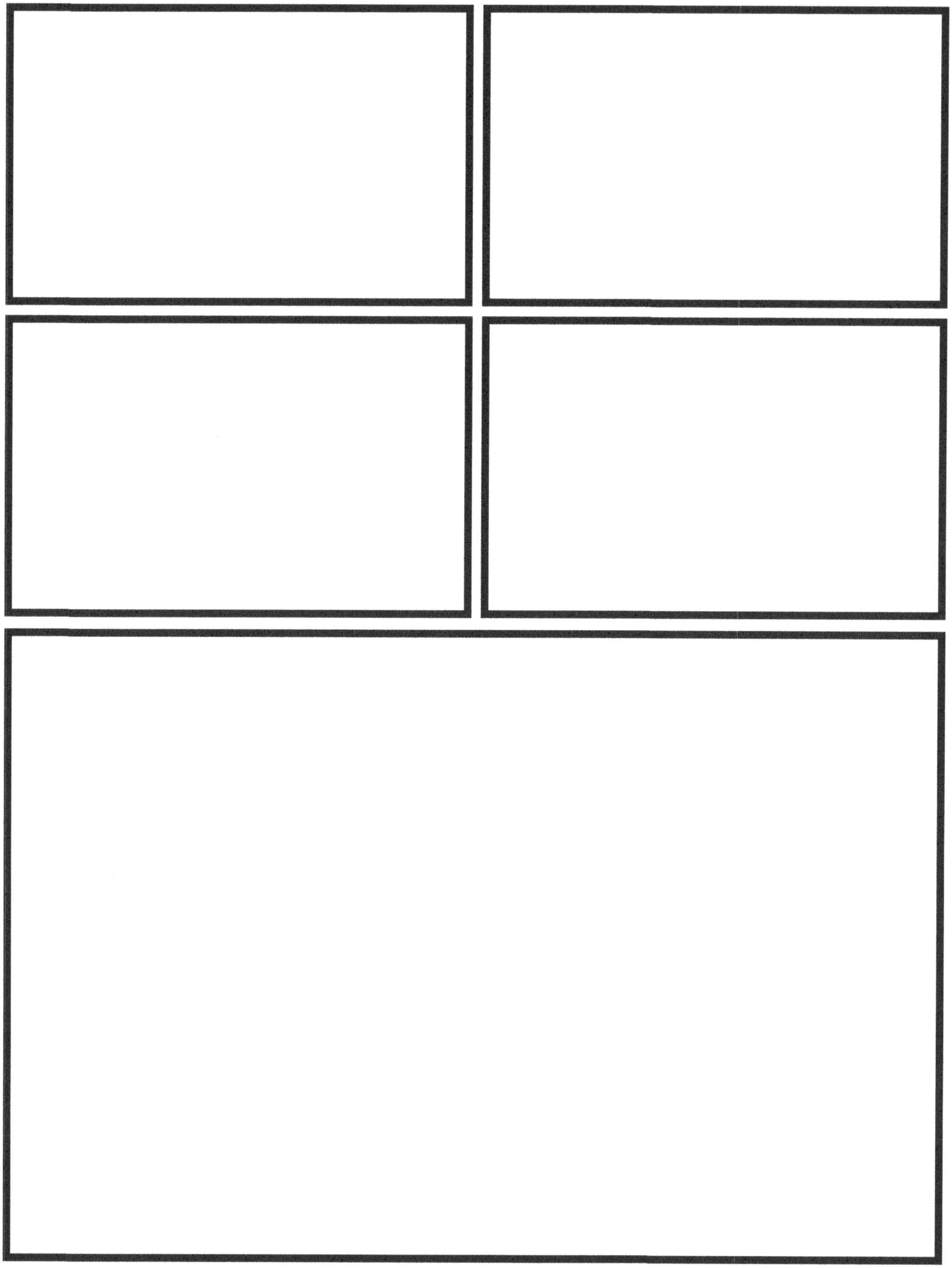

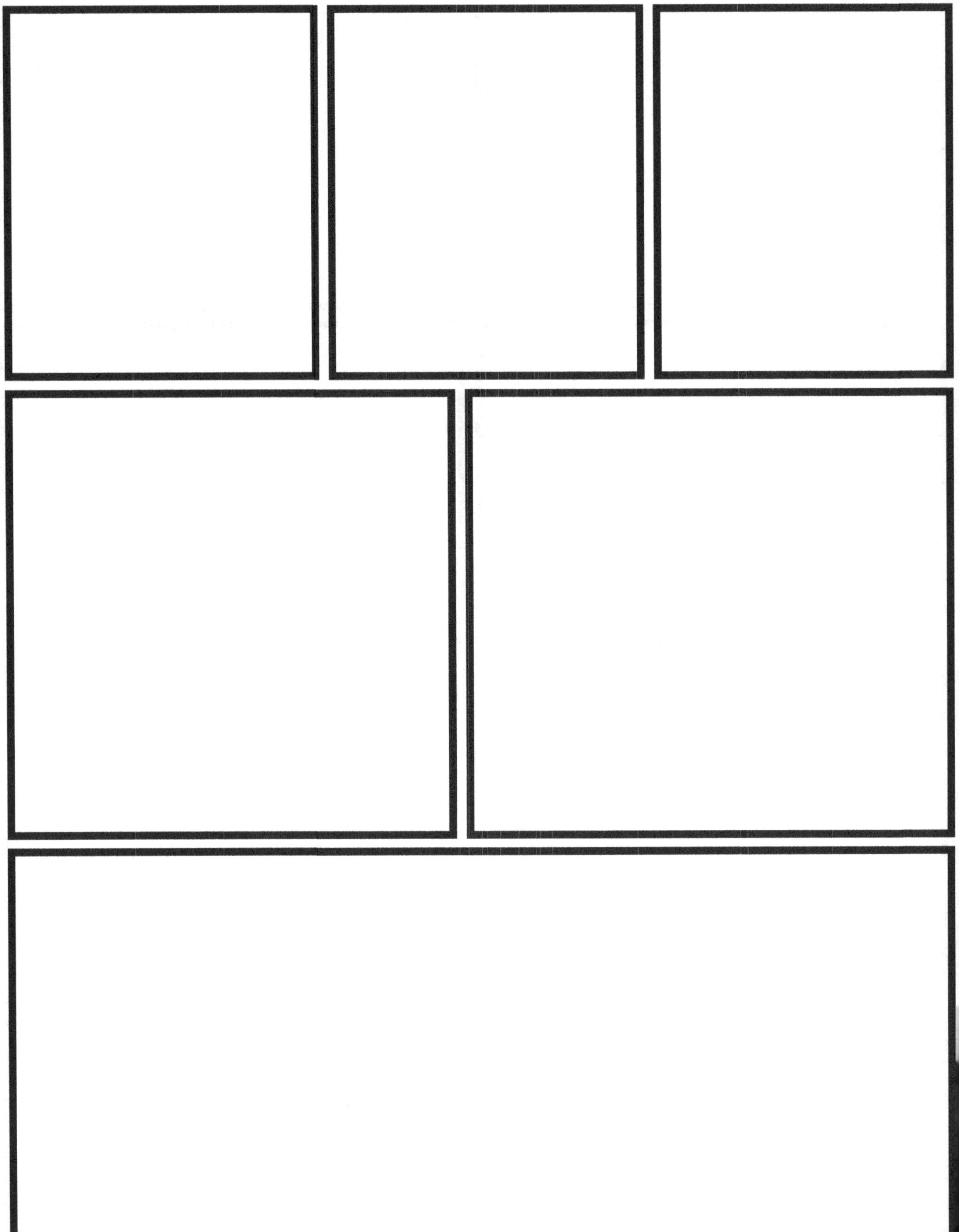

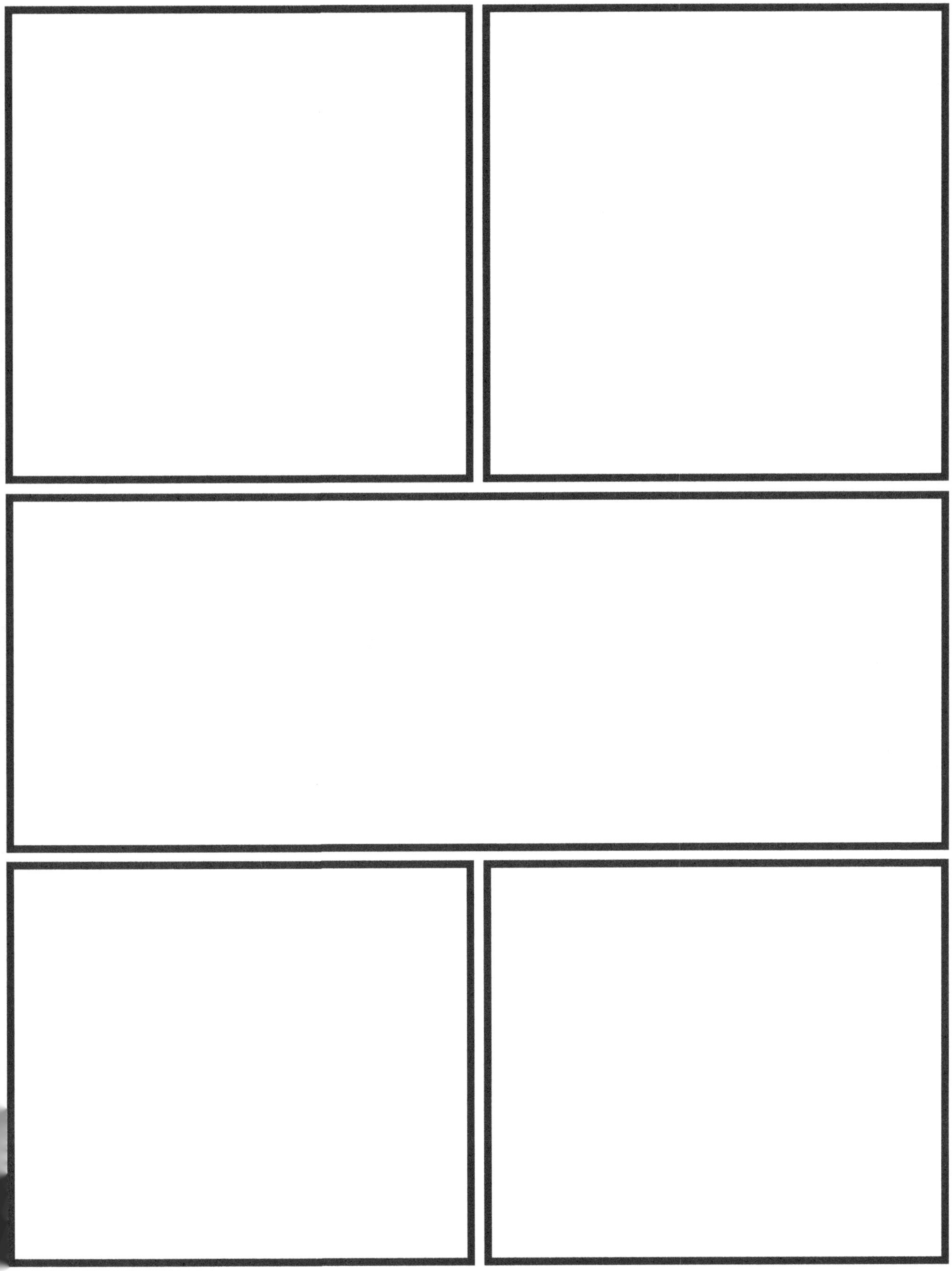

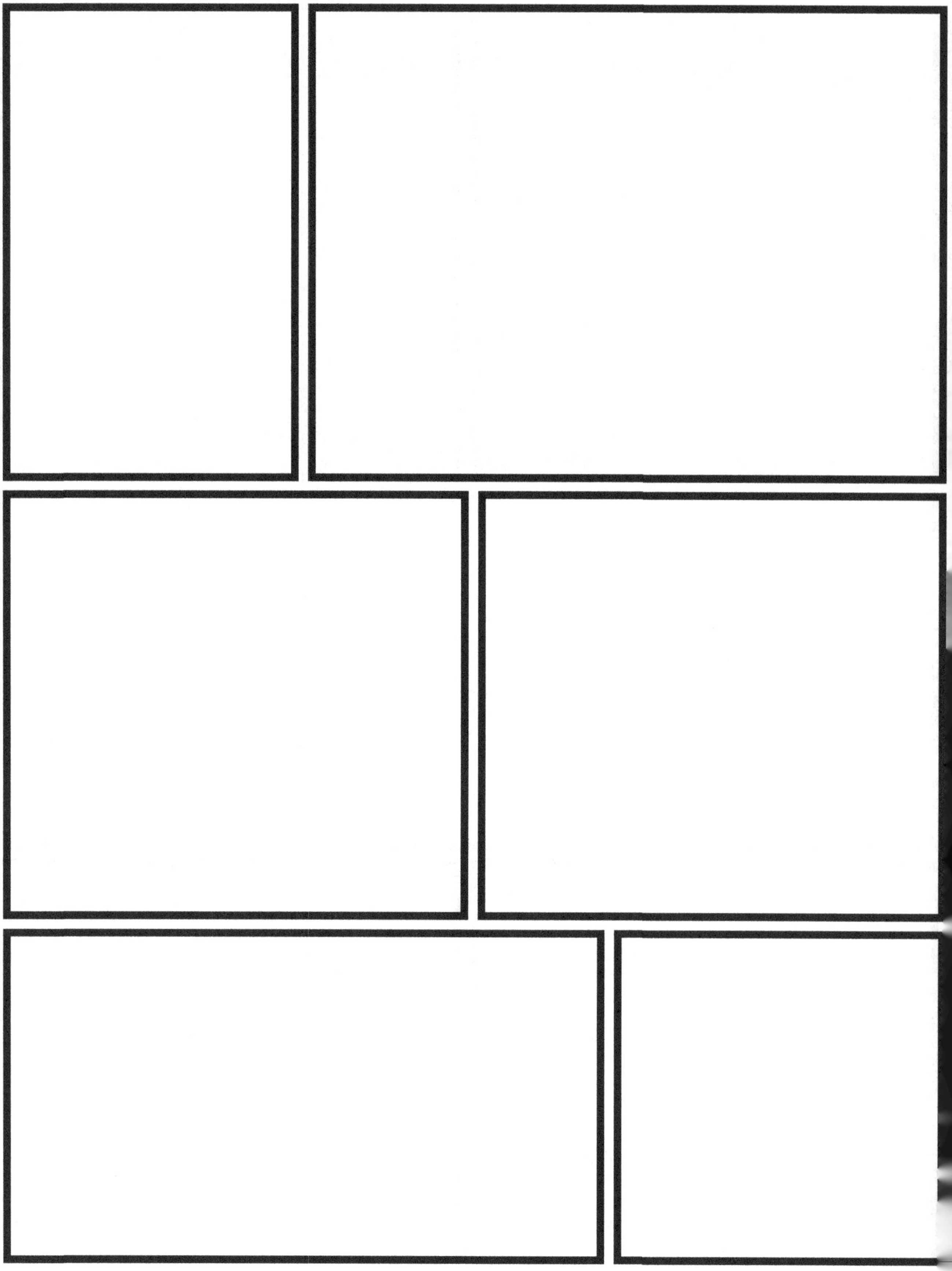

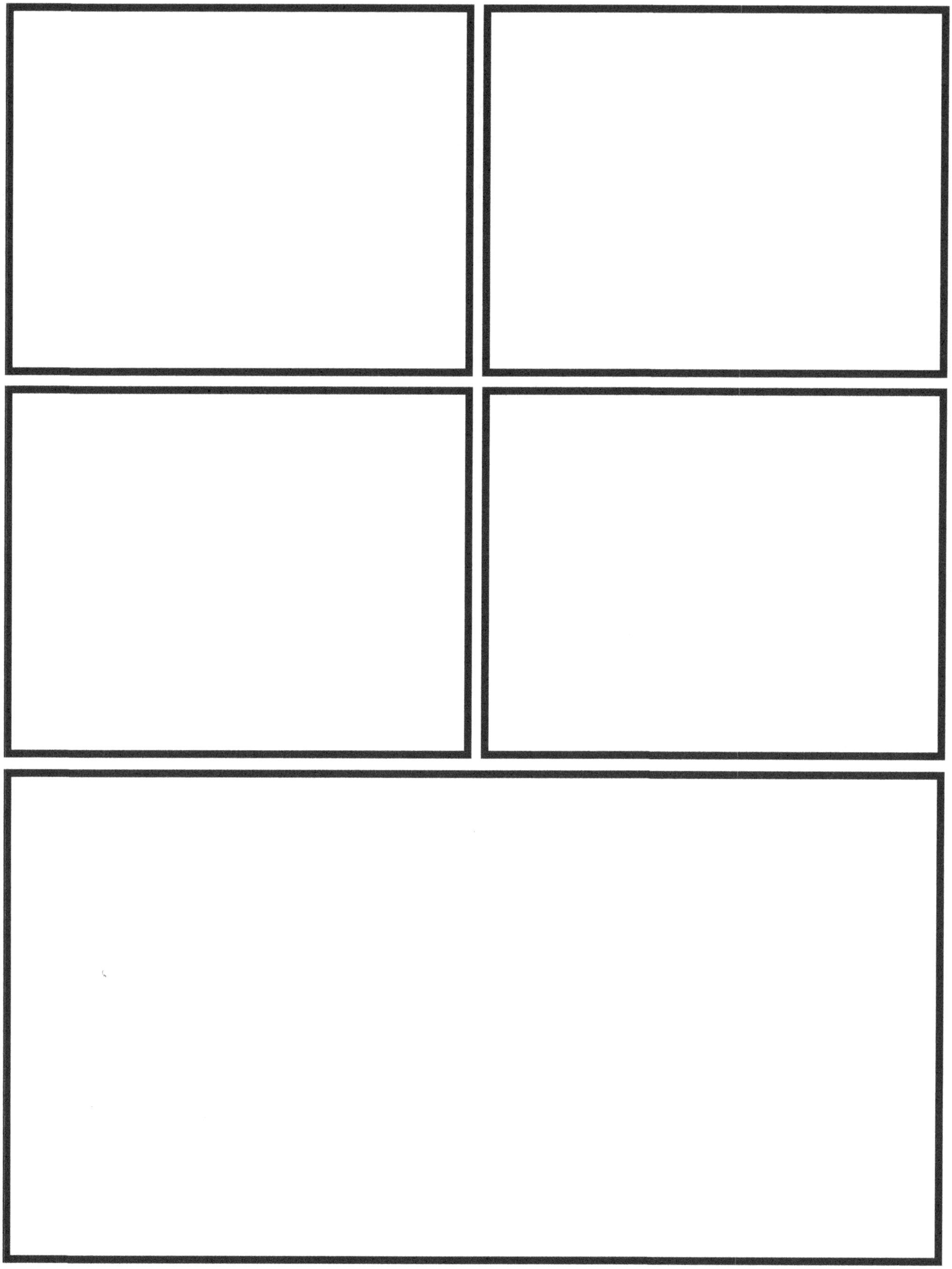

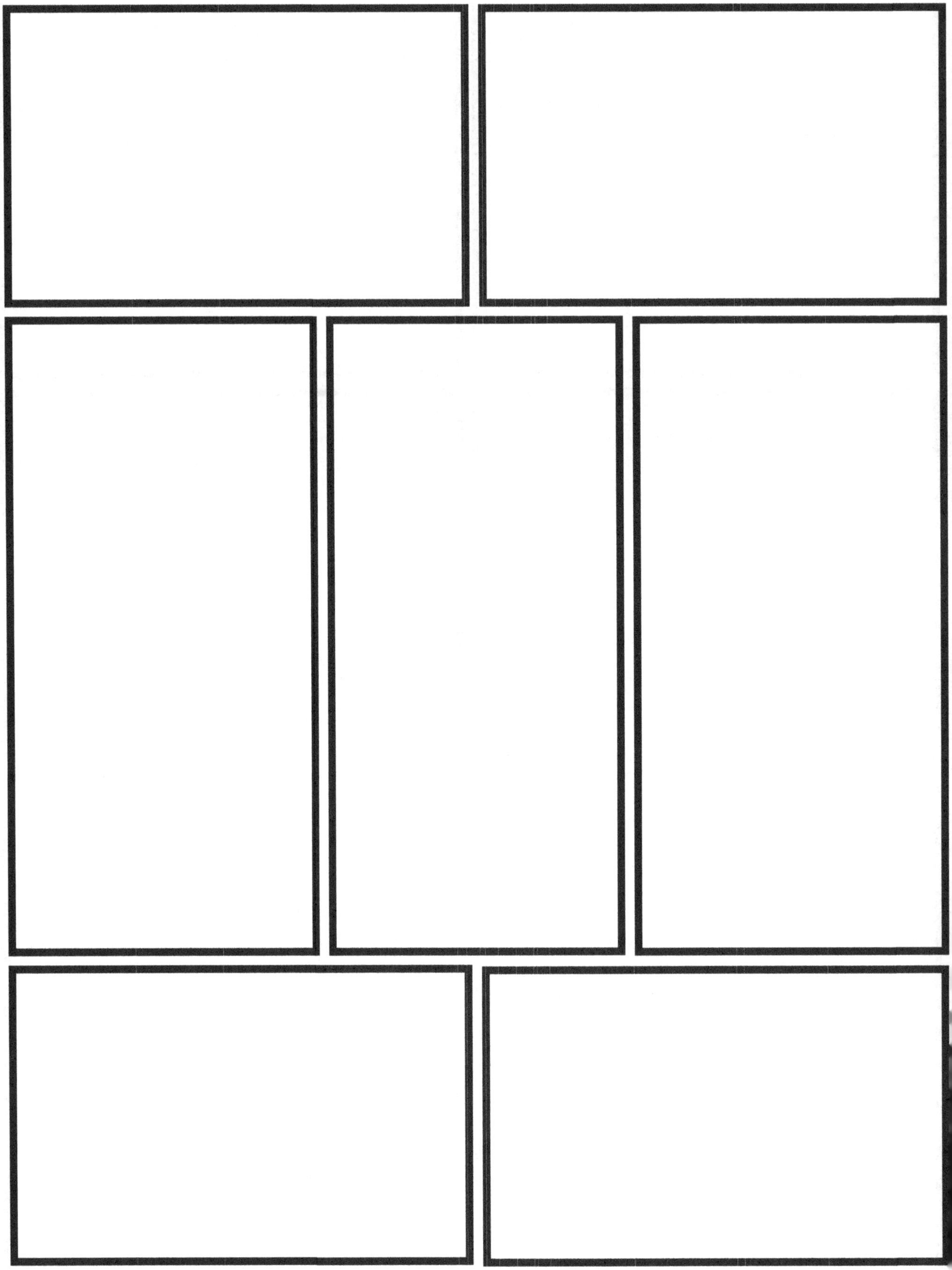

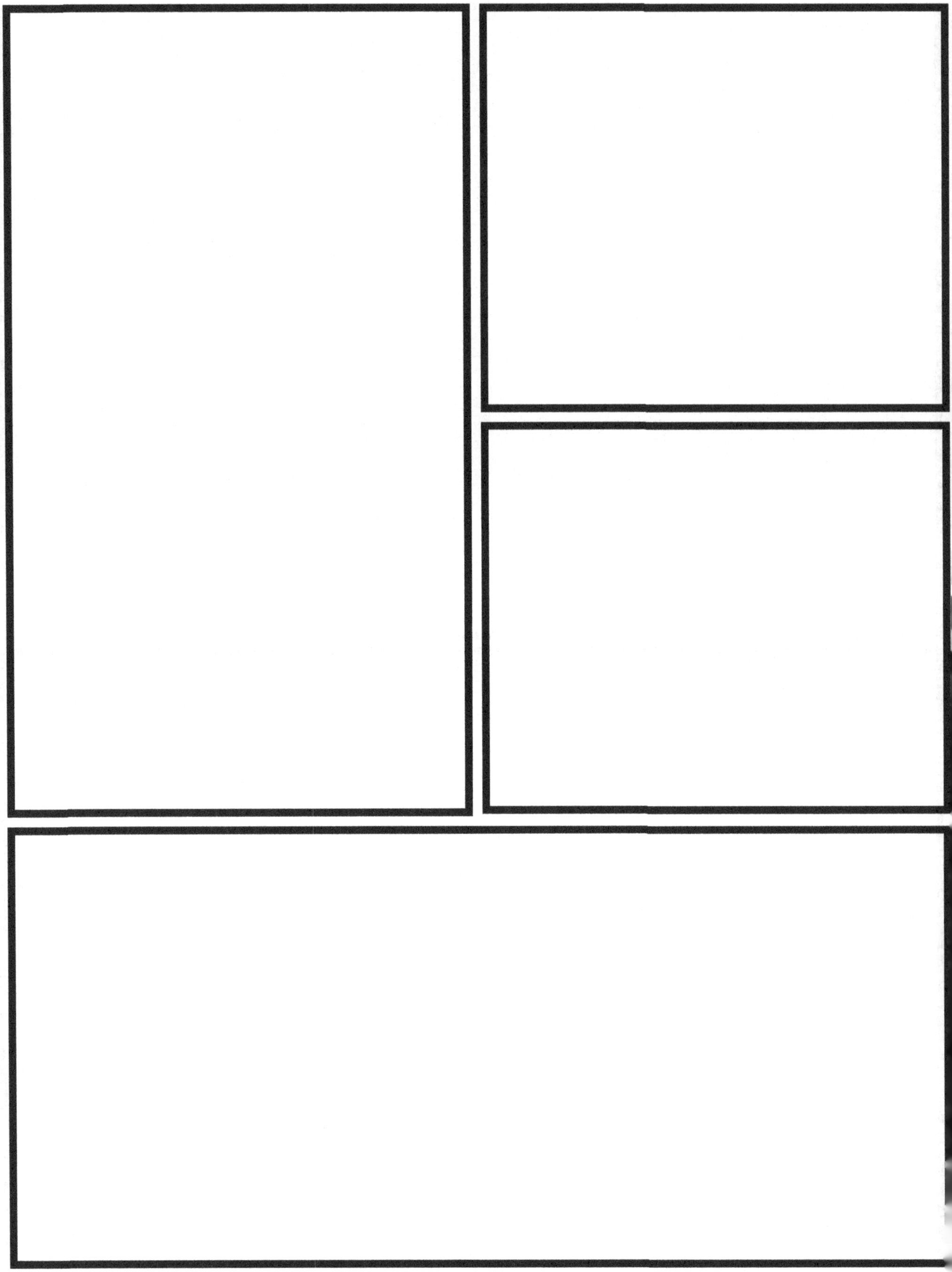

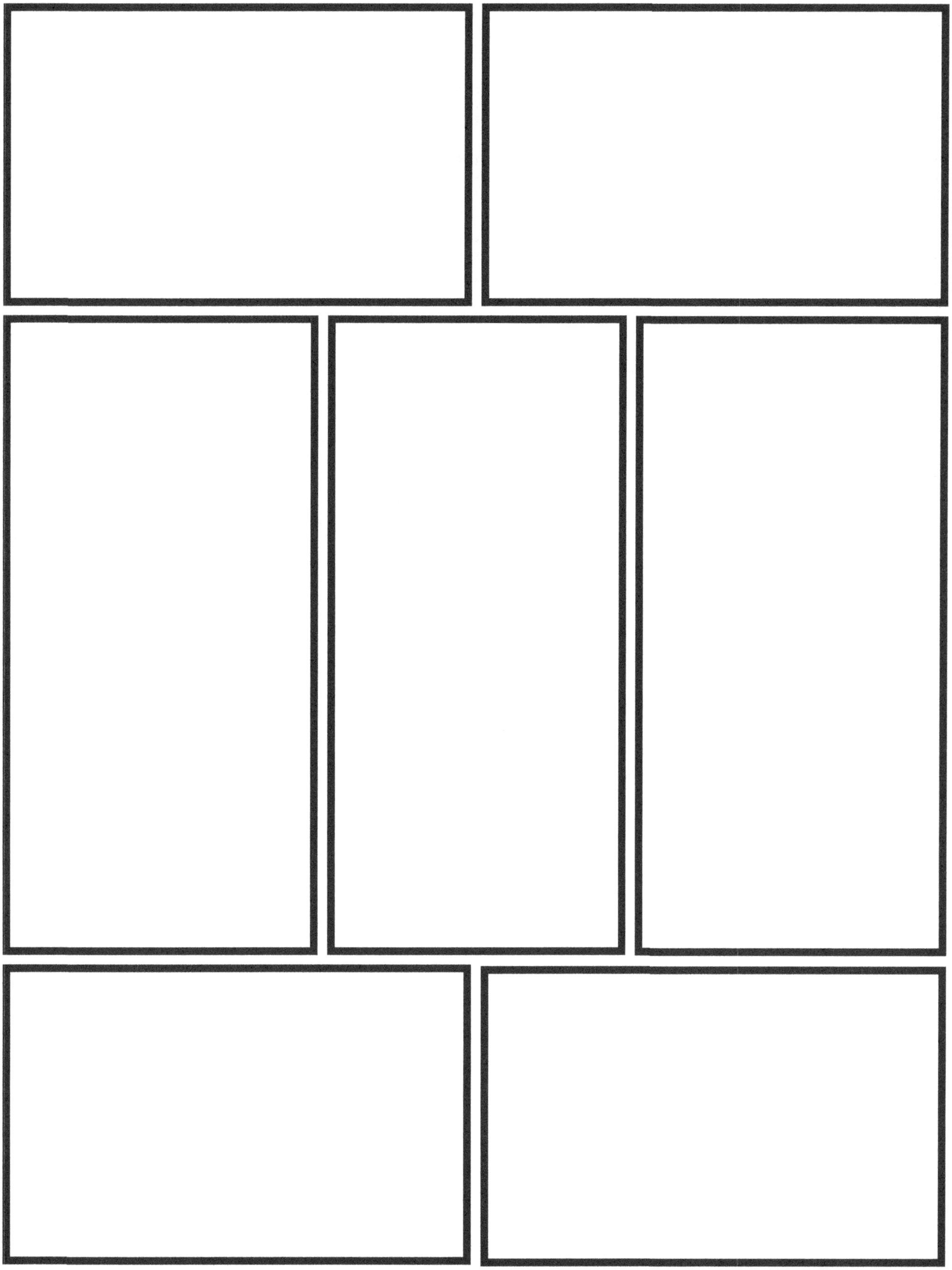

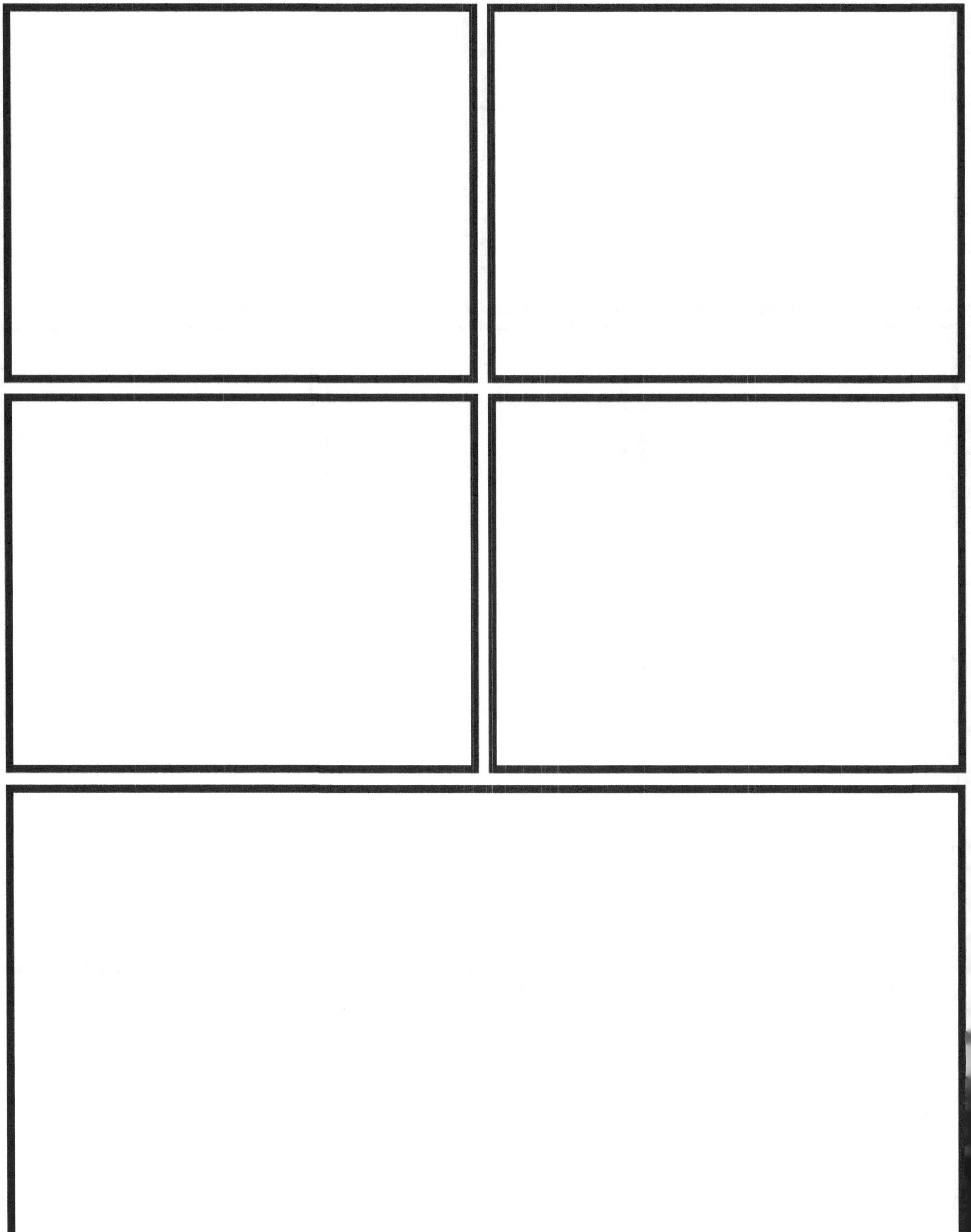

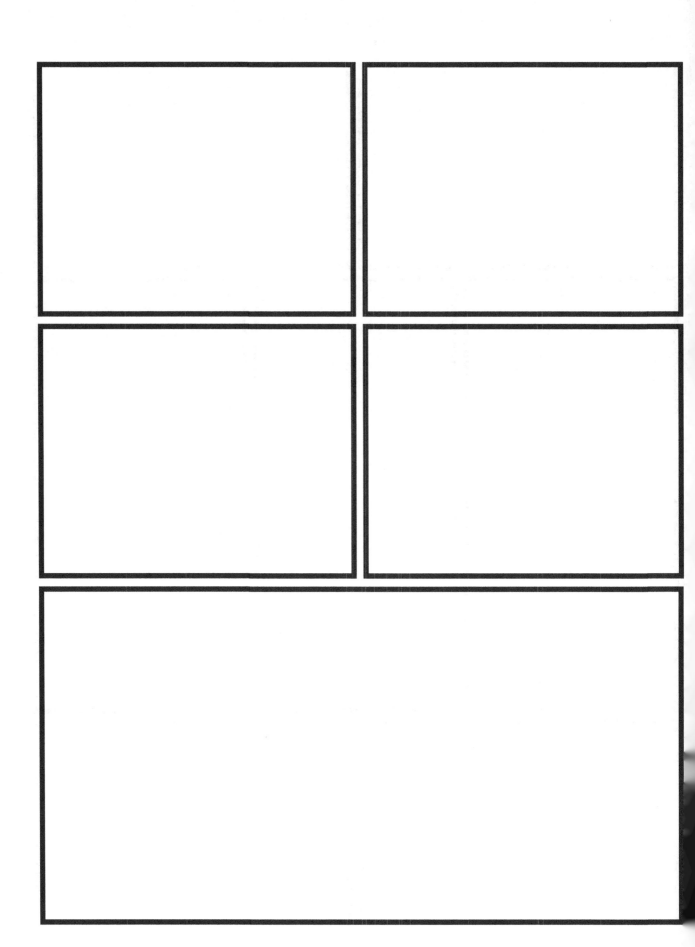

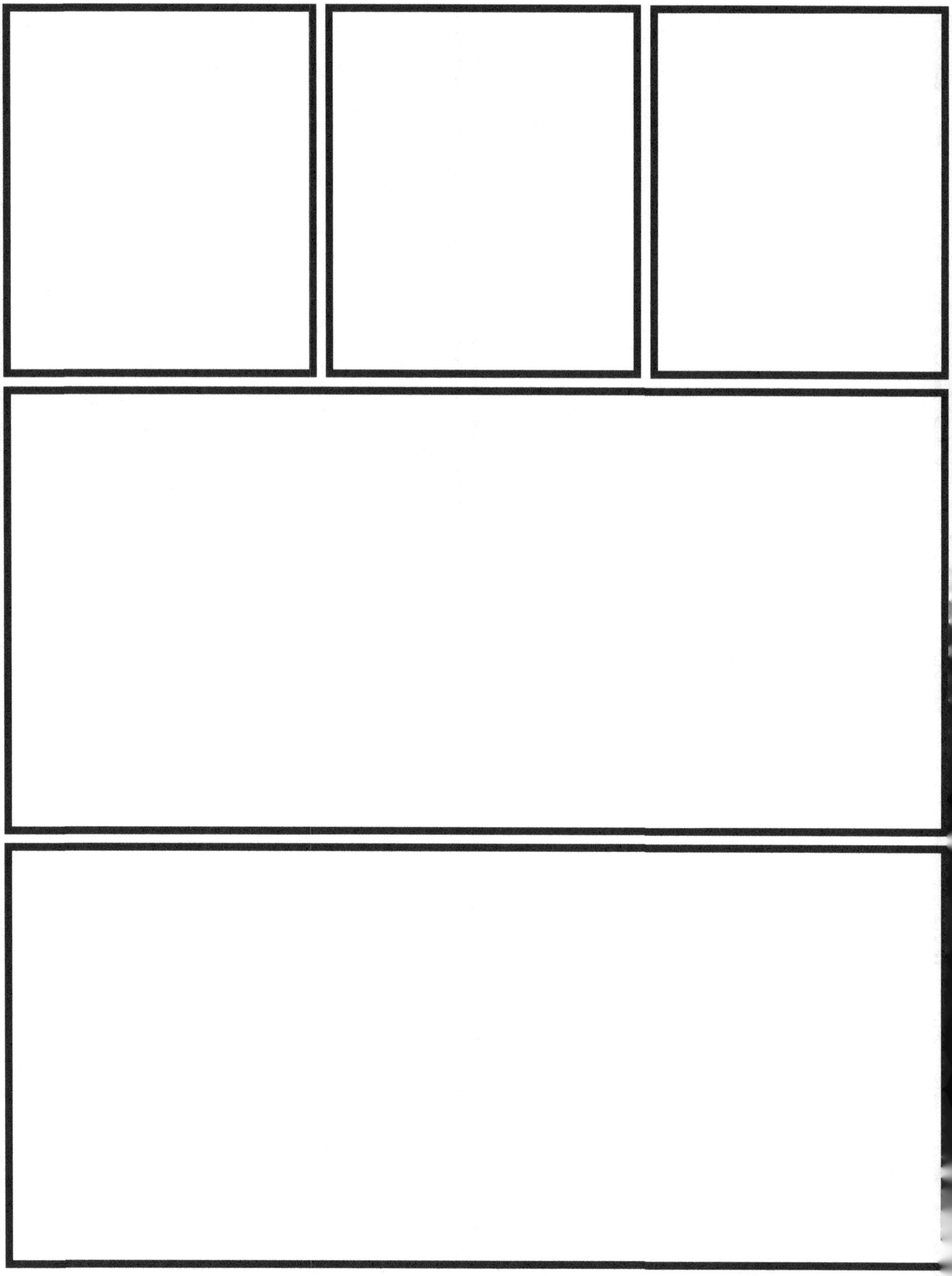

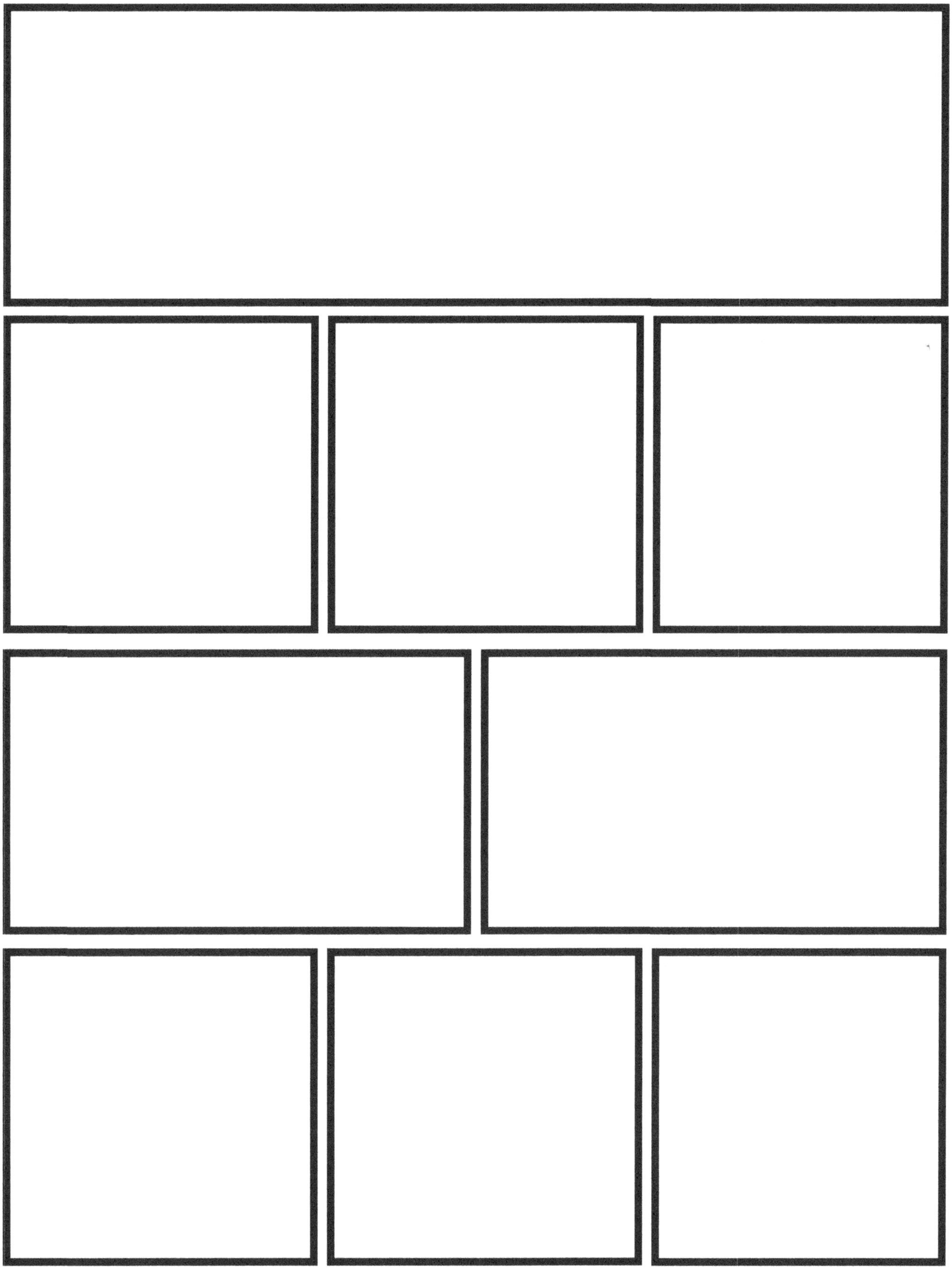

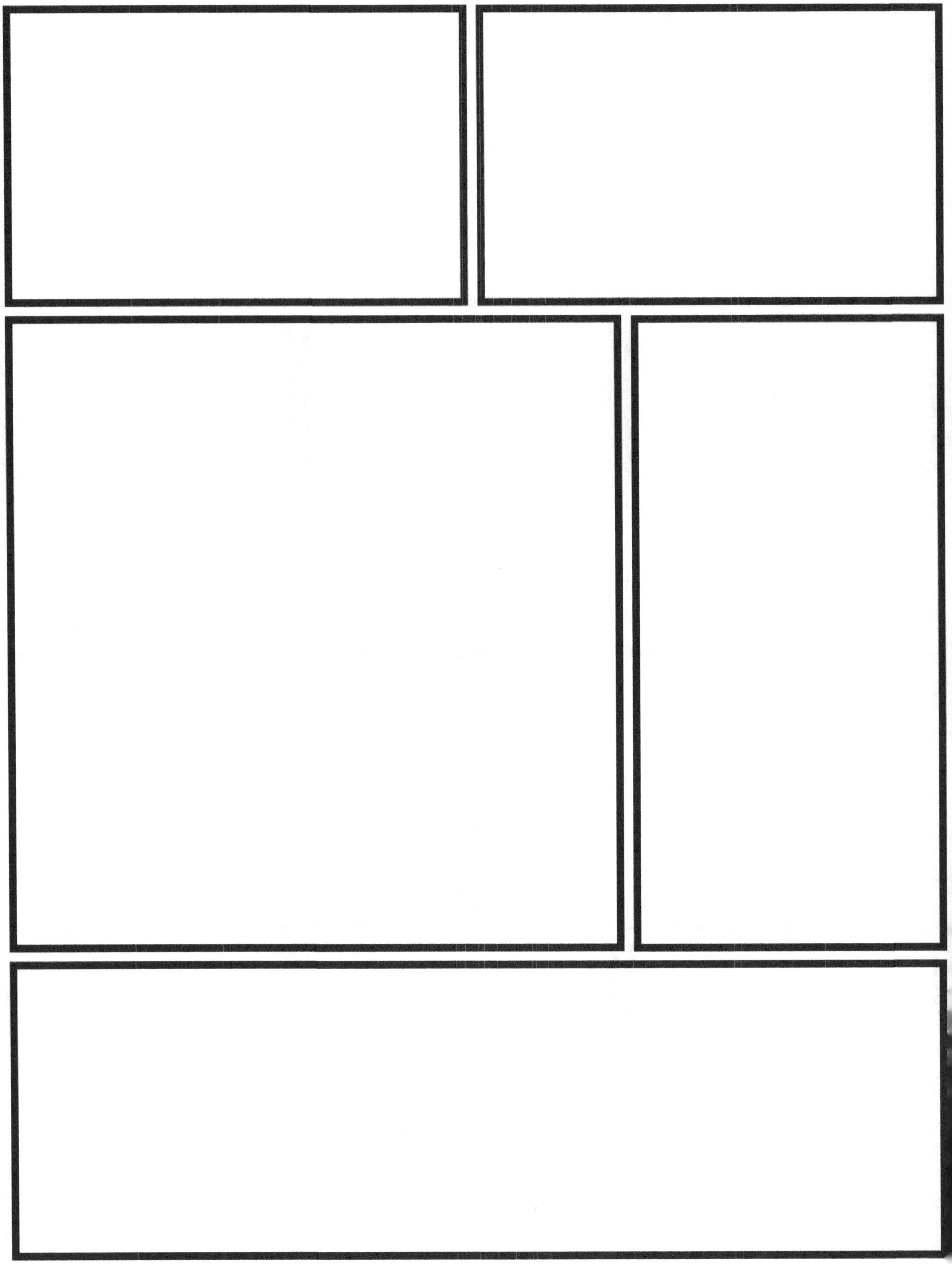

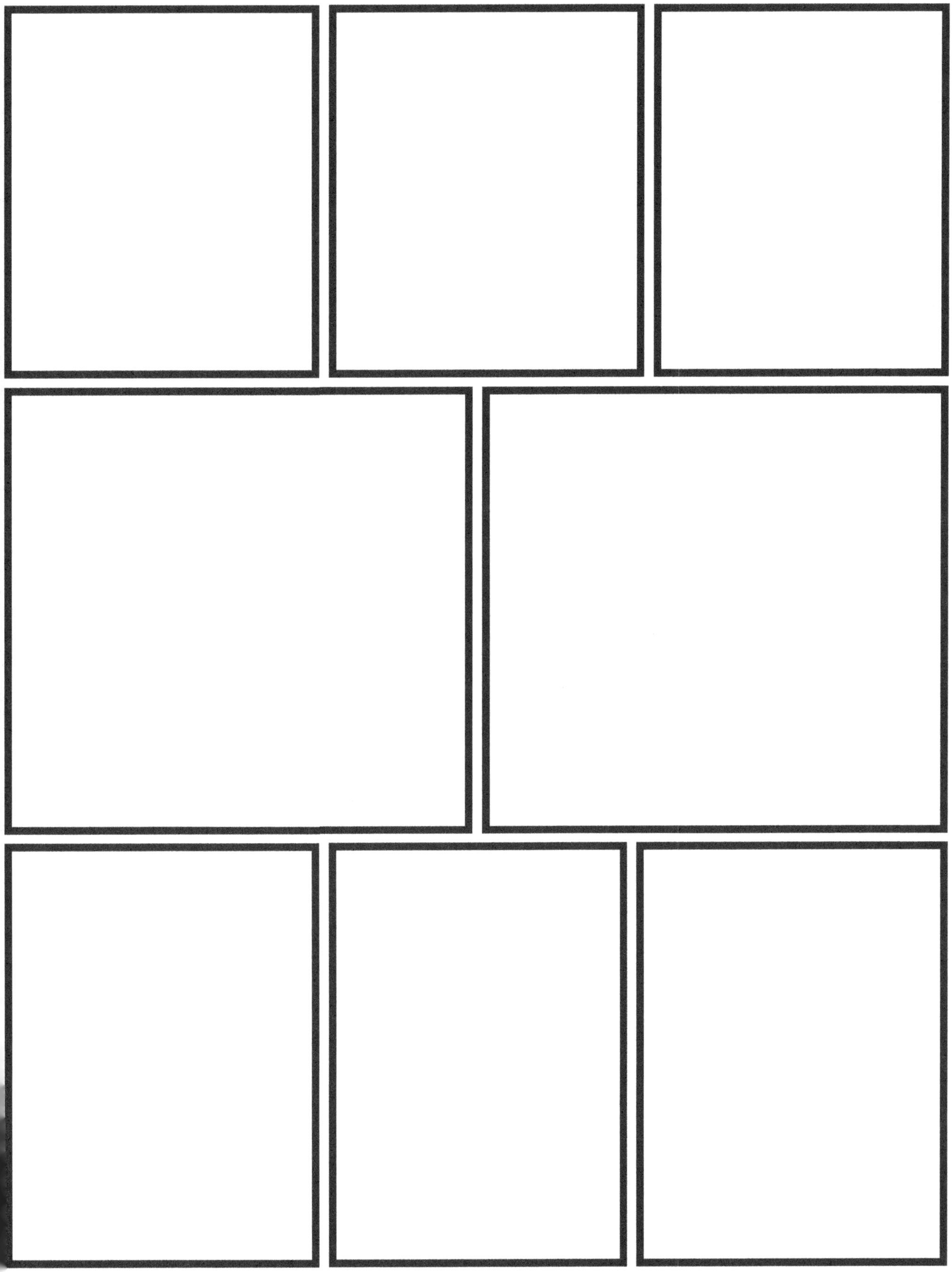

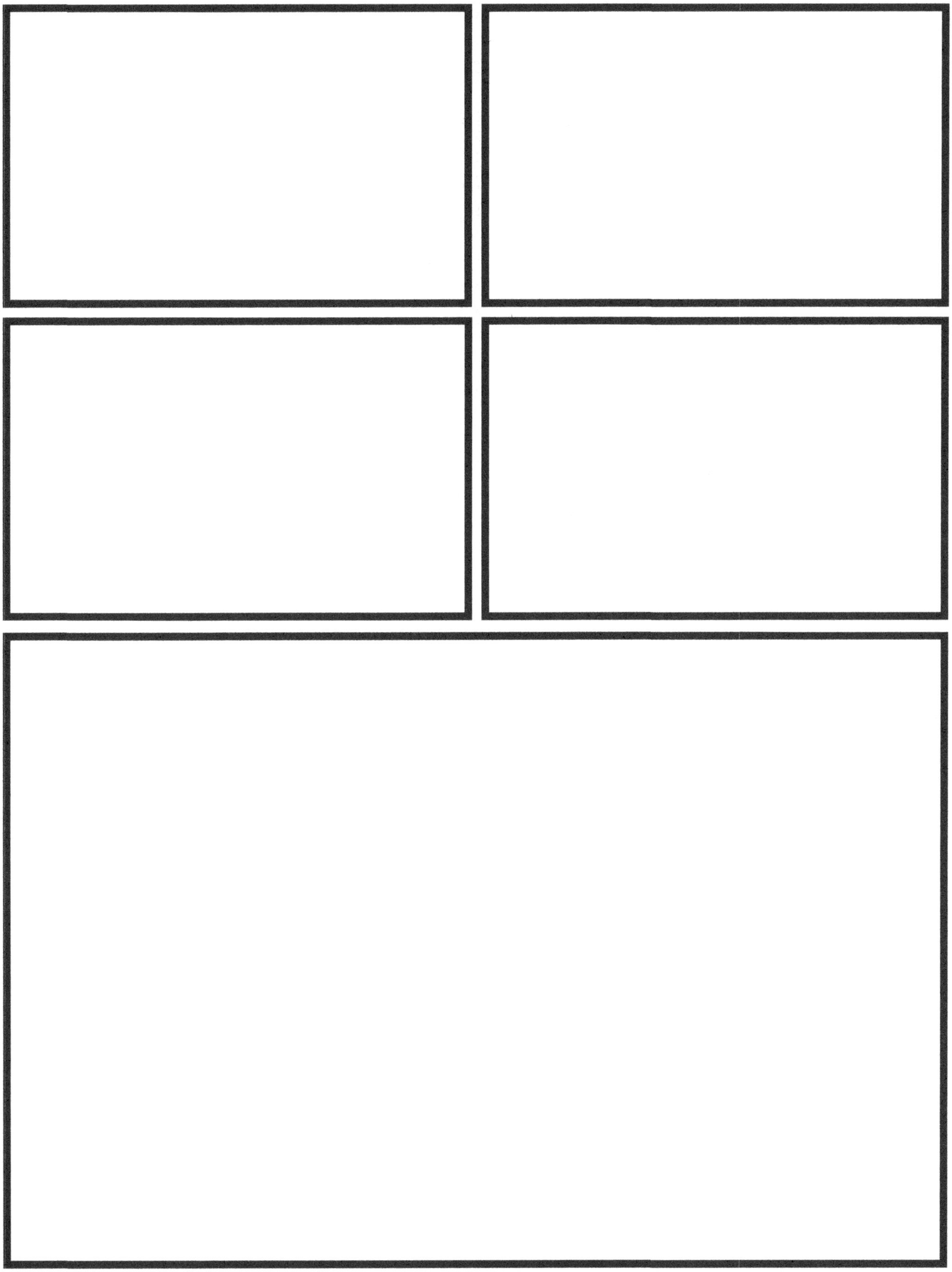

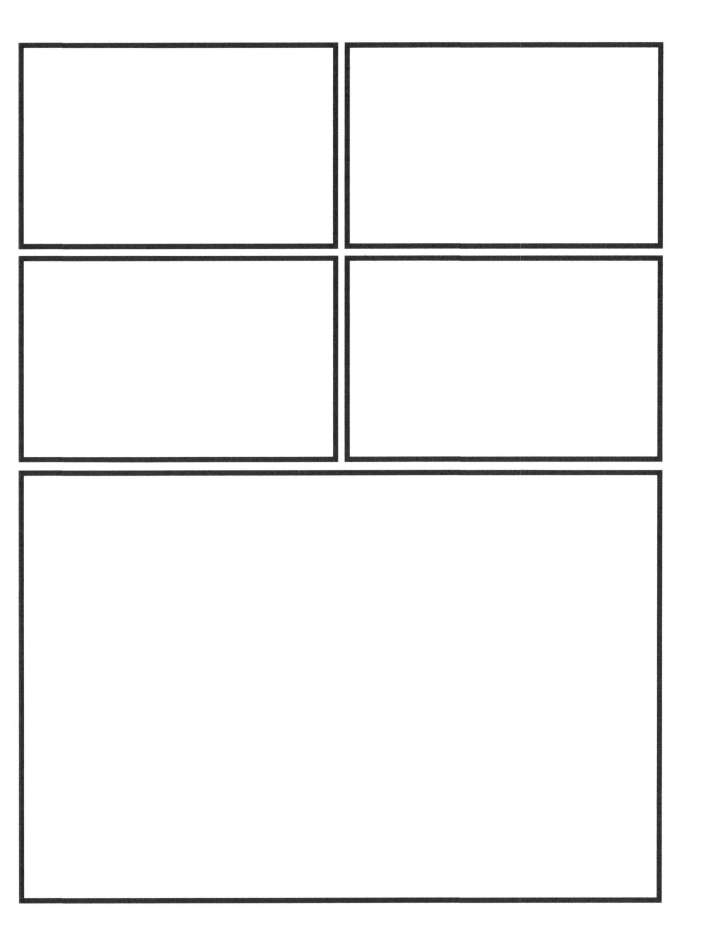

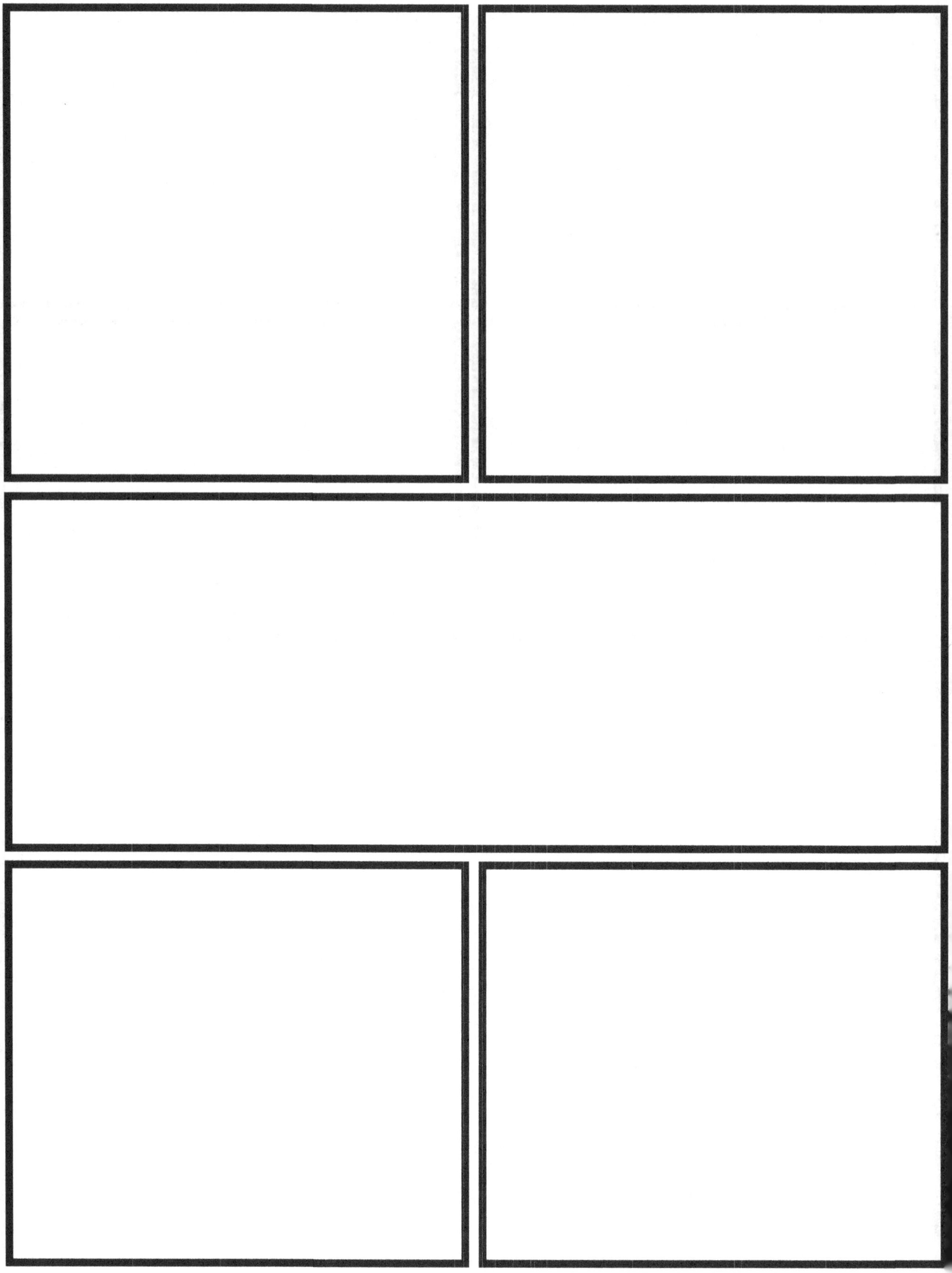

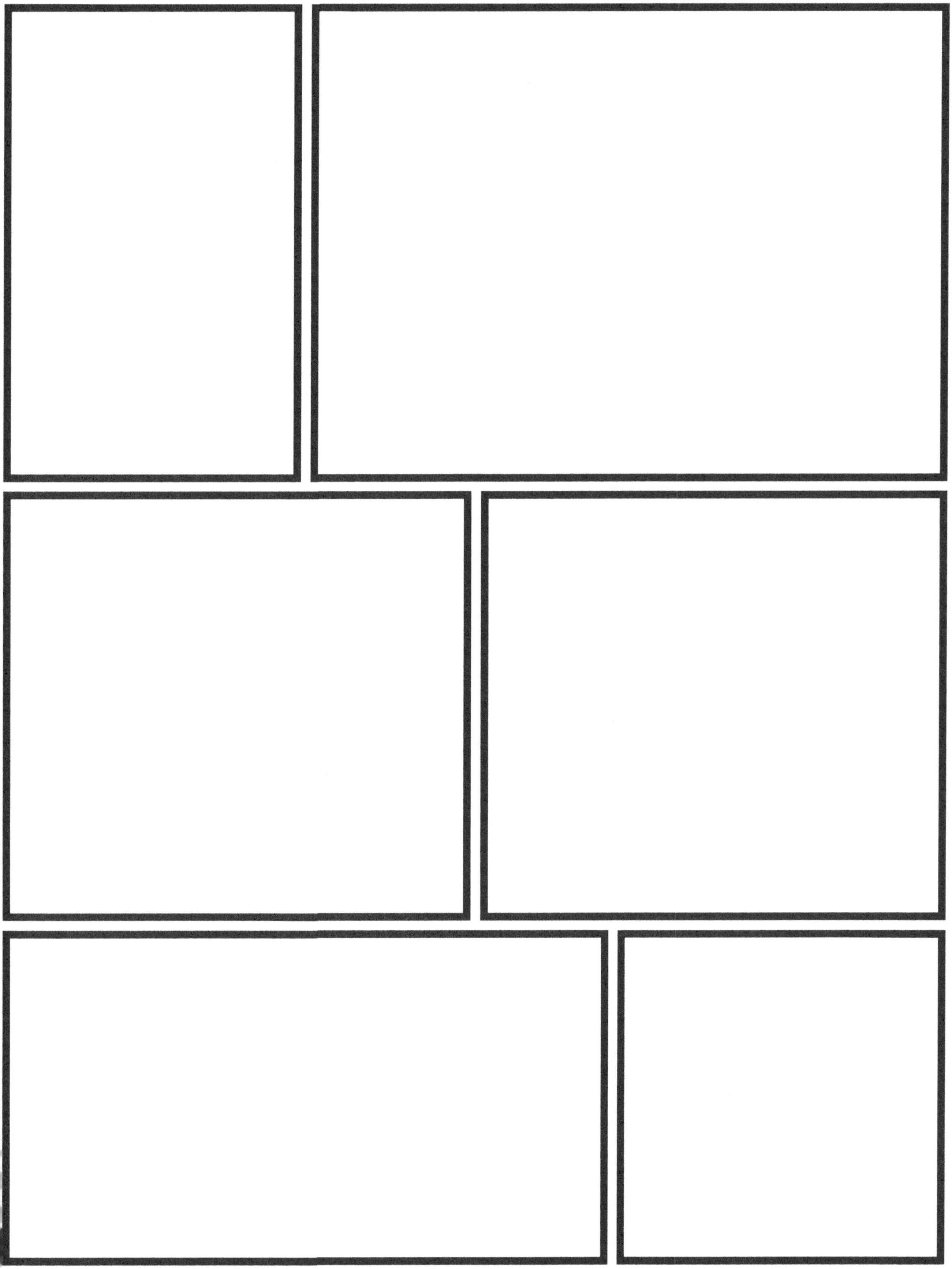

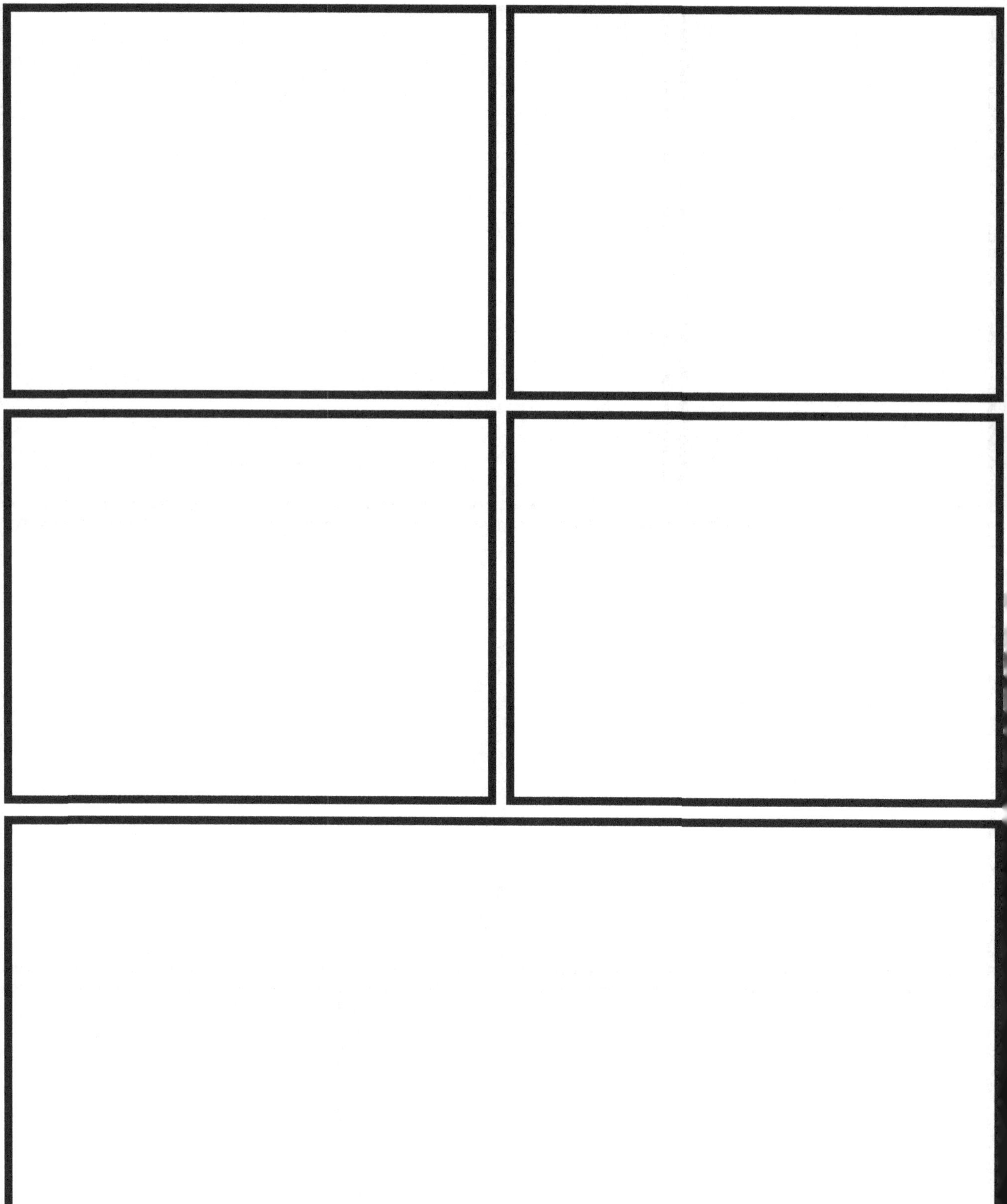

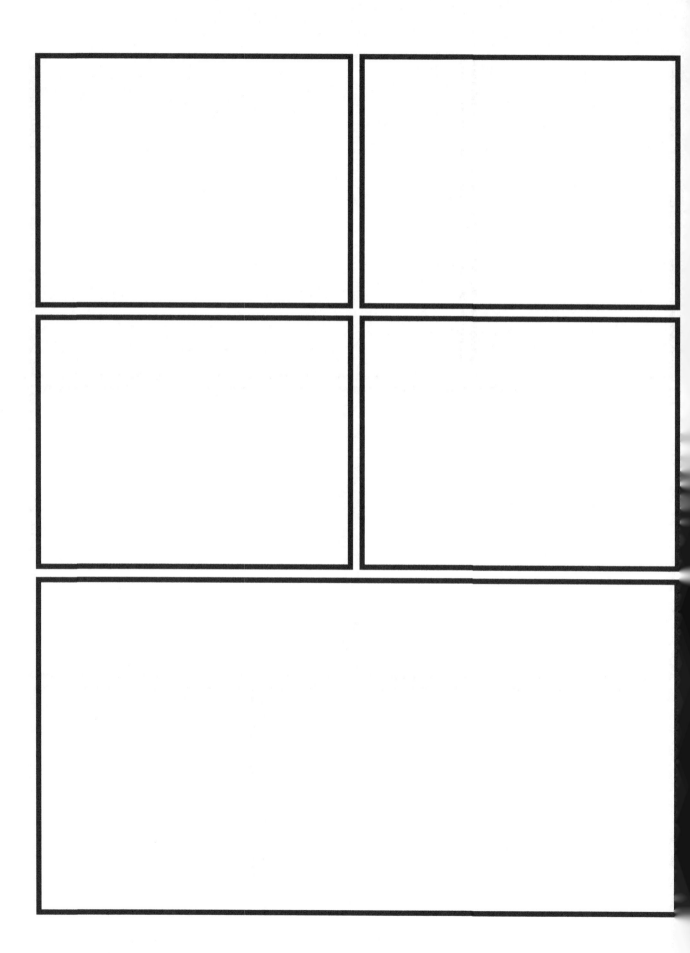

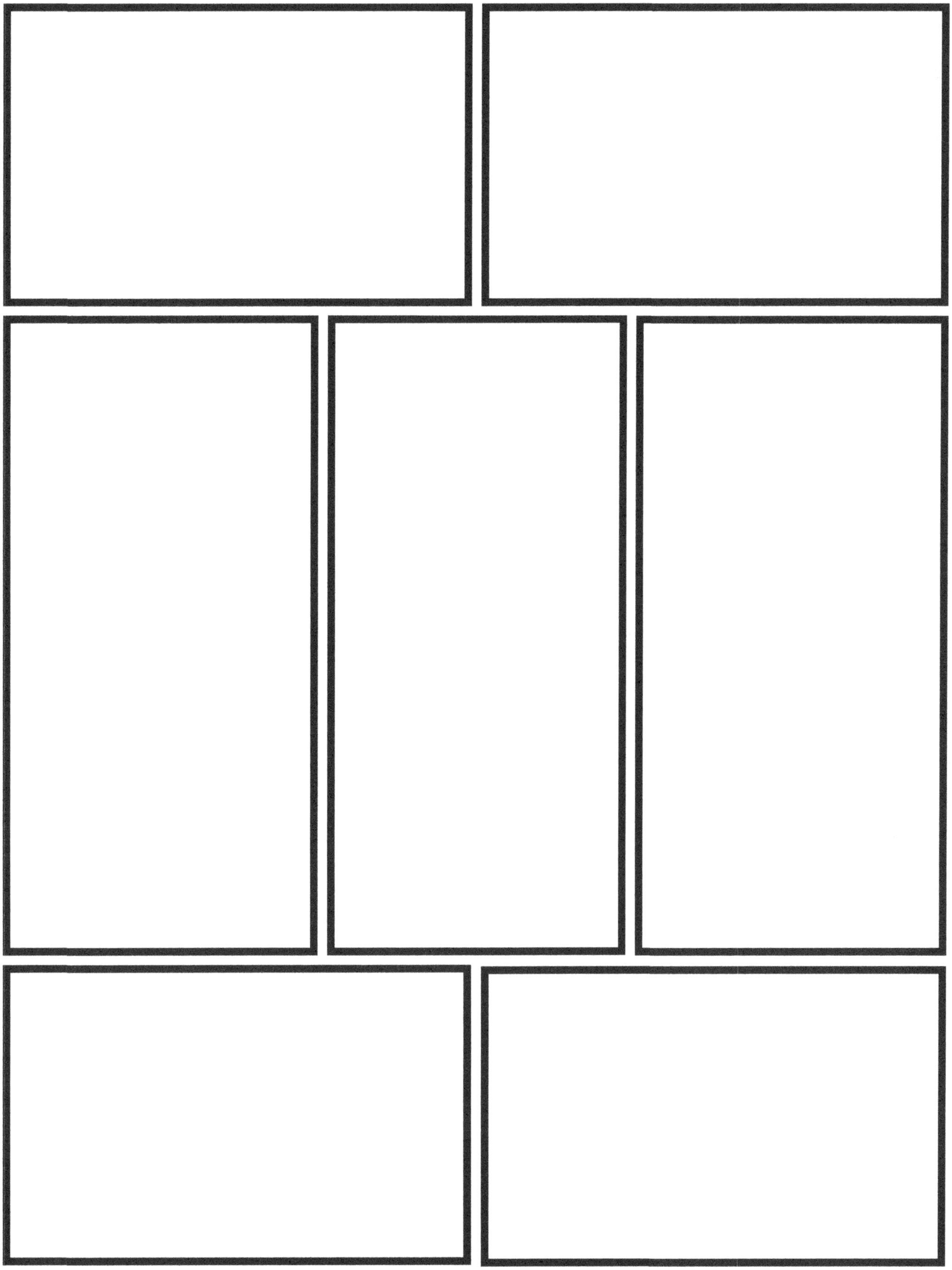

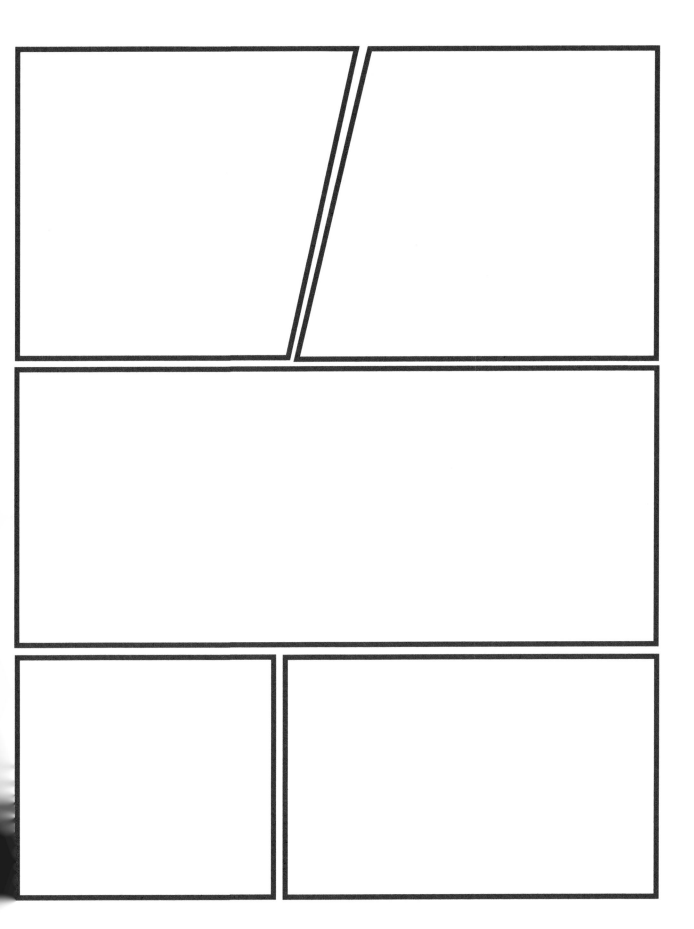

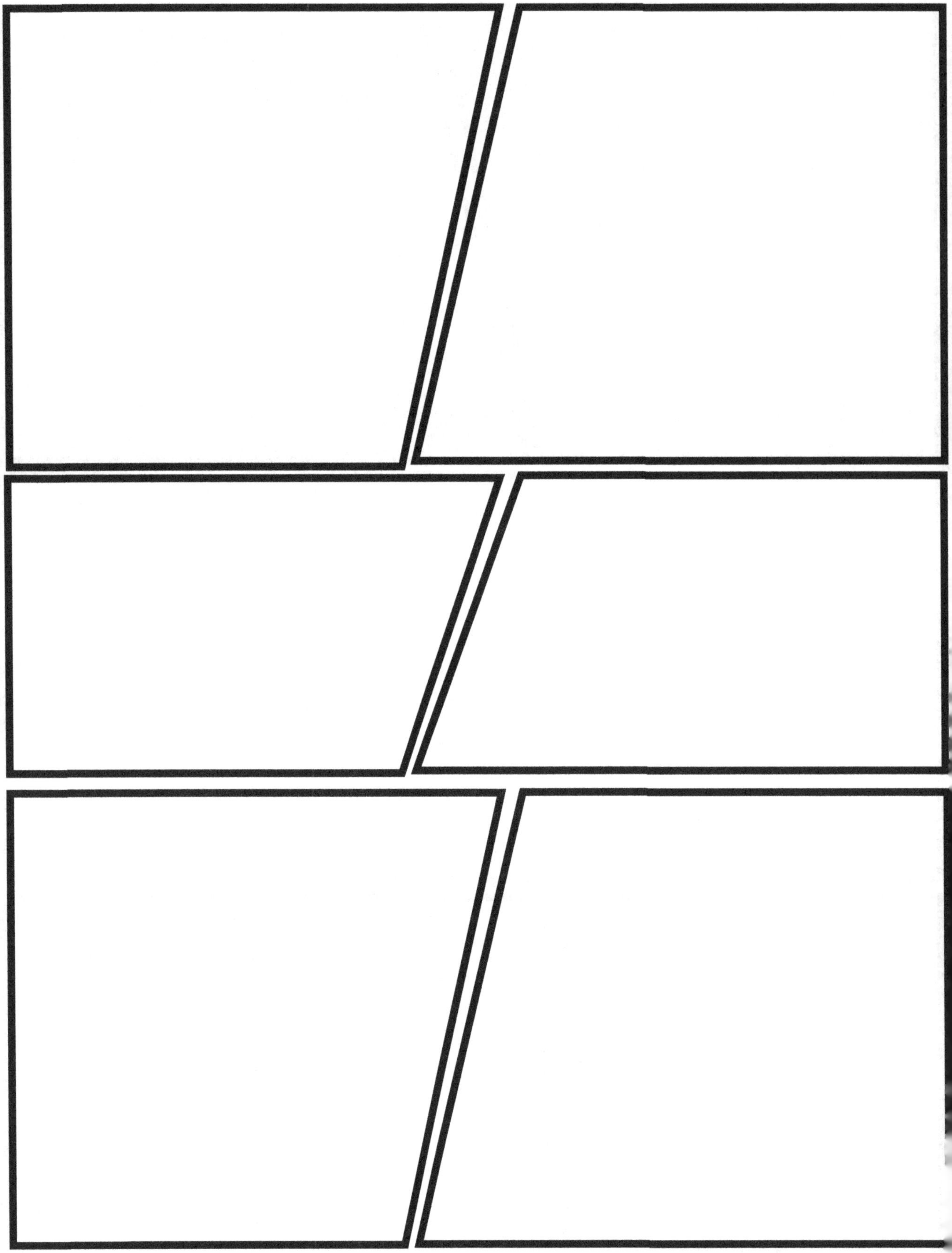

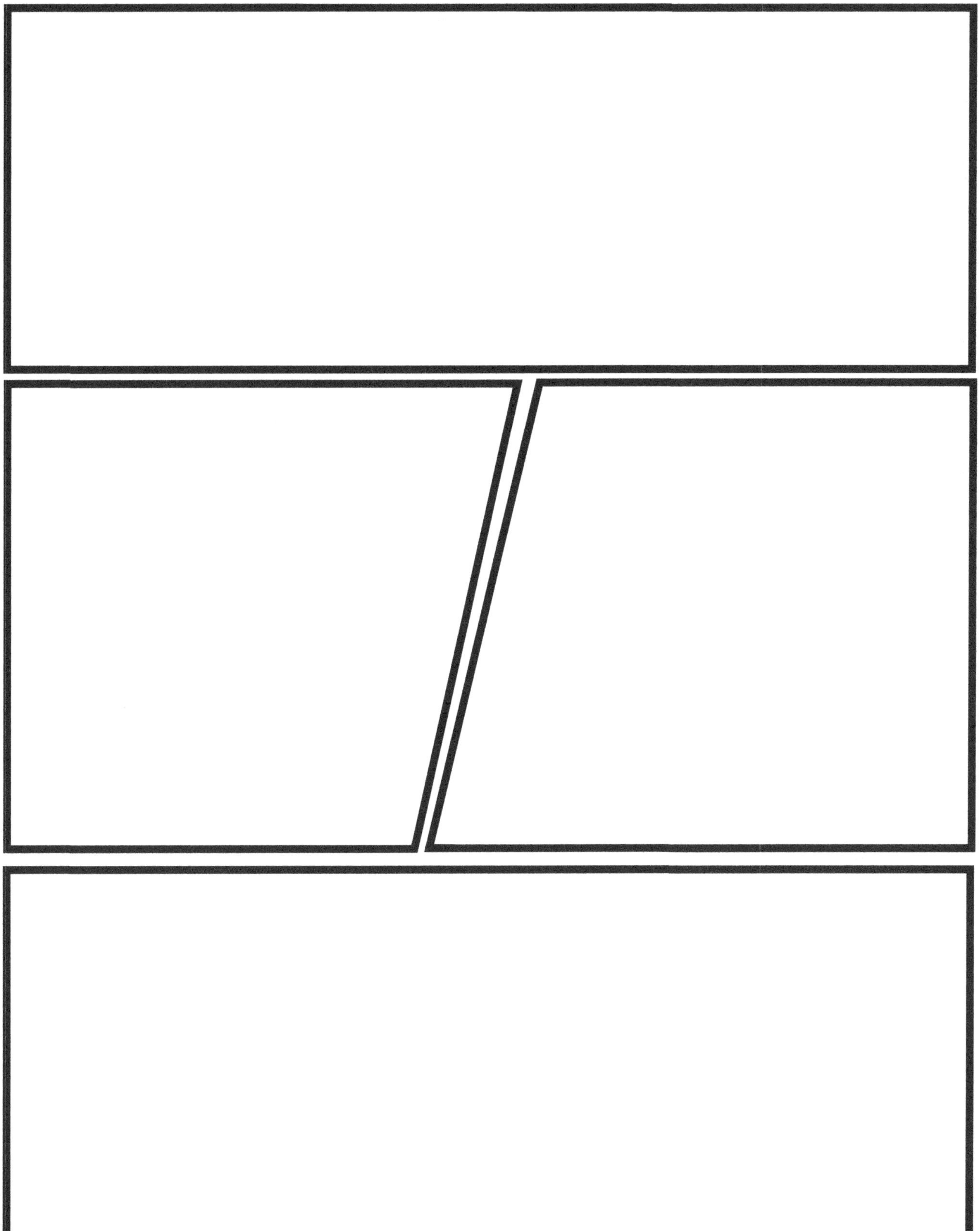

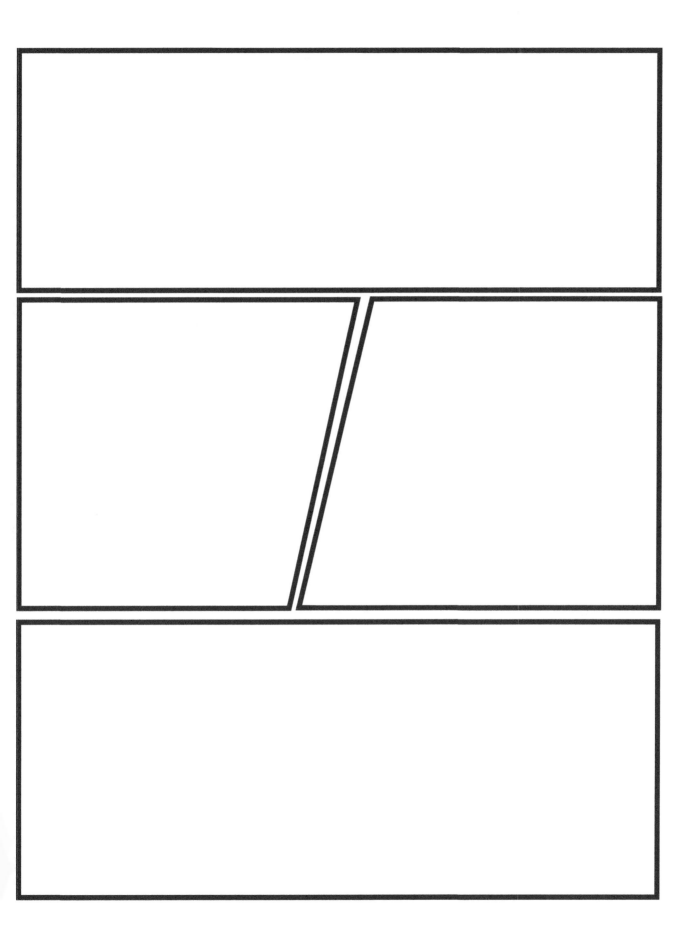

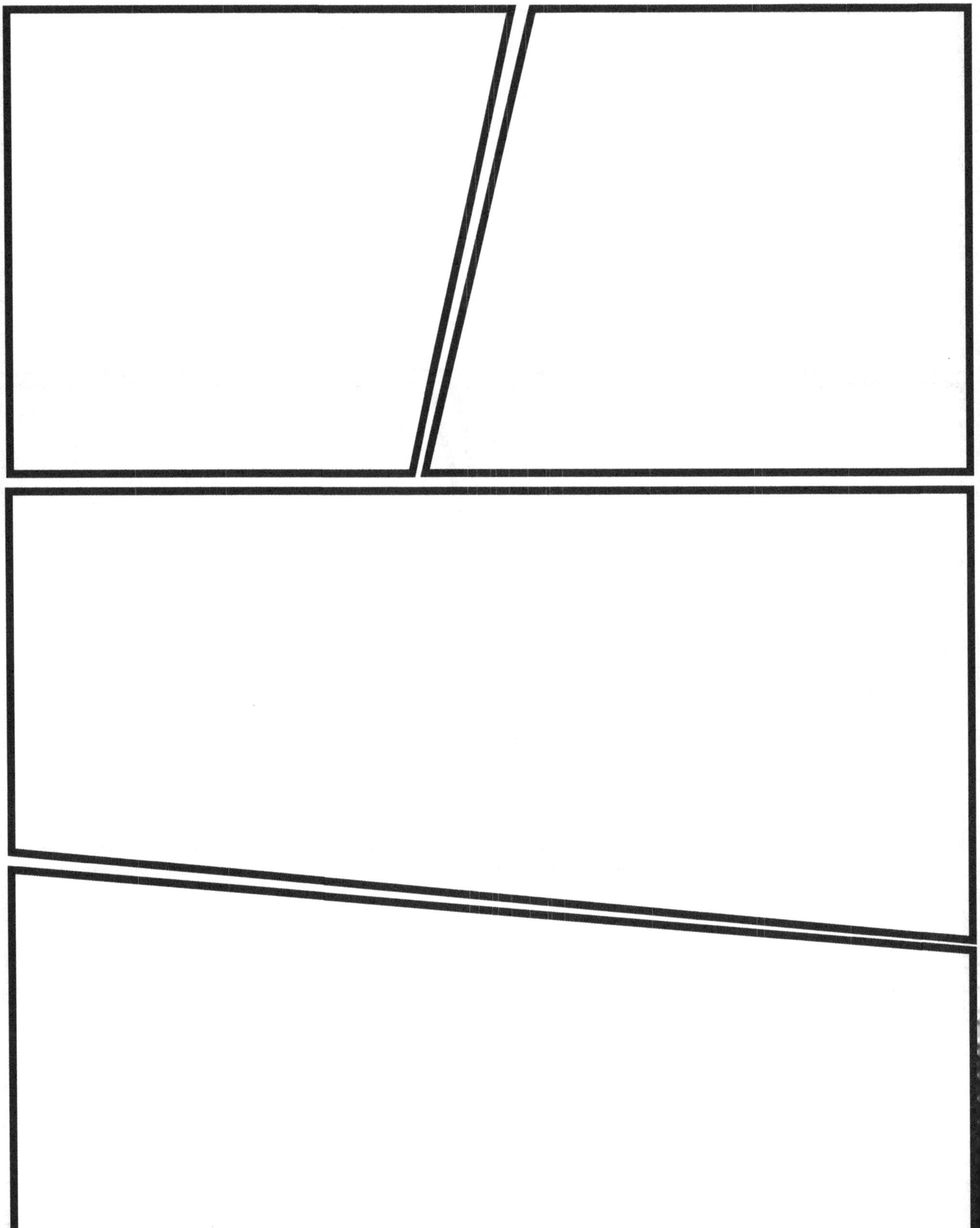

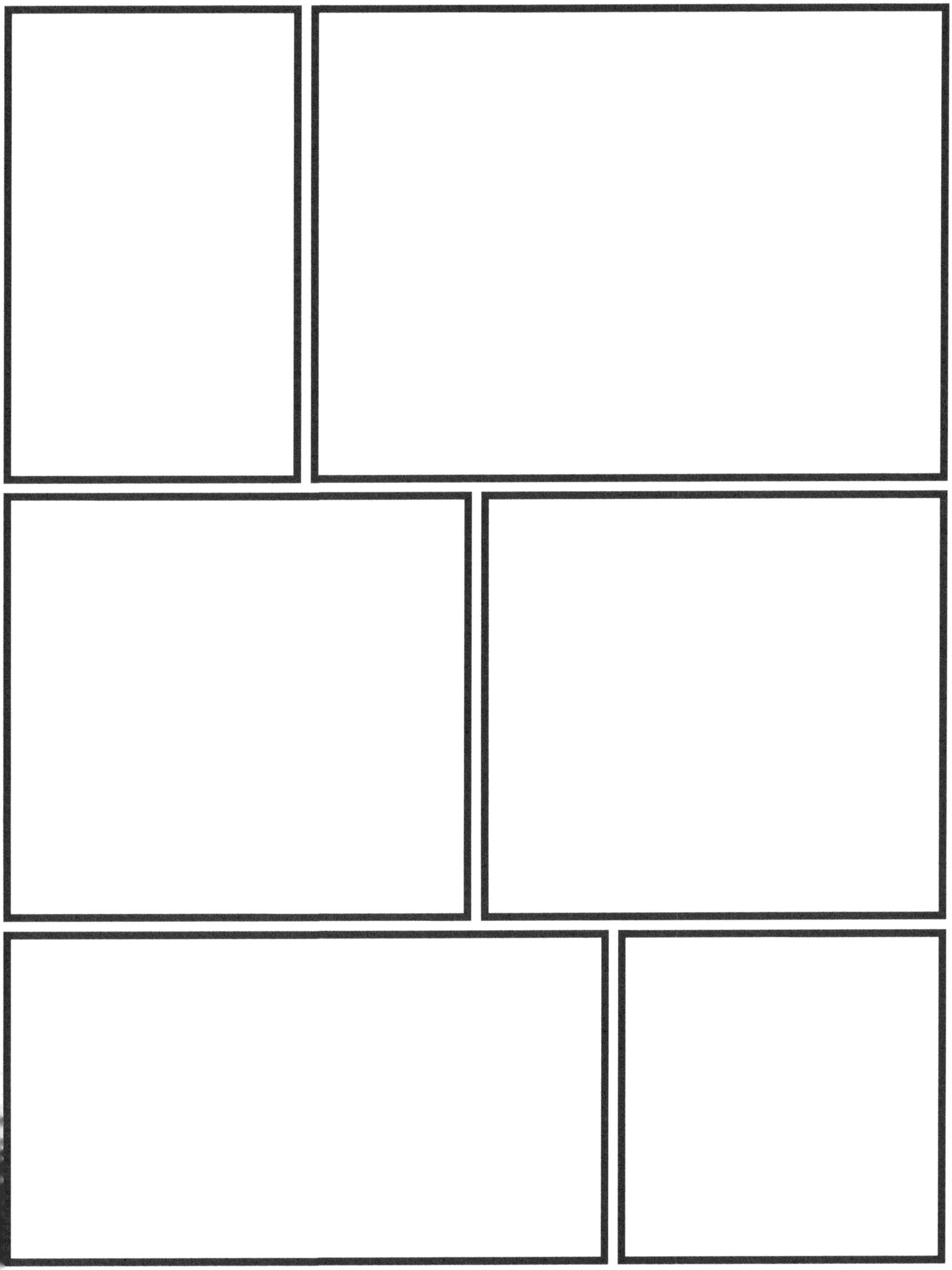

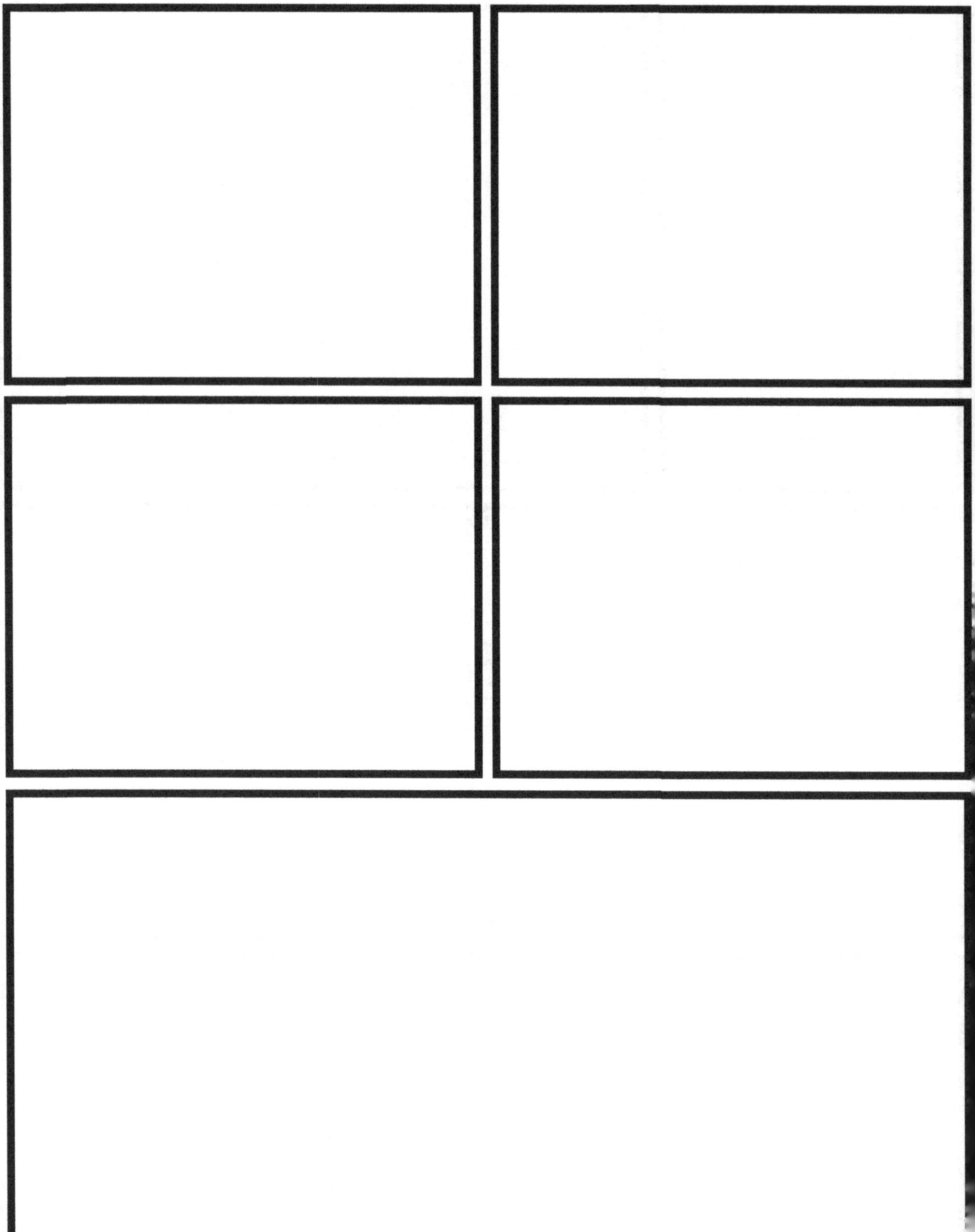

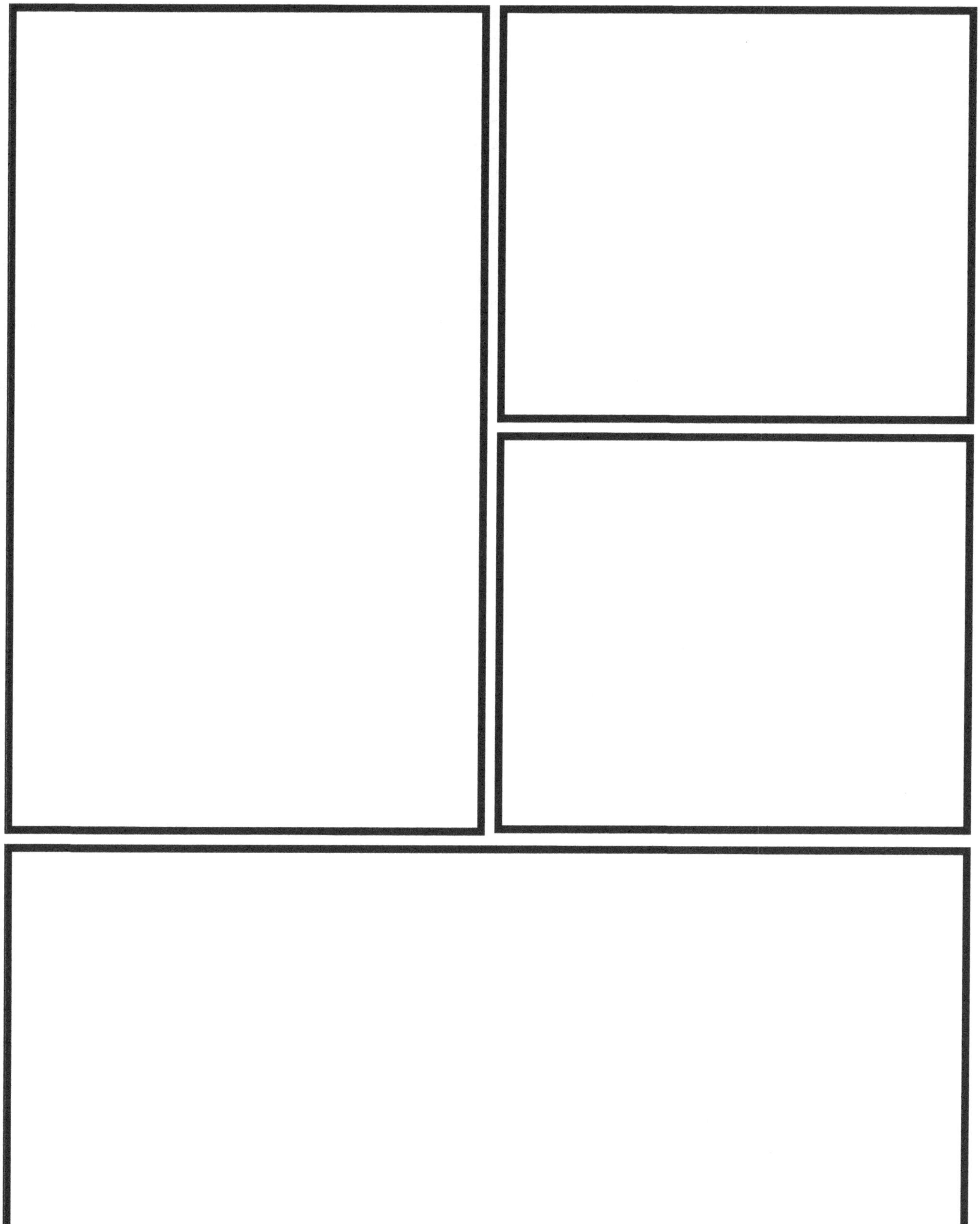

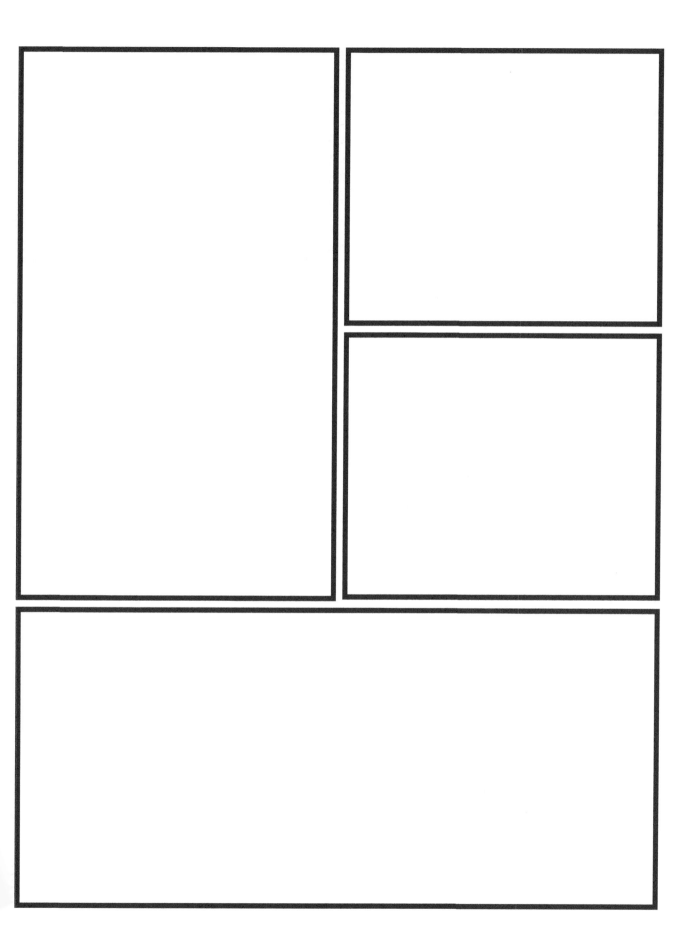

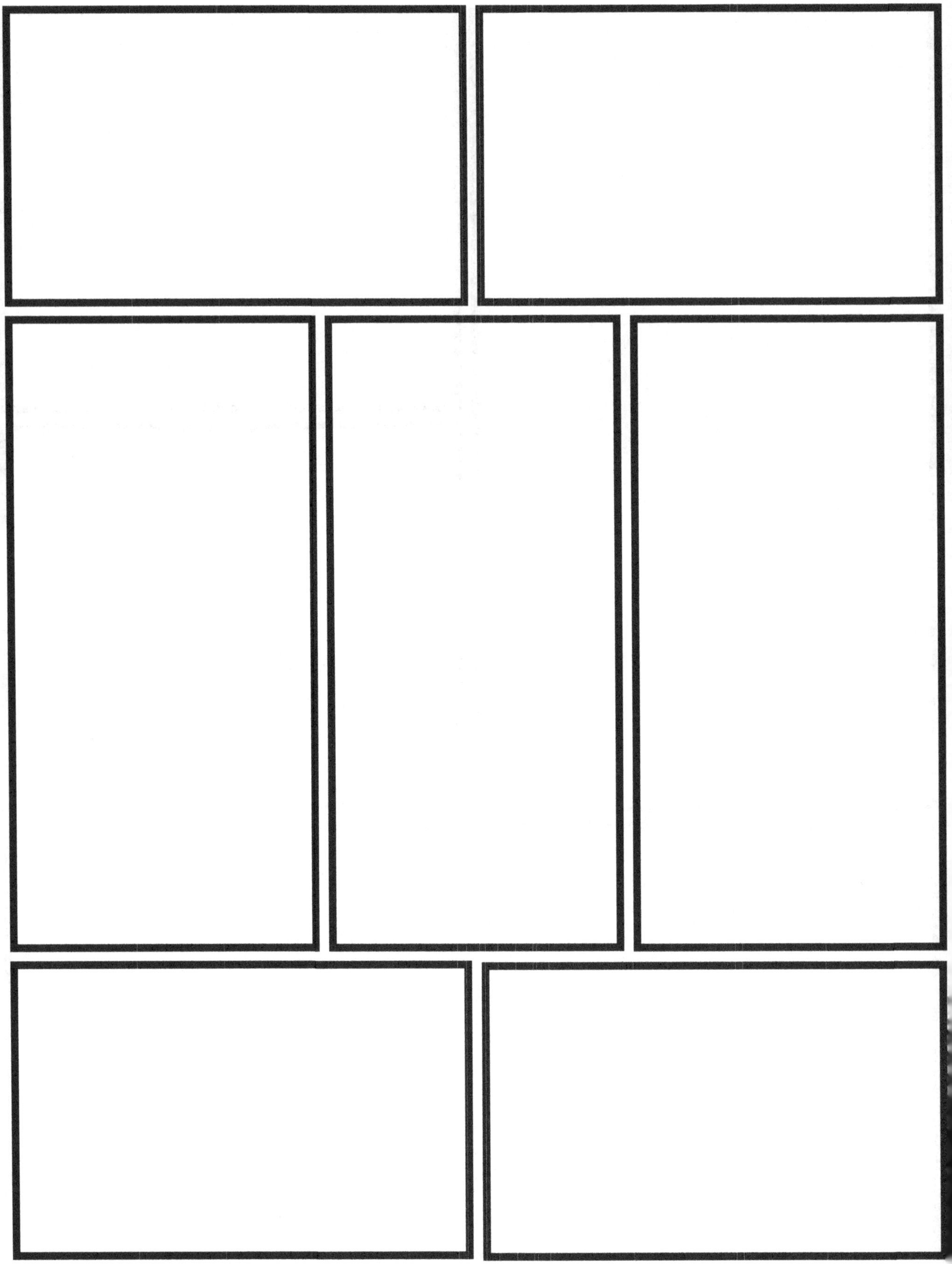

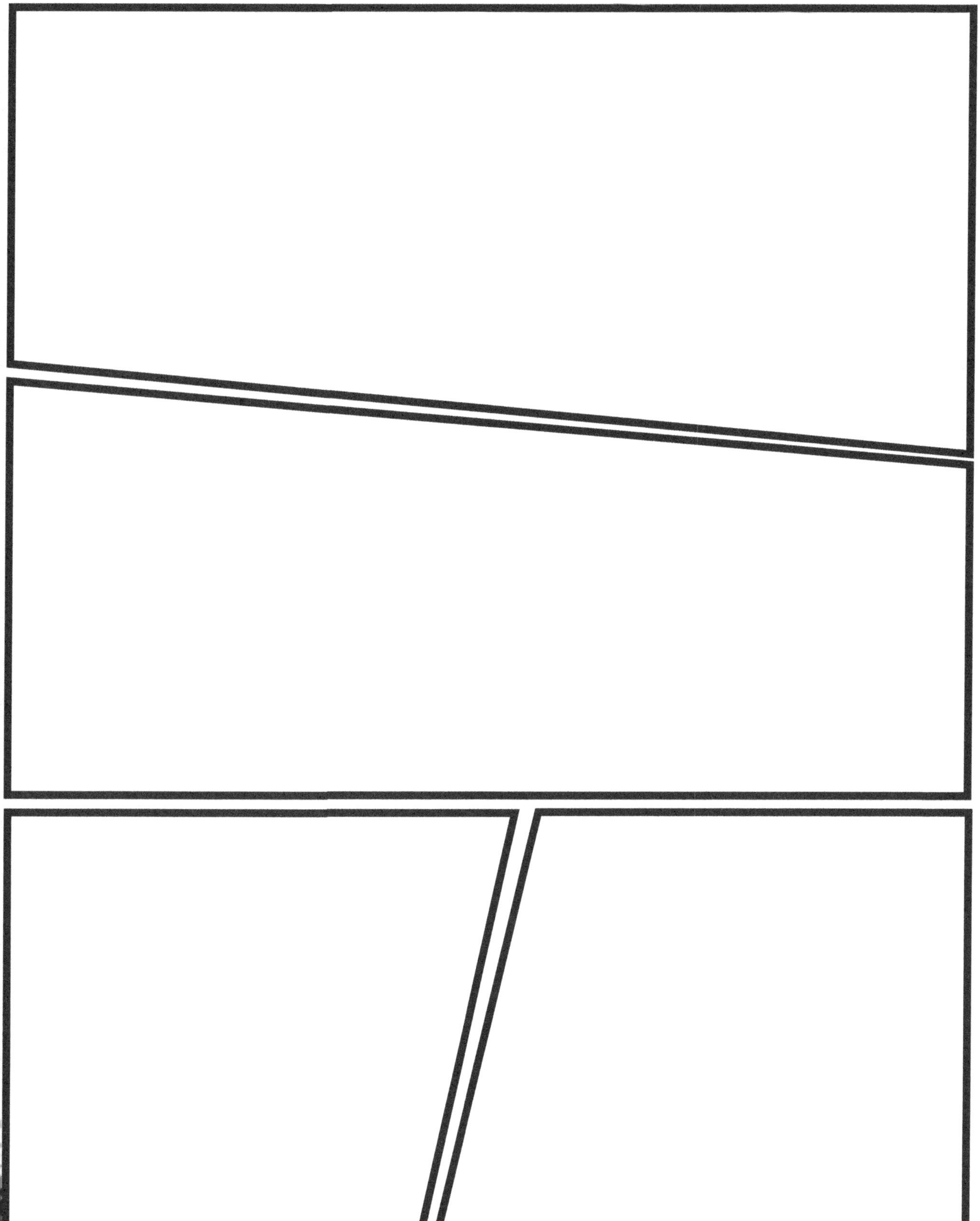

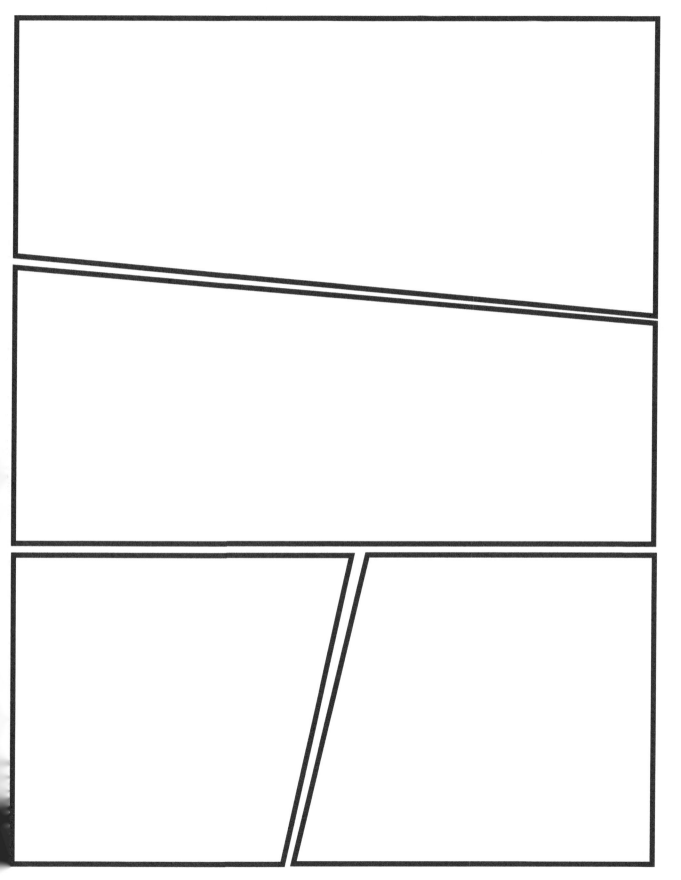

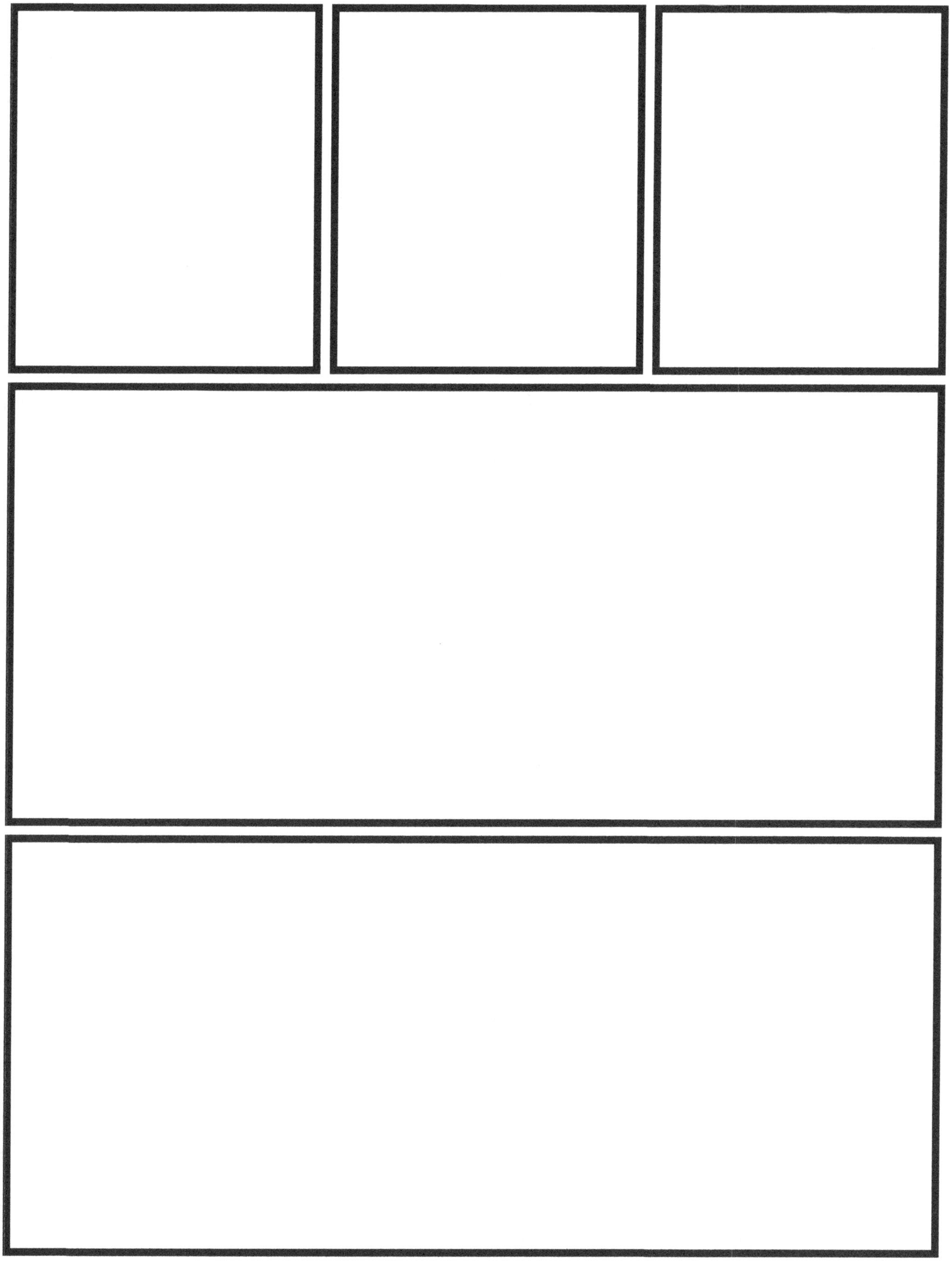

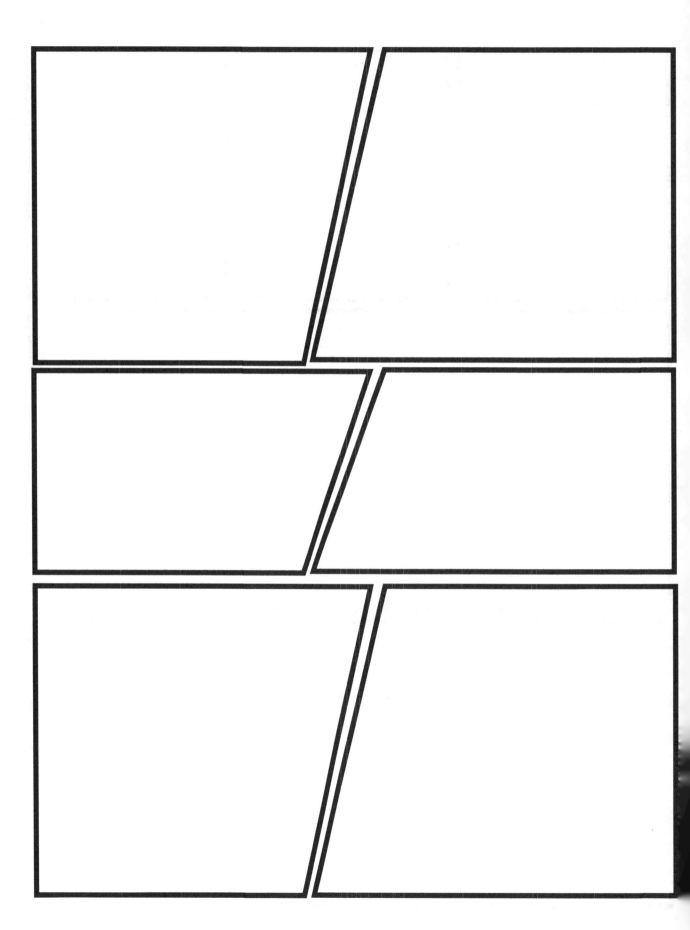

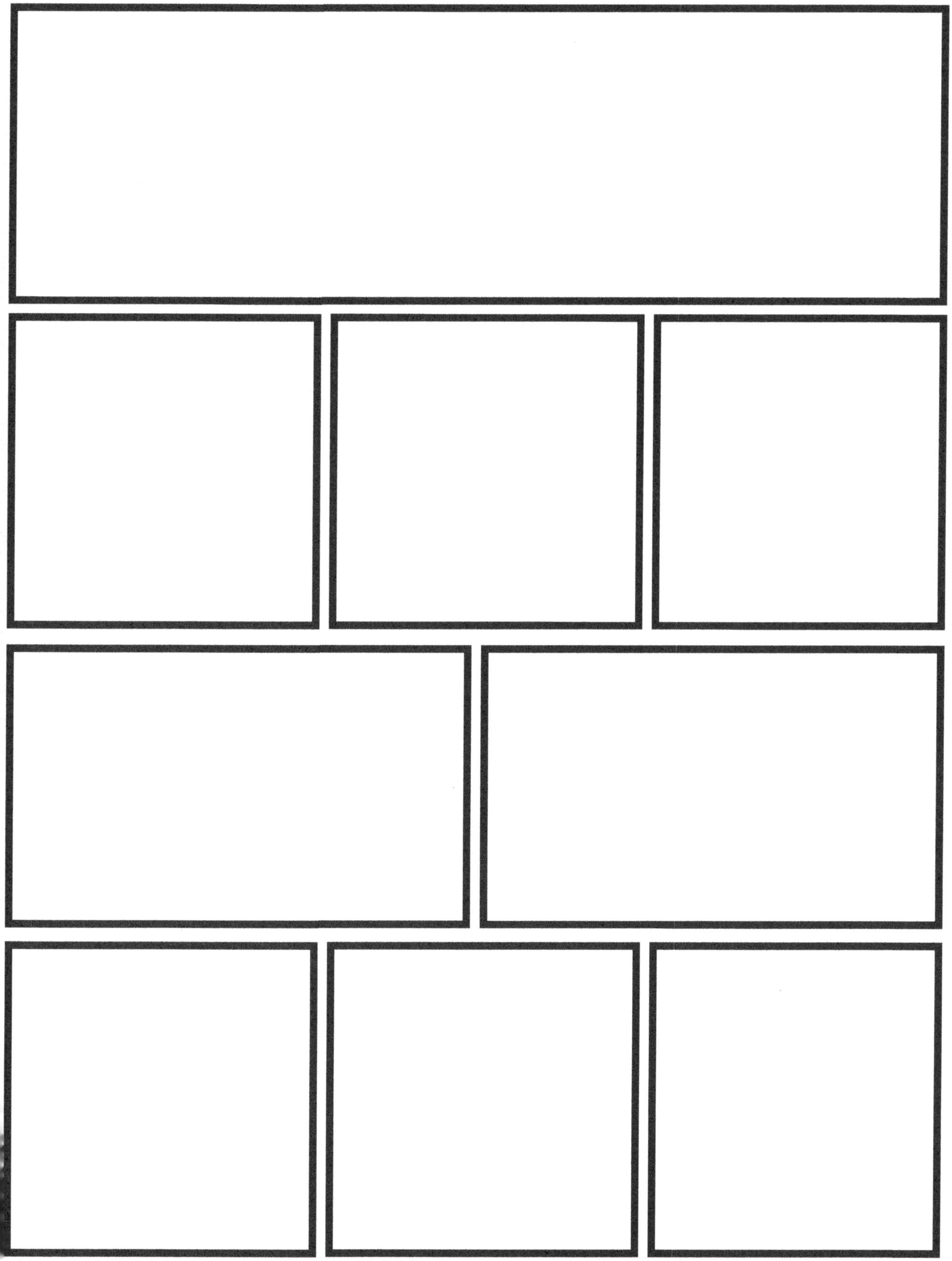

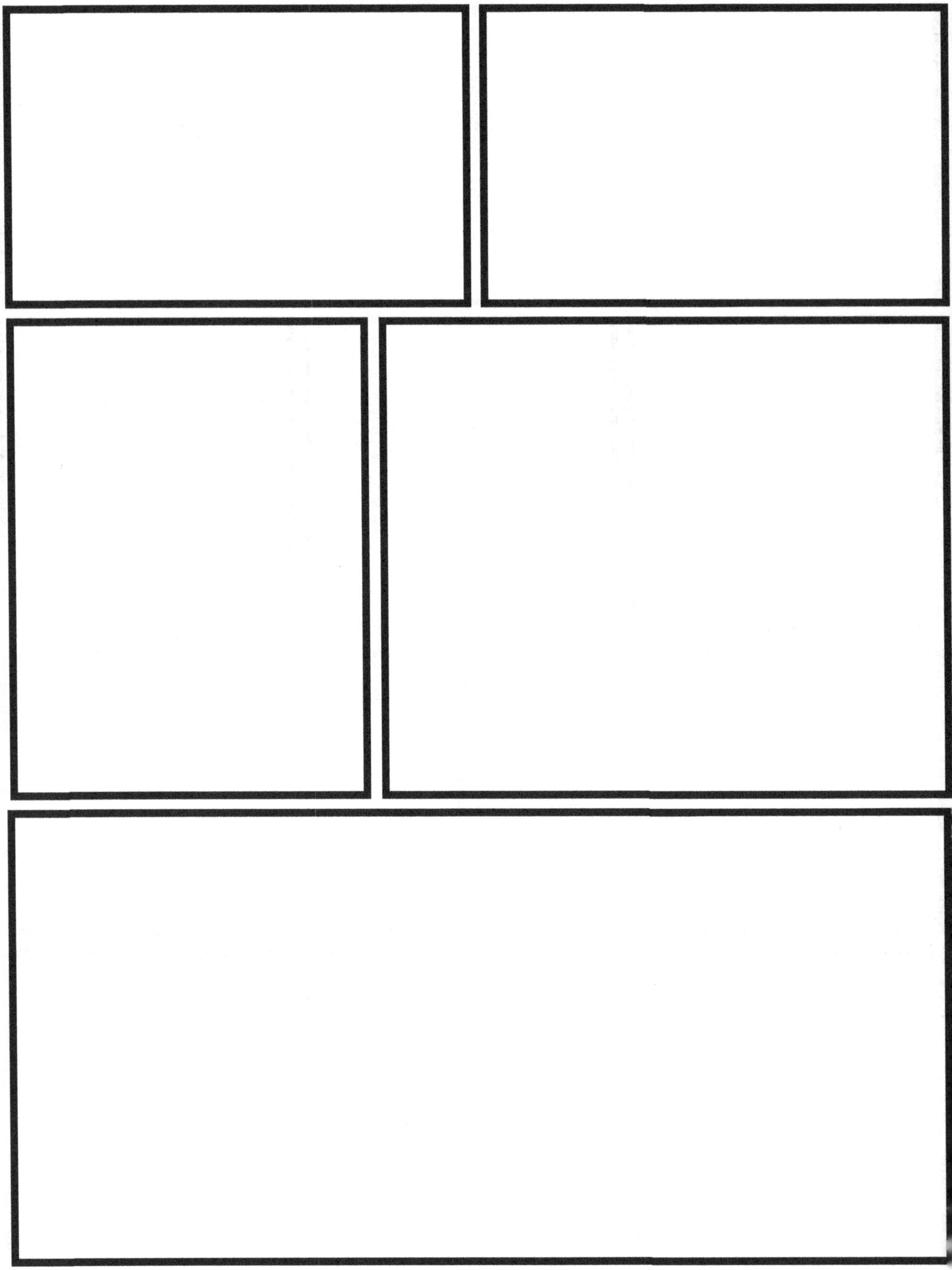

Made in the USA
Las Vegas, NV
20 February 2024

86045642R00079